MARY BERRY
at Home

MARY BERRY

at Home

....

OVER 150 RECIPES
FOR EVERY OCCASION

This book was first published to accompany the television series entitled
Mary Berry at Home
which was first broadcast in 1996
Executive Producer Frances Whitaker
Produced and directed by Mandy Temple

Published by
BBC Worldwide Ltd, Woodlands,
80 Wood Lane, London W12 0TT

First published 1996
Reprinted 1996, 1997
First published in paperback 2001
© Mary Berry 1996
ISBN 0 563 38738 6 (hardback)
ISBN 0 563 53776 0 (paperback)
The moral right of the author has been asserted

Edited by Wendy Hobson
Designed by Tim Higgins
Photographs by Philip Webb
Dishes prepared for photography by:
Caroline Liddell (home economist)
Helen Payne (stylist)
Illustrations by Kate Simunek

Set in Aldus by Ace Filmsetting Ltd, Frome, Somerset
Printed and bound in Great Britain by Butler & Tanner Ltd, Frome, Somerset
Colour separations by Radstock Reproductions, Midsomer Norton
Jacket printed by Lawrence Allen Ltd, Weston-super-Mare

ACKNOWLEDGEMENTS

I couldn't have done this book without a great back-up team.

Special thanks are due firstly to Frances Whitaker of Hawkshead, whose televisual eye was such a help when making up the programme content. She could cut out unnecessary complications at the same time as being aware of the material that would inspire viewers.

Thank you also to Caroline Liddell, with whom I have worked so closely over the past year, testing all the recipes. She is a joy to work with, and there was much laughter amid all the professionalism. Caroline went to great lengths seeking perfection for the recipes in the photography with Philip Webb.

Lucy Young (Luc for short!) has worked with me now for six years, efficiently organizing the Aga Workshops. A talented cook herself, her sense of presentation and style is second to none. When we thought we'd got something just right, Luc would add that little last-minute touch to make it extra special. Without her, my working life would be impossible to manage.

I'd also like to say thank you to Nicky Copeland and Frank Phillips of BBC Books for their enthusiasm which has not waned from the very moment we started the book and series.

CONTENTS

INTRODUCTION

I always like to think of my cooking as being Cordon Bleu made easy. I have cut out all the long processes, yet I do not need to rely on packets and convenience foods. I always like to use fresh seasonal ingredients, as I think this is the best and healthiest way in which to feed my family and friends at home.

Cooking has changed throughout the years. Quick-frying or stir-frying are relatively new techniques, and sauces are lighter now – more than anything because of new ingredients like low-fat crème fraîche and fromage frais. These, plus the new yoghurts, have added so much to the flavours of foods and to the general excitement of eating. However, do not worry; before I even put pen to paper on this book, I went round all the big shops in London and major super-markets near and far just to see what was available, and where. To me there is no point in writing a book if the ingredients I use are only available from rarefied sources. Everything I mention and cook with here should be readily available in your local good shops or supermarkets.

My own style of cooking has changed as well. It's become simpler, quicker and healthier. We have always eaten a good, balanced diet at home, but now I've cut down even further on things like fats and flour (although we indulge every now and again). Even my style of entertaining has changed. When I was first married, we were much more formal, and we hardly ever ate in the kitchen. Now we rarely use the dining room, except for entertaining in the winter. In the summer we're generally outside, clustering around the barbecue, or in the kitchen with a couple of friends, having a quick and easy kitchen supper (a stir-fry or a pasta which I would have partially prepared earlier) after a game of tennis, perhaps.

With such a busy life – children popping in and out, a husband and family to feed, books to write, recipes to test and Aga workshops to run – my cooking has also become much more organized. I may not *cook* for the freezer now as I once did, but I certainly cook with the fridge and freezer very firmly in the background. This saves me running to the shops all the time (not so easy when you live out of town). And I have an efficient store-cupboard (see page 13) which I keep stocked with things that are used frequently, such as tinned tomatoes, or the little luxuries that can make such a difference to a dish, or which can form the basis for something delicious when a friend drops in unexpectedly, for example, unusual pasta.

My cooking these days divides itself roughly into two areas: cooking for the family and cooking for guests and parties. For the family I cook what I know they enjoy, so there are familiar elements in the way we eat – meat or fish perhaps four or five times a week, salads and fruit every day, lots of lightly cooked vegetables, rice and pasta. As our daughter Annabel is vegetarian, I often cook a vegetarian dish midweek that we can all enjoy, and I reproduce a number of those recipes here. All these family-type recipes have very generous portions, simply because I have a very hungry family! And, anyway, one should never worry about making too much, because it's nice to have left-overs to enjoy the next day and they often seem to taste better.

When I cook for guests, the same principles must apply – you should always cook what people enjoy or are likely to enjoy, and prior menu planning is very important. A barbecue is now one of my favourite ways of entertaining, as these days simpler foods seem to be preferred, with sausages, kebabs, butterflied lamb, perhaps – even Judy's Thighs (the explanation of which you will find on page 211). This to me is the essence of entertaining: I can be with my guests while the cooking is actually being done and, with any luck, someone else (usually a man) might take over! However, good planning and careful choice of recipes and ingredients will make a more formal entertaining occasion equally successful – from everyone's point of view – and again will enable you to spend more time with your guests rather than being imprisoned in the kitchen while they all have a good time elsewhere. If you have planned the menu well ahead, prepared and cooked a proportion of it in advance, and then follow some of my tips and suggestions, entertaining at home, whether for six or sixty, should be a joy, not a chore.

About This Book

Mary Berry at Home contains my favourite new recipes. It differs in format from all my other books because I've tried to include as much helpful information as I can. I'm always asked questions, such as what can be frozen, what can be prepared ahead, how something can be re-heated, and how to adapt recipes for a fan oven or an Aga. So I answer all those questions in each recipe. And because I have treated the recipes individually, you won't have the bother of checking and adapting some generalized instructions.

The ingredients for each recipe are given in metric and imperial; as always, use one or the other, do not mix them. I then go through all the stages of the recipe in detail in the conventional way, as if cooking with an ordinary cooker, and assuming that you will serve the dish immediately you have finished. Then, in little notes at the end, I give instructions – all of them tried and tested – on various aspects of the preparation and cooking process. I tell you what elements you can prepare ahead; how to cool, cover and store the dish. I then detail how and at what stage you can freeze it. Then I explain how you can thaw and re-heat a frozen or chilled dish. A dish that is very cold – just out of the fridge, say – can take longer to re-heat than one at room temperature. Usually I try to thaw frozen dishes in the fridge overnight, but I specify in the individual recipes.

Because fan or convection ovens cook much faster than most ovens, I've given temperatures and timings for them. Cooking with an Aga is yet another technique, and I give separate instructions for this as well, based on appliances with two ovens as this is what most people have (with the occasional mention of the baking oven in the four-oven Aga). If the recipe is cooked on top of the stove, I have not given Aga instructions specifically. I've been cooking with an Aga for twenty years now, and give classes at my home, so I'm well aware of what people need to know.

I would like you to view this book as a working manual. I have tried to cover every eventuality I can possibly think of, but all cooks change things slightly (although it's best that you do the recipes as printed first of all), and cook in slightly different ways according to their circumstances. If you want to add more basil than I have specified somewhere, for instance, do so and mark it on a yellow Post-it note on the recipe itself. If you do this sort of thing with all the recipes, you'll know the next time that another recipe was 'plenty for ten, not quite enough for twelve'. By adding notes in this way, you make your recipe book into your totally reliable friend.

Ingredients

Ingredients, whether fresh or bought packaged, canned or bottled, form the backbone of all our cooking.

Fresh ingredients – meat, fish, vegetables and fruit – I hardly need to discuss, as we all know how important these foods are in our diet. A knowledgeable and reliable butcher, fishmonger and greengrocer are vital to all of us, and if you are loyal to them they will be loyal to you, ordering or preparing foods especially for you. Your relationship with a supermarket can never be so personal, but many have special counters where trained butchers or fishmongers can help you and cut or trim to your requirements.

With fresh ingredients, seasonality is the most important element. I know we can buy strawberries all year round now, but there is nothing to beat the flavour of the English strawberries of June and July. We are rather spoiled at home in that we grow so much of our own produce and this, I suppose, is why I'm so passionate about food in the right season. Ideally, one should look at the produce available before one plans a specific recipe or menu. (If I were making a fish pie, for instance, I would look at what was in the fishmongers and a good price rather than going out with a firm idea in my head of what I wanted.)

Mary Berry prepares Danish-style Open Sandwiches. Also shown (clockwise from top) are Cranberry and Apricot Fruit Cake, Very Best Chocolate Cake, Anzac Crunch Biscuits and The Very Best Scones. Recipes for all these are in 'Super Sandwiches, Cakes and Baking'.

Many fresh meats and vegetables around now are 'new' in a sense, and these have influenced me in my cooking, especially in the recipes in this book. I remember when chicken was a very special Sunday treat. This was usually roasted whole, and if you wanted it in pieces, you would have to joint it yourself. Now packets of thighs or breasts or drumsticks are readily available with or without skin, and can be cooked in an infinite number of ways. Similarly, packets of seafood or game are now to be found in most good supermarkets. All these can simplify the chopping, preparing and cooking of many wonderful dishes. Packs of mixed mushrooms are also new, and these are very useful, particularly the *big* field mushrooms (I have invented quite a few recipes using these).

However, other ingredients are important too. If you have a well-stocked fridge, freezer and store-cupboard, you can relax in the knowledge that there's always something on hand with which to make a meal for the family or to feed unexpected guests.

FATS AND OILS

There are three oils I use most – sunflower, olive and virgin olive – and which one of those I opt for depends on the finished flavour I want. The sunflower is best if I want a neutral flavour; I'll use the olive oil in something to which its flavour can contribute.

I also use goose fat occasionally. If I've roasted a goose, I keep all that fat rendered out like gold dust, straining it, freezing it, and using it for roasting (potatoes usually). There's nothing like it. Duck fat comes a close second. Chicken fat is useful too, and I keep it in the fridge or freezer. It's most handy when doing the pre-frying of a chicken casserole. I rarely use dripping these days, saving it only for the birds!

But there is nothing like real butter. I wouldn't dream of making an omelette, shortbread or butter biscuits without it. It has its own unique flavour whether eating it 'raw' (unsalted on toast), or cooking with it (salted). I never bother with clarified butter: to prevent butter burning when frying (because of the milk solids), I simply add a little oil.

However, having said all that, when I'm using strong flavours like ginger or cocoa, I wouldn't hesitate to use margarine. The ones I use for cakes are soft baking margarines (such as Stork SB, Blue Band or Flora Baking). These have at least 80 per cent fat in them, and can be used in all-in-one mixtures straight from the fridge. (But in hot summers, if left out, they become too runny, and results have been disappointing.) Never confuse these baking margarines with spreads, which are fats with a quantity of water in them to make them low in calories and which are suitable only for spreading on bread or toast, or perhaps putting in an uncooked fish pâté made from, say, smoked salmon or canned fish.

All fats, apart from oils, can be kept in the freezer.

DAIRY PRODUCE

Because of the children, I am completely incapable these days of judging how much milk I will need – they might drink none, or two pints in one go – so I keep some homogenized milk in the freezer. Milk comes in many grades – Channel Islands, whole, homogenized, semi-skimmed and skimmed (in descending order of fat content). I tend to buy semi-skimmed: it has less than half the fat content of whole milk and, in most cases, it has about the same amount of vitamins. (It contains more calcium than whole milk.)

Yoghurt We used to have only plain full-fat and fruit yoghurts, but now we have a selection: plain low-fat, very low-fat, whole milk, bio, set and Greek yoghurts. Yoghurt is a cultured or fermented milk product, and it is formed by friendly bacteria which can digest the lactose in milk (whether cows', sheep's or goats'). Yoghurts in Britain are also divided into 'stirred' and 'set'. The majority on sale are 'stirred' (fermented in a tank and then transferred to pots); 'set' yoghurts are fermented in the pot. I love these thicker, richer yoghurts, and use them a lot (although they're not low calorie, containing considerably more fat than the dietary type of yoghurt). If I cook with them, actually applying heat, I add a teaspoon of cornflour per 150 g (5 oz) yoghurt to prevent it curdling.

Fromage Frais These used only to be factory-made types like Petit Suisse, but now we have a choice. The name literally means 'fresh cheese', and it originated in France. It has a yoghurt-like texture, and a similar mild, slightly sharp flavour. The fat content varies from less than 1 per cent to about 8 per cent. The low-fat type can be used a lot in cold dishes with added flavourings such as herbs. It's good, too, as a cream-like topping. This is one of the really useful new ingredients available to us, as is Quark, a very similar soft cheese.

Creams Seven main types of fresh cream are available. These are, in a rough ascending order of fat content: half, single, soured, crème fraîche, whipping, double and clotted. Only those with a high fat content can be frozen.

Half cream is light, similar to the 'top of the milk', and contains 12 per cent fat. It cannot be whipped or frozen.

Single cream is usually a pouring cream, not a whipping cream, and contains 18 per cent fat. It cannot be frozen unless included in a dish. If used in cooking, it can separate when boiled, particularly if anything acid, such as lemon juice, is used in the recipe. It's better to use double cream or crème fraîche.

Soured cream is made from single cream, therefore has the same fat content, but has a natural culture added to it to 'sour' it, rather like yoghurt. It cannot be whipped or frozen.

Crème fraîche is one of the new creams available, the name meaning literally 'fresh cream'. It has a slightly fresh, piquant taste, generally contains 30 per cent fat, and cannot be whipped or frozen. It comes in two types: a richer one (a little less rich than double cream) and a lower fat one. Both become runny when heated and need to be reduced if you want a sauce consistency, especially the low-fat one. This low-fat crème fraîche is absolutely ideal either to enrich something, or to make mayonnaise *less* rich, and it adds a nice sharpness and bite. I often use the rich one to de-glaze the meat juices in a pan to make a very quick and simple sauce.

Whipping cream is a higher fat cream (35 per cent) which means that it can be whipped to double its original volume, and can be frozen. I would choose to use this for desserts as it gives so much volume, but not so much fat as double cream. (To make a home-made whipping cream, whip two-thirds of double and one-third of single together.)

Double cream, though, is wonderful stuff, and very versatile. It contains 48 per cent fat, and can be whipped very quickly to a large volume. It can also be frozen. Double cream also comes in thick, extra thick and pouring; they all, however, have the same consistency when you heat them.

Clotted cream is wonderful for cream teas, although it has a fat content of 55 per cent. I don't use it in cooking. It may be frozen.

UHT and *Long-life creams* are available. I don't use these as a general rule, but they are useful on the larder shelf for emergencies.

Always keep yoghurts and fresh creams in the fridge. Follow the sell-by date, and use your nose to check that everything is as it should be.

FLOURS

I buy plain, self-raising, strong flour for bread, wholemeal and wholemeal self-raising. For all-in-one cakes I add baking powder to self-raising, but never be over-generous; a mixture can rise up in the oven, then fall back again. Measure ingredients carefully for baking.

Flours these days are sifted before going into the bag, so I don't bother sifting them at home, except when I'm making a whisked sponge. That *extra* sifting makes sure that no flour lumps appear in the whisked mixture.

SUGARS

I prefer natural sugars. Granulated is used for general sweetening, caster when a finer texture is required. I also have icing, light muscovado and demerara.

If you have a problem storing soft brown sugar in your larder – in other words it becomes a solid block in its bag – you'll find that a clean damp J-cloth in the bag will keep the grains separate.

HERBS

Fresh herbs are now available, cut and as plants, in supermarkets, and we should use them as often as we can for their unique flavours. These little seedlings from the supermarket can be planted in the herb garden (best near the back door or the kitchen) or in a windowbox. Often the perennials don't need the most perfect soil, as they originate in the fairly poor soils of the Mediterranean. Watering is the prime requisite, though; never let them dry out. And give them a good feed every now and again.

I have planted a wonderful traditional herb garden at home, and I find it invaluable throughout the year. When working with Caroline Liddell on this book, she mentioned to me that the tarragon that came from our garden was much more powerful in flavour than the tarragon she could get in her supermarket in central London. I was amazed by this, but have since discovered that growing conditions have a considerable effect on the pungency of this herb. My herbs gently come up in their own time, and all I do is cut them back when needed; the herbs sold throughout the year are forced along in poly-tunnels with a gentle heat, so therefore their flavour will not be as intense as it might be.

Some herbs can be dried – freeze-dried are best – and some can be preserved in oil, particularly basil. In my store-cupboard list (opposite), you'll see the freeze-dried herbs I keep. If you buy basil plants to grow on the windowsill or in the greenhouse cut them back and water and feed them when you have picked every single leaf off them; they will come back with renewed vigour.

STOCKS

Not so much of a 'basic ingredient' as some of the others mentioned here, perhaps, but when you are trying to organize yourself well, stocks are vital. I know we all think we are too busy to spend time on making something like stock, but really the rewards are so great and the outlay and effort so little. We've always got a pot on the go in the Aga at home – it cooks overnight in the simmering oven. I make beef or chicken stock and, occasionally, fish stock (but there are some very good fish stock cubes). The most important thing is a good supply of raw bones, and so you need to be loyal to your butcher and he will keep you the bones you need (when he's cutting breasts off chicken carcasses, or stewing steak from the leg). My butcher keeps poultry carcasses for me, and I either use them immediately or I chop them up small and store them in the freezer. Overleaf are recipes for basic chicken, game and beef stocks. Both can be cooled, sealed and labelled, then kept in the freezer for up to 6 months in 150–300 ml (5–10 fl oz) cream or yoghurt cartons. Thaw at room temperature for 4 hours.

There is a very good vegetable stock on page 58; it's best to make it a day ahead.

The Store-cupboard

I have a cool walk-in larder just to one side of the kitchen which I love. There's so much space there, and I can arrange things on the narrow shelves so that they are easily visible. When it is well stocked, I can often rustle up a meal purely from store-cupboard ingredients.

Perhaps it might be helpful if I were just simply to list what I had in it the day we were writing this piece.

Tins
whole plum tomatoes,
    and chopped
    tomatoes
a few fruits
    (white peaches,
    mandarins, etc.)
anchovies
tuna in oil
olives (green and black)
syrup
treacle
beans (kidney,
    flageolet, baked)

Packets
flour
sugar
salt
bicarbonate of soda
baking powder
various pastas
various rices
dried fruits
    (including apricots
    and cranberries)
coffees
teas
dried porcini
Long-life milk
dry mustard powder

Jars
wild mushrooms
pesto
tomato passata
sun-dried tomatoes
stem ginger
mango chutney
mustards
home-made jams
    and jellies
home-made marmalade
honey

Bottles
oils
vinegars
brandy and rum
vermouth
Cassis
gravy browning
    (it adds wonderful
    colour)
soy sauce
Worcestershire sauce
vanilla and almond
    extracts

Spices
mixed spice
pickling spice
cumin (whole and ground)
coriander (whole and
    ground)
turmeric
nutmeg (whole)
peppercorns
cinnamon (whole and
    ground)
paprika
cayenne
ginger (ground)
cardamom (whole)
curry powder
garam masala
saffron

Herbs (freeze-dried)
basil
tarragon
marjoram
dill tops
bay leaves
rosemary
thyme

Chicken or Game Stock

Makes 2.5 litres (4 pints)

1.5 kg (3 lb) carcasses, trimmings or bones, cooked or uncooked, from chicken or game	3 carrots, chopped
	3 sticks celery, chopped
2–3 halved, unpeeled onions	Bouquet garni (bay leaves, thyme, parsley)
4 litres (7 pints) water	½ teaspoon black peppercorns

Put the bones into a stockpot with the onions and cook until browned.

Pour in the water and bring to the boil, skimming off any scum that forms on the surface. Add the remaining vegetables, and the bouquet garni and peppercorns. Half cover with a pan lid and simmer for 2½–3 hours, or 5 hours if the bones are uncooked.

Strain the contents of the pan into a large bowl, cool, skim, then decant into pots for freezing, or for use in a soup or sauce. When cold, scrape the set fat off the surface – much easier than earlier skimming.

Beef Stock

Makes 1.75 litres (3 pints)

2 kg (4 lb) beef marrow bones, sawn in 6 cm (2½ in) pieces	4 litres (7 pints) water
2–3 onions, coarsely chopped	Bouquet garni (bay leaves, thyme, parsley)
2–3 carrots, coarsely chopped	½ teaspoon black peppercorns
2–3 sticks celery, coarsely chopped	

You will need a large roasting tin and a large pan or stockpot.

Pre-heat the oven to 230°c/450°f/gas 8.

Put the bones in a roasting tin and roast for 30 minutes. Add the chopped vegetables and turn them in the fat in the tin. Return the bones and vegetables to the oven to roast for a further 30 minutes.

Tip the contents of the roasting tin into a large pan or stockpot then pour in the water and bring to the boil skimming off any scum that forms on the surface. Add the herbs and peppercorns then leave to simmer very gently for 6–8 hours.

Strain the contents of the pan into a large bowl, cool, skim, then decant into pots for freezing, or for use in a soup or sauce. When cold, scrape the set fat off the surface – much easier than earlier skimming.

Using Your Freezer

I like to think I'm always ready with something home-made to offer if people appear at short notice. And this is where the freezer comes in. Nowadays when so many women go out to work, it's good to know you have something in stock. For instance, I often have certain foods in a box in the freezer – something like French bread slices spread with Boursin then grated Cheddar (see page 220) – which I can put in the oven to have with drinks. I also have home-made biscuits ready prepared, but I never keep these in a tin as the family would eat them: I keep them in the freezer and judiciously dole them out! They only need refreshing in the oven, or cut sections of the mixture just need a brief baking in the oven from frozen.

Years ago I worked for *Home and Freezer Digest*, then the bible of the new domestic technique of freezing. Today freezing is very much a fixed part of our lives, and we all recognize it as the very best method of preservation – and the very best way of ensuring quick, fresh and easy meals. I am not going to go into details about how to freeze as there are many excellent books on the market, but a basic principle must always be, if you take something perfect and freeze it correctly then that's the way it will come out; by the same token, if you freeze something that's a little tatty, it will come out like that too.

Most foods freeze, but some just *won't*. Salads do not freeze successfully, as most salad vegetables contain too much water. Cooked vegetables don't freeze well for the same reason (although when freezing most green vegetables, an initial quick blanching in boiling water is recommended). Among other foods that will not freeze are hard-boiled eggs (they go leathery), mayonnaise (it curdles) and low-fat creams (they separate out).

I freeze vegetables and fruits when they are in season, and when I have a surplus, either from the garden or when they are on offer in the local shops or supermarket. I love the freedom this gives me: broad beans fresh from the freezer six months after their all-too-brief season in June; home-grown July raspberries (a fruit that freezes very well indeed) with yoghurt as a winter breakfast, or with ice-cream as the finale to a winter supper. I have emphasized my love of eating in season, but when it's out of the freezer, it's all right; I just wouldn't buy imported green beans or raspberries in the winter.

You can also freeze newly caught fresh fish: a whole salmon, for instance, gutted and well wrapped, I will keep for up to a year. Usually, though, I buy fish which has already been frozen and store it in the freezer until needed. Game will keep well in the freezer too – a hung pheasant for a year. The bigger the piece of meat, the better it will keep (but do not freeze salted or smoked meat for long.)

There are a large number of basics which I freeze, just in case. I always have a little butter in the freezer, as well as a couple of loaves of bread, some Cheddar cheese, and homogenized milk. I freeze orange juice in cartons for the same reason as I do milk (slightly more long-term than the larder shelf). Cream is handy in the freezer as well. Remember, though, that its condition before freezing is the prime consideration: if a clotted cream is solid when you put it in the freezer, it will come out that way too. Stocks are one of the things I could not do without in the freezer. With a good tasty stock there, you have the basis for a well-flavoured soup, sauce, risotto or any number of dishes. Store stock in the quantities you think you will make most use of: in 300 ml (10 fl oz) containers for a sauce or gravy, for instance, or larger containers for soups. The soups themselves freeze well too.

It's amazing the things I have discovered you can freeze. I have actually evolved recipes for two fruit salads that can be frozen; specific fruits – cut in larger chunks – are still crisp when they thaw, and they don't discolour. I also freeze fresh ginger: well wrapped, it comes out in perfect condition, infinitely preferable to those shrivelled nuggets I used to find in the larder or fridge. And I also freeze nuts because of their high oil content: these can go rancid if left in their packets even in a cool larder.

Many cooked dishes freeze well. Those that don't are fairly obvious. Cooked vegetables I've mentioned already, and pasta often absorbs more liquid in the freezer; pies with potato toppings don't freeze very successfully either. I've outlined throughout the book which individual dishes can be frozen, and at what stage of their preparation this will be best.

So far as freezing containers are concerned, you can freeze a lasagne or fish pie in the cooking dish, then re-heat and serve, all from the same dish. Or you can line the dish with foil, fill it with the cooked food and freeze until solid. You then remove the dish from the freezer, allow it to thaw enough to slip the block of foil-wrapped food out, and then re-wrap and re-freeze. When you want to thaw and re-heat it, you can slip the block of food (out of the foil, of course) back into the same dish. If you're doing this with tins – spring-form tins, for example – line them with clingfilm before putting something in them to freeze; I don't like the metallic taste you can otherwise get, and anyway some fruits and other ingredients react with metal.

Another idea is to use large yoghurt pots, ice-cream containers and plastic boxes. These are handy for smaller quantities: a small yoghurt container topped with clingfilm is ideal for left-over sauce or gravy (I always save these; I've put so much effort into them, why should I waste them?). Don't fill the boxes too full, because frozen liquid expands, and don't put a casserole, say, into a container that's too big, as it will take up unnecessary space in the freezer. A really useful tip from Caroline Liddell, who has helped me enormously with this book, is to freeze stocks or soups in those 1–2 litre (1¾–3½ pint) mineral water plastic bottles; you can stack them neatly in your freezer then, to get the stock or soup out when thawed, simply cut off the top of the plastic bottle.

Always keep cooked foods with other cooked foods in the freezer, and uncooked foods with uncooked foods. Label the packets or containers very well. One of the girls I used to share a flat with before I was married had a box, basket or shelf in the freezer which she kept for things she knew needed to be used up quickly – that half of fish pie, those two portions of casserole, two sausages, or three slices of cake. They're more accessible and easier to remember kept there than in the bulk of the freezer. I work to this principle still, all these years later, and it's amazing how often I can come up with something for supper from this section of the freezer alone.

I never now cook specifically for the freezer, as we all used to do. But while I'm cooking for one meal – if friends are coming for supper, say – I'll cook double the quantity and freeze half for another meal I've arranged for the future (when I expect different guests, of course!). The container should be well marked; also add the date on which you want to use it. I then mark in my diary that I need to take the food out of the freezer the day before to allow it to defrost. It's a wonderful feeling having at least one part of a future party organized well in advance.

One of the questions I'm always asked is whether one can re-freeze foods. You can do with certain things, but only if they are absolutely fresh, and only you can know this. If you've thawed best-quality frozen mince, then cooked it into a moussaka or lasagne, then of course you can freeze it. However, if a dish were to contain cooked frozen peas, they wouldn't come out so well the second time around. And if you are selling home-made cakes at a school fête or bazaar, it's a good idea to tell people if they have been frozen.

Equipment

Apart from the fridge and freezer, which should be bought in accordance with the needs of your family, the other large piece of equipment needed for trouble-free family cooking and entertaining is a good cooker. Certain other gadgets are useful as well.

Mushroom and Goats' Cheese Tiers from 'To Begin With'
are prepared for baking.

COOKERS

There are many different types of cooker – electric, gas, conventional, fan or convection and Agas – and all vary. Even two of the same make can perform differently. Years ago I worked for the Electricity Board, and the standard thing then was to send people like me out to test the cookers once they had been installed. The recipe we used was a Victoria sandwich. Once I tested two ovens of the same make that had been delivered the same week to two houses in the same street. To get exactly the right colour on one of the sponges, I had to cook it for 8 minutes longer than the other!

It's for this reason that I always say, 'cook it for *about* so many minutes'. Mediterranean Tuna en Croûte may take 10 minutes longer in *your* oven, so note this on a Post-it note on the recipe, so that you remember next time. My recipes work for me, and will for you, but there may be just a few variants because of the nature of your particular oven.

Every instruction manual will note that fan or convection ovens are, as a general rule, about 20–25 per cent hotter than a conventional oven; because the air is circulating, the cooking will also be faster. In the recipes here, I have given cooking times for a conventional oven in the recipe method, but with notes at the end about what to do in a fan oven. Often with a fan oven you can start a recipe from cold, as it heats up so quickly, so for recipes with a cooking time longer than 30 minutes, I have suggested there is no need to pre-heat the fan oven. I also find that I have to lower the temperature and cover the food with foil to prevent it over-browning.

I have also given instructions for cooking in Agas. This only involves the oven – the roasting and simmering oven – as cooking on top of an Aga is just the same principle as an electric, gas or halogen hob. One really useful tip concerns how to lower the heat of the roasting oven for baking: simply slot in the cold plain shelf provided with the Aga above the food. This will lower the temperature below the shelf to a baking temperature for 20 minutes or so.

Microwave ovens vary too, in wattage, and in what they can do. But most now have a turntable and a browning element, so you should consult your own handbook for more specific instructions. Microwaves are very useful for re-heating, thawing, melting and many other kitchen tasks.

You can buy oven thermometers to check the heat of your oven. Another recommendation is that you make sure you have the right pans and cooking pots for your particular cooker. And, a tip which applies to all cookers, you must remember that if you use a different dish to the type recommended in the recipe, then the timing and sometimes even the result will be different. Food in a shallow 1.75 litre (3 pint) dish will take much less time to cook than food in a deep dish of the same volume. (To be honest, I always prefer to cook in shallower dishes. There's more surface area to be crisped and browned nicely, and more topping to be shared!) The more foods you put in an oven to cook at the same time, the longer they will take, as the temperature of the oven is reduced.

Electric Aids in the Kitchen

Whatever help you have in the kitchen in the way of machinery, you need to have it easily available. I'm lucky as I have a rise and fall shelf that I can tuck away in a cupboard for my food processor. I keep my large free-standing mixer on a shelf in the larder beside my scales; as I weigh things out, I can put them straight into the mixer.

My food processor I use a lot, and I bought the largest one I could find. In it I do all the jobs like chopping nuts or vegetables, cutting meat for a pâté, and chopping herbs (the last of the parsley when the plant is finished, all chopped to go into the freezer). Processors always work better with fairly dry foods, whereas blenders work best with a lot of liquid. So when making a puréed soup in a processor, strain off all the liquid first and purée the vegetables alone; the results will be so much more satisfactory.

Processors are not suitable for making meringues – far better to use a hand or electric whisk. You can make pastry and bread in the processor, but I usually prefer to do that in my mixer, as the processor can over-process.

Hand mixers are invaluable – they're portable, quick and, best of all, quiet!

Knives

Good sharp knives are absolutely essential, and you should sharpen them every three months or so. I got quite worried recently when I couldn't seem to get the same sharpness on my knives. (I sharpen them myself, having been taught how to do it properly by my butcher.) It was only when I looked at my sharpening steel that I realized what was wrong. That steel had been a wedding present, and as I have been married for 28 or so years, it had worn completely smooth!

Pans and Dishes

You will know what you need for family and entertaining purposes, and what sort of pans to buy to suit your cooker. A set of good pans, in different sizes and with lids, is a necessity for every cook. If these can be non-stick, so much the better, as non-stick surfaces are so good now. I particularly couldn't operate without my large lidded preserving pan which I use for both stocks and for home-made jams and jellies. Another vital thing in my kitchen is a really big non-stick frying pan with deep sides and a lid; I use this for stir-fries, and for browning meat for casseroles.

I have shallow baking dishes for lasagne; I could use a roasting tin, but it's nicer to bring a proper dish to the table. And I have deeper, sturdy casseroles. Mixing bowls are useful in all sizes, and I couldn't do without a couple of reliable measuring jugs.

As far as measuring is concerned, I much prefer a scale with weights at one side and the scale pan on the other. I have found that these are much more accurate for small amounts than the spring-balance ones or those battery ones.

You can acquire a certain amount of confidence if you are truly familiar with the dishes at your disposal. If your lasagne dish holds more than enough for your hungry family of four, then you can happily make the same up for six guests! I have one particular bowl that can be used for a pudding or a salad, and I'll always try to think up something to put in it because not only does it hold a lot, but it also looks good.

LIFT-OFF

This graphite paper used to be called 'magic paper', and I *do* think it is magic. It replaces silicone paper and is wonderful because you can use it again and again. It's very thick gauge, you put it on your baking tray, use it in the oven, then wash and store until the next time. I like recycling things rather than throwing them away, and Lift-Off seems to last endlessly – it's guaranteed for three years, but I have been using the same pieces for about twelve! (See mail-order information on page 284.)

Health and Safety

We're all becoming much more aware of health and safety in the kitchen. Cleanliness is very important, and great boons nowadays are the dishwasher and washing machine. The hot cycles on both of these can efficiently clean plates and cloths respectively. It's a good idea to have separate chopping boards in the kitchen for cooked and uncooked meats; this avoids cross contamination, particularly when cutting something like chicken.

One of my firmest rules in the kitchen is never to leave anything out overnight. Foods are always placed in the fridge. After all, our kitchens are very much warmer now than in our grandmothers' days; we have central heating, and very much more efficient draught-proofing. This is particularly important when you're cooking for a big party. If you've got a big pan of chicken in a sauce, it's imperative to cool the chicken quickly by sitting the covered pan in cold water, and then put it in the fridge. It's so easy for a big bulk of food to go off.

Remember, too, that children and the elderly, pregnant women and anyone in ill-health should avoid recipes that contain raw eggs.

Menu Planning

When planning a menu, whether for a lunch or dinner or a barbecue, for a buffet or drinks party, there are several points to be taken into consideration. First of all, try to organize things as far in advance as possible. Use your freezer by pre-preparing, perhaps even totally pre-cooking, parts of a meal. If you know that certain elements of the menu just need to be thawed the day before your party, you'll feel very much more relaxed. Make lists of what needs to be done, get someone to help you with some of the chores, and have the shopping, cleaning and preparation done well in advance.

It's always nice to try new things, but perhaps you should try them out on the family first – just in case! If you have a speciality, however, and people obviously enjoy eating it, then do it often. At Christmas time I always serve open sandwiches for meals following

Chilled Celebration Salmon with Fresh Herb Sauce, from 'Buffets and Large Parties', makes a striking centrepiece for a party meal.

the big day; people have had so much to eat that smaller and more elegant offerings seem to be just the thing, and everyone can help themselves. There are certain soups, too, that I always make if a few of us are going to a rugby match and I am organizing a picnic lunch; everyone seems to like them, and they're hot and satisfying. I even think their familiarity is an added bonus!

You also have to consider the type of meal you are contemplating. Some of us can push the boat out occasionally and not worry about how expensive basic ingredients are, while many are desperate to keep to a budget. It's still possible, however, to entertain friends and eat well if you have very little money! Some of the recipes to which my assistant Luc has introduced me are very clear indicators of that. Luc has great style in her cooking, and I have included many of her recipes and ideas.

When you are choosing the actual recipes to cook for the meal, there are a few 'rules'. If the first course is fishy, you don't want to have fish as a main course. If you have pastry in the first course, you should not offer a pastry dessert. Cheese should not appear in both the savoury courses, particularly if you were thinking of offering a cheeseboard as well. Cream, too, should appear in one of the courses only. Think about texture as well. If you have a crunchy salad to begin with, offer something smoother later on; but a smooth creamy soup, followed by a savoury mousse, then a creamy pudding is not a good idea! Colour is also important. After all, we *see* the food first.

You also have to think about the work involved. If you have a lot to do at the last minute for one course – the main course, say – make sure that there is nothing left to be done on the first and final courses. I nearly always have a cold first course that I can arrange on individual plates. These I stack in the fridge, ready to go. I would follow that with a hot main course which, depending on the occasion and on numbers, I would either leave in the kitchen on a side table for people to help themselves, or I would help them to the meat or fish, and vegetables would be handed around.

In most cases, you will know what your guests will eat, and I always keep a note of special likes and dislikes. (My brother loves treacle suet pudding, for instance, which he only has on his birthday at home. He gets it when he comes to me!) I think you should avoid certain types of food if you're not sure of guests' tastes. Be wary of serving fish or shellfish; kidneys and other offal are also debatable, as many people just don't like the idea, let alone the flavour. If I were very unsure about someone's taste, and was serving something fishy, I think I would have a piece of melon in the background, already prepared.

So far as choice is concerned, offer more than one thing only in vegetable accompaniments and at the dessert stage, at a lunch or dinner party. (Barbecues and buffets are slightly different. I usually have no choice for a first course, unless unsure of taste (see above), and none for the main course. I would offer at least two vegetables, both very much in season – one prepared in a different way and one last-minute idea – along with potatoes. I nearly always offer two puddings, one rather special and rich, and the other, one of my fruit salads.

Finally, I think it's best not to over-feed one's guests. Try to balance the meal so that your guests are still hungry after the first course – this must never be too substantial. It's far better too to offer a helping that's on the small side at first, which allows guests to have seconds if they want. This applies particularly to puddings, especially rich ones; offer a tiny slice or helping to begin with. No one's going to thank you if they've been to supper on Saturday night and get up regretting it on the Sunday morning. Let the choice be theirs.

Food for a Crowd

It's always difficult to think in terms of exact quantities when cooking for a crowd. The more people you have, often the less they will eat (why that should be so, I just don't know), and sometimes a quartet of teenagers can demolish enough to feed ten people!

The time of day is important, too. If the party is held after work, say, your guests could be starving; if it is a post-Christmas do, appetites could be a little jaded after all the festivities.

These lists below offer only the most general guidelines.

Sandwiches

1 large sandwich loaf *thin cut*	about 24 slices
1 large sandwich loaf *medium cut*	about 20 slices
1 large sandwich loaf *thick cut*	about 16 slices
1 long French loaf cuts into	about 20 slices

Butter: About 100 g (4 oz) per large sandwich loaf or 12 bread rolls. (Always have it soft and spreadable – it goes further!)

Sandwich Fillings per 10 rounds of 1 large medium-cut sandwich loaf

Cheese and chutney	300 g (10 oz) grated cheese, plus 4 tablespoons chutney.
Salmon	450 g (1 lb) canned salmon, drained and flaked then mixed with mayonnaise.
Egg	6 chopped hard-boiled eggs bound with mayonnaise.
Meat	350 g (12 oz) thinly sliced meat with salad.
Cucumber	1 cucumber, thinly sliced.

Liquids

Milk for tea	600 ml (1 pint) per 20 cups.
Milk for coffee	900 ml (1½ pints) per 20 cups.
Cream for fruit salads	600 ml (1 pint) per about 12 portions.
Wine/champagne	6 glasses per bottle.

Savoury Dishes per person

Salted nuts	15 g (½ oz).	Salmon	100–125 g (4–5 oz).
Potato crisps	25 g (1 oz).	Rice, uncooked	40–50 g (1½–2 oz).
Meat for casseroles	175 g (6 oz).	Pasta, uncooked	75–100 g (3–4 oz).
Joint with bone	175–225 g (6–8 oz).	Soup	600 ml (1 pint) will
Joint without bone	100–175 g (4–6 oz).		serve 3 people.
Steak	175 g (6 oz).		

Sweet Dishes per person

Strawberries	100 g (4 oz).
Raspberries	75–100 g (3–4 oz).
Meringues	6 egg whites and 350 g (12 oz) caster sugar will make about 30 small meringues.
Cakes	A 25 cm (10 in) sponge will serve 16 people.

Food and Drinks per person at parties

Drinks parties	5–6 savoury items, plus nuts and crisp	3–4 drinks.
Finger buffets	8–10 items (a couple of them sweet)	3–4 drinks.
Fork buffet	1 first course, 1 main course with accompaniments (vegetables, salads, etc), and 2 desserts and/or cheese.	

To Begin With

TO BEGIN WITH

Choosing the right dish to begin with, whether the meal is for guests or for the family, is important. People will be hungry, so you want to satisfy that hunger – but not too much, or they won't have room for the rest of the meal. You also want to satisfy their eyes, because if the first thing you offer them looks inviting on the plate as well, of course, as tasting special, the meal is off to a good start.

Some of these recipes can be prepared at least a few hours ahead of the meal, but most can be prepared and/or cooked and stored in the fridge for as long as three days, while a number can be cooked a couple of weeks in advance and frozen. The most important thing to remember in these cases is to allow time once the foods are out of fridge or freezer for them to come to room temperature or to thaw, whichever is relevant.

There's a real sense of getting ahead with soups, and most of those here can be made in advance and freeze well. We often think we're too busy these days, but a good, flavourful, home-made stock doesn't take up much actual work time, and it does make all the difference to a soup, giving such depth of flavour. It is not difficult or expensive to coax flavour from beef, veal or chicken bones, vegetables, herbs and spices (see pages 14 and 58). Once a soup is cooked, cool it quickly and freeze it – perfect. Don't add any garnishes at this stage: things like cream should be added only when the soup is re-heating (although you can freeze your croûtons separately so they are ready and waiting). Another soup hint is that most vegetable soups should not be kept hot for too long; they can lose their colour, and several of them will lose their fresh taste. And, most importantly, don't ever make a *small* amount of soup. If there's some left, who cares? Enjoy it the next day!

PREVIOUS PAGE
Duck Terrine with Orange Confit
(page 28).

The Duck Terrine I think is to die for! I first tasted the original recipe when having supper with great friends of my mother in her village. I've made a few amendments since, but I owe the inspiration to Graham. The Filo Purses Stuffed with Spinach, Mushrooms and Goats' Cheese were inspired by something I tasted when having lunch in a five-star London hotel with a girlfriend. I came straight home and copied the idea. I still find it amazing that one layer of filo will do, instead of the usual three or four. The Swiss Cheese and Chives Soufflé Tarts, the other filo pastry recipe, look wonderful and taste equally delicious. Pâtés are a good standby, and the Three-fish Pâté is made purely from store-cupboard ingredients – so easy, and so tasty.

I like to invent recipes that make use of what is newly available, and the Bruschetta Marinara uses the handy packs of mixed seafood some of the supermarkets are now offering. The same thing is true of the two mushroom dishes. I love the huge, flat mushrooms you can now buy; they make a handy 'plate' for other ingredients. These individual 'portions' of mushrooms would also look good on a platter on a buffet table.

With an authentic Gravadlax recipe, a stir-fry chicken liver salad, and rolls to accompany your starters, I think you have quite a considerable – and delicious – selection to choose from. And don't forget, two of these starter dishes could quite happily provide a light lunch or supper – a soup and bread, followed perhaps by a filo dish or a mushroom dish.

This sign indicates recipes that are suitable
for vegetarians, but please note that some of them
include dairy products.

Duck Terrine with Orange Confit

SERVES 8–10 AS A FIRST COURSE OR 6–8 AS A MAIN COURSE

An unusual and delicious combination of duck, pork, orange and pistachio nuts that is straightforward to make, this dish can be prepared several days ahead and kept in the fridge with the orange confit. We also tested this with ten stewed, stoned prunes cooked in orange juice instead of the pistachio nuts. Keeping in the fridge is preferable to freezing, which is only satisfactory short-term for most pâtés and terrines.

3 large bay leaves	Grated rind and juice of 1 large
About 8 long, thin slices of streaky	orange
bacon, rinded	2 tablespoons dry vermouth or
1 large garlic clove, chopped	white wine
450 g (1 lb) belly pork, rinded and	150 g (5 oz) fresh white
cut in pieces	breadcrumbs
About 1½ teaspoons salt	100 g (4 oz) shelled pistachio nuts
Freshly ground black pepper	2 large duck breasts

You will need a non-stick loaf tin 23 × 11.5 cm (9 × 4½ in), greased.

Pre-heat the oven to 200°C/400°F/gas 6.

Lay the bay leaves down the centre of the loaf tin. With the flat side of a kitchen knife, spread and stretch out each bacon slice thinly on a board, then arrange the slices so they overlap across the length of the loaf tin, on top of the bay leaves. Leave any surplus bacon hanging over the edge of the tin. This can be folded in over the meat mixture when the tin is full. Cut a bacon slice into 3 to line each short end of the tin.

Process the garlic briefly, then add the pork pieces and process for a further 20 seconds. Do this in batches if necessary. Add the salt, a generous amount of pepper, the orange rind and juice, vermouth or wine and breadcrumbs. Process again, just enough to mix together thoroughly. Press half the mixture into the lined tin, level with the back of a spoon then sprinkle in half the pistachio nuts. Skin the duck breasts, reserving the skin, then cut the meat in 5 mm (¼ in) strips down the length of the breasts and arrange these lengthways in the tin. Season well with salt and pepper before sprinkling in the remaining nuts. Press the remaining meat mixture on top, level, and fold the bacon strips in over the meat. Cover the meat with the skins from the duck breasts to keep the terrine moist, cover with foil, then put the tin in a small roasting tin on the centre shelf of the oven. Carefully pour in sufficient boiling water to come half-way up the side of the loaf tin. Bake for 1¼ hours, then remove the foil and discard the duck skin. To make sure the terrine is cooked, insert a thin skewer in the centre. When the skewer is removed the juices should flow clear; if not, bake for a further 15 minutes. Remove the loaf tin from the water bath and leave to cool for about 2 hours.

When the terrine is cold cover the surface with a sheet of freezer film and put a matching size loaf tin on top. Put weights inside the second loaf tin, put the whole thing in a dish to catch any juices, then transfer to the fridge for 24–48 hours to become firm.

To turn out the terrine, run a knife around the edge to loosen the meat from the sides of the tin. Position a serving plate on top and invert so the tin can be lifted free of the terrine. Only dip the tin in hot water if the terrine will not come out of the tin.

To prepare ahead: *The covered, weighted terrine can be kept in the fridge for up to 1 week.*

To freeze: *Not recommended, but if you must 2 weeks only.*

To cook in a fan oven: *Do not pre-heat oven. Put the small roasting tin in the oven and pour in sufficient boiling water to come half-way up the side of the tin. Bake at 190°C for about 1¼ hours; discard the duck skin and check if done; if not bake for a further 10 minutes or until the terrine is cooked.*

To cook in the Aga: *Cook the terrine for 1¼ hours in the roasting tin half-filled with boiling water on the grid shelf on the floor of the roasting oven with the cold plain shelf on the second set of runners. The juices should run clear when the centre of the meat mixture is pierced with a skewer.*

Orange Confit

FILLS A 500 ML (17 FL OZ) JAR

3 medium-sized seedless oranges	225 g (8 oz) sugar
	4 cloves
85 ml (3 fl oz) white wine or cider vinegar	1 teaspoon allspice berries
	7.5 cm (3 in) cinnamon stick

Scrub the oranges with a brush in warm, soapy water. Using a very sharp knife, slice each one into 5 mm (¼ in) slices, discarding the ends. Lay the slices flat in a medium-sized pan and add just sufficient cold water to cover. Bring to simmering point, then cover and continue to cook very gently for about 1 hour or until the rind is tender. Use a draining spoon to transfer the slices to a bowl, then discard the liquid left in the pan.

Measure the vinegar, sugar and spices into the same pan and warm over a low heat until the sugar has dissolved. Return the orange slices to the pan and bring to the boil. Tilt a lid over the top of the pan and boil gently until the juices take on a slightly caramelized appearance and the orange slices are translucent. Spoon into a hot, clean preserving jar. Cover and leave to cool. Seal, label and keep in the fridge for several weeks before using.

To cook in the Aga: *Put the sliced oranges in a pan with just sufficient water to cover. Bring to simmering point then cover and transfer to the floor of the simmering oven for about 1 hour or until the rind is tender. Cook the slices in the spiced vinegar, uncovered, on the floor of the simmering oven for about 30 minutes. Use a draining spoon to transfer the orange slices to a preserving jar. Boil the remaining pan juices for about 5–10 minutes or until the juice has become syrupy, then pour over the fruit. There should be just sufficient liquid to cover the fruit.*

Warm Chicken Liver Salad with Crisply Fried Sage Leaves

SERVES 6 AS A FIRST COURSE OR 4 FOR A LIGHT LUNCH

If you can, get chicken livers from the butcher as they are easier to handle. If not, frozen chicken livers are available in most supermarkets in 250 g tubs. Give these plenty of time to thaw out; overnight in the fridge is best. Drain and dry the livers thoroughly before you fry them, so they can then be seared briefly in a very hot pan and emerge tinged pink and tender.

450 g (1 lb) chicken livers
½ crisp lettuce or 2 small round lettuces
1 bunch of watercress
3 tablespoons sunflower oil
About 12 large sage leaves
175 g (6 oz) thick slices of streaky bacon, rinded and cut into thin strips
3 × 1 cm (½ in) thick slices wholemeal bread, crusts removed and cubed

4 tablespoons French Dressing (see page 129) made with wholegrain mustard
25 g (1 oz) butter
1 tablespoon balsamic vinegar
Salt and freshly ground black pepper

Put the chicken livers to drain in a sieve over a bowl. Using a pair of kitchen scissors, cut the larger pieces of liver in half and remove any stringy bits. Transfer the prepared livers to a double thickness of kitchen paper to absorb any remaining juices.

Tear the lettuce leaves into pieces and discard any large watercress stalks. Divide the leaves between 6 serving plates, cover with clingfilm and chill in the fridge until ready to serve.

Heat the oil in a large frying-pan until very hot. Fry a few sage leaves at a time for a few seconds only. The leaves should turn a darker green, but not brown. Lift them carefully from the pan with a fork and leave aside to drain on kitchen paper. Now add the bacon strips to the pan, and when they start to brown, stir in the bread cubes. Fry together until crisp and brown, then drain on kitchen paper.

Just before serving, remove the salads from the fridge, uncover and spoon a little French dressing over each portion. Re-heat the oil in the pan and let it get very hot before adding the butter. As soon as the foam subsides, put the chicken livers into the pan. Sauté for up to 3 minutes over a high heat, then pull the pan aside, add the vinegar and season with salt and pepper. Swirl the livers in the pan juices, then spoon the contents of the pan over the salads. Quickly sprinkle with the bacon and croûtons and top with the fried sage leaves. Serve immediately.

To prepare ahead: *Fry the sage leaves, drain and leave aside. Fry the bacon strips and bread cubes. At this stage the recipe can be left for up to 6 hours.*

To freeze: *Not suitable, except that you can use croûtons that you have frozen earlier. Just add them to the pan for 1–2 minutes once the bacon has become crisp.*

Ⓥ
Mushroom and Goats' Cheese Tiers

SERVES 6 AS A STARTER OR 3 AS A MAIN COURSE

A delicious, highly adaptable recipe that goes down well with vegetarians. In the recipe it is served hot, but it is also very successful served at room temperature, sprinkled with a little balsamic vinegar. Smaller, cup mushrooms and medium-sized tomatoes served this way make a well-behaved and good-looking dish for a summer buffet.

6 × 13 cm (5 in) flat mushrooms	*Salt and freshly ground black*
2 tablespoons olive oil, plus extra	*pepper*
for brushing	*2 beefsteak tomatoes*
2 medium onions, thinly sliced	*1 × 150 g tub fresh soft goats'*
2 tablespoons pesto	*cheese*

To garnish
A little mild paprika

To serve
Crusty bread

Pre-heat the oven to 200°c/400°f/gas 6. Select a shallow baking dish just the right size to contain the mushrooms in a single layer.

Twist the central stalks from the mushrooms and reserve. Wipe the caps with kitchen paper then lightly brush the tops of the mushrooms with oil. Brush the base of the baking dish with oil and arrange the mushrooms, gill-side up, in the dish.

Heat the 2 tablespoons oil in a large frying-pan. Fry the onions over a moderate heat, stirring frequently, for 10 minutes until they are beginning to soften and brown. Stir in the chopped mushroom stalks and cook for a further 2 minutes. Remove the pan from the heat and stir in the pesto. Taste and season with salt and pepper if necessary. Spoon an equal quantity of onion mixture into each mushroom. Cut a thin slice from the stem and base of each tomato and discard. Slice each one into 3 thick slices, put one on top of each mushroom and season again.

If the cheese is firm enough, slice it into 6 and lay the slices on top of the tomato. If very soft, spoon a little on top of each tomato then flatten and spread it slightly with a knife. Sprinkle each cheese-topped mushroom with a little paprika. Cover the dish with foil. Bake for 10 minutes, then uncover and bake for a further 15–20 minute until piping hot. To serve, lift the mushrooms from the dish with the aid of a fish slice and eat them with hot crusty bread to mop up any juices.

To prepare ahead: *The foil-covered dish of prepared mushrooms can be stored in the fridge for up to 24 hours before baking.*

To cook: *Cook following the recipe above.*

To freeze: *Not suitable.*

To cook in a fan oven: *Pre-heat the oven to 190°c. Bake for 10 minutes, remove the foil covering and bake for another 10 minutes.*

To cook in the Aga: *Cover loosely with foil, then bake on the grid shelf on the floor of the roasting oven for about 15 minutes, removing the foil for the last 5 minutes.*

Ⓥ
Designer Mushrooms on Field Mushrooms

SERVES 4

This makes a delicious and unusual starter and is ideal as a supper dish for vegetarians. Use this recipe to take full advantage of some of the wonderful mixtures of mushrooms some supermarkets are selling in a single pack.

4 × 10 cm (4 in) diameter flat
    mushrooms
About 2 tablespoons olive oil
Salt and freshly ground black
    pepper
15 g (½ oz) butter
1 shallot, finely chopped
1 garlic clove, finely chopped
100 g (4 oz) shiitake mushrooms,
    sliced

100 g (4 oz) oyster mushrooms,
    sliced
100 g (4 oz) chestnut mushrooms,
    quartered
1 × 200 ml carton crème
    fraîche
Juice of ½ lemon
1 tablespoon chopped fresh
    parsley

To serve
Honey-glazed Walnut Bread
(see page 236)

You will need a shallow ovenproof baking dish, just large enough to hold the mushrooms in a single layer.

Pre-heat the oven to 180°C/350°F/gas 4.

Twist the central stalks from the flat mushrooms, slice the stalks and reserve. Wipe the caps with kitchen paper. Meanwhile, heat the olive oil in a frying-pan. Fry the mushrooms gill-side down for 5 minutes, turning them over half-way through the cooking time. Place them in the baking dish, season with salt and pepper, then put in the oven. Put the plates at the bottom of the oven at the same time to keep warm. Add the butter to the pan, stir in the shallot and cook over a moderate heat for 3 minutes or until the shallot begins to soften and colour. Add the garlic and continue cooking for 1 minute. Add the shiitake, oyster and chestnut mushrooms, the sliced mushroom stalks then the crème fraîche. Turn down the heat to low and cook gently for about 5 minutes, then uncover and continue to cook until the mushrooms are tender and the sauce has reduced to a nice coating consistency. Add the lemon juice and season to taste with salt and pepper. Remove the pan from the heat. Spoon an equal amount of the mushrooms and sauce over each flat mushroom, sprinkle with parsley and serve with toasted walnut bread or good brown bread.

To prepare ahead: *Arrange the fried large mushrooms on a flat baking dish, cover and put in the fridge. Cook the other mushrooms completely, cover and put in the fridge. Keep for up to 24 hours.*

To freeze: *Not suitable.*

To re-heat: *Pile the mushrooms in cream on to the large mushrooms, stirring in any juice that might have run out of the large mushrooms. Re-heat for about 10 minutes in a pre-heated oven at 220°C/425°F/gas 7. Sprinkle with the parsley.*

To cook in the Aga: *Prepare following the recipe above, then re-heat in the roasting oven for about 10 minutes. Serve sprinkled with parsley.*

ⓥ
Swiss Cheese and Chive Soufflé Tarts

Makes 8

A lovely light starter, this is a cheese soufflé baked in a thin, filo pastry tart shell. This recipe has proved to be remarkably adaptable: crisp bacon pieces, chopped sautéed mushrooms, or sautéed spinach can be put in the base of the tarts before the soufflé filling goes in if a slightly more substantial dish is wanted. As they stand, the tarts can be baked in mini-muffin tins to make delicious bites to serve with drinks. There is no need for any nerve-racking, last-minute preparation of the soufflé mixture. The made-up, uncooked tarts freeze, thaw and bake rapidly and successfully.

About 4 sheets of filo pastry
About 25 g (1 oz) butter, melted

For the soufflé
50 g (2 oz) butter
40 g (1½ oz) plain white flour
300 ml (10 fl oz) milk
4 eggs, separated
A little freshly grated nutmeg
1 teaspoon Dijon mustard
100 g (4 oz) Gruyère or Emmenthal,
　　grated
2 tablespoons snipped fresh chives
　　or chopped spring onions
Salt and freshly ground black
　　pepper

You will need 2 × 4-hole Yorkshire pudding trays, greased.

Pre-heat the oven to 180°c/350°F/gas 4.

To make the soufflé, melt the butter in a medium-sized pan, then stir in the flour and cook for 1 minute. Pull the pan away from the heat and gradually stir in the milk. Return the

Designer Mushrooms on Field Mushrooms
(page 32)

pan to the heat and bring to the boil, still stirring. Simmer gently for 1–2 minutes, then add the egg yolks, nutmeg, mustard, two-thirds of the cheese, the chives or spring onions, salt and pepper. Stir briskly, then cover and leave aside until cool.

Work on one sheet of filo at a time so the pastry does not dry and crumble. Keep the rest of the pastry covered with a damp cloth. Brush the sheet with melted butter then cut in half lengthways and into 3 widthways to give 6 rectangles each about 10 × 9 cm (4 × 3½ in). Lay 3 squares on top of each other so the corners form a star shape. Press gently into one of the buttered Yorkshire pudding tins. Repeat with each sheet of pastry to line the 8 individual shapes.

Put the egg whites into a clean, grease-free bowl and whisk until stiff but not dry. Stir 2 tablespoons of egg white into the sauce to thin it a little, then fold in the rest of the egg whites. Spoon an equal quantity of the mixture into each tart shell, then sprinkle with the remaining cheese. Bake in the oven for 10–15 minutes until well risen and pale golden at the edges. Serve instantly, if not sooner!

To prepare ahead: *Have the soufflé mixture ready to the stage just before folding in the egg whites. Lay a piece of clingfilm directly down on top of the sauce. Line the Yorkshire pudding tins with the pastry. Both sauce and pastry can be kept in the fridge for up to 8 hours. Then follow the recipe.*

To freeze: *Freeze the filled, uncooked tarts open in their tart tins. Once they have frozen, slip into a plastic bag, seal, label and freeze for up to 1 month.*

To thaw: *Thaw for 1½ hours at room temperature.*

To cook: *Cook following the recipe.*

To cook in a fan oven: *Pre-heat the oven to 160°c. Bake for about 10–12 minutes.*

To cook in the Aga: *Place the trays on the grid shelf on the floor of the roasting oven for about 8–12 minutes until well risen and pale golden at the edges.*

HOME-MADE MARINATED OLIVES
For delicious flavoured olives to serve at any time, drain cheap brined olives, then pack in a jar and top up with a good olive oil and a combination of herbs, garlic, chillies, pickling spice, bay leaves or cardamom seeds. After two weeks they will be better than anything you can buy. The flavoured olive oil is excellent for salad dressings.

Ⓥ

Filo Purses Stuffed with Spinach, Mushrooms and Goats' Cheese

MAKES 8 PURSES

These are small, fragile, crisp little parcels, packed with really piquant flavours. Watch them carefully as they bake because the single thickness of filo around the filling cooks quickly. Don't worry about cutting the filo pastry squares accurately. If you don't use all the goats' cheese, use it up as a sandwich filling.

1 × 225 g bag frozen leaf spinach, thawed or 225 g (8 oz) fresh young spinach leaves	Juice of 1 lemon
1 tablespoon oil	1 fat garlic clove, crushed
75 g (3 oz) butter	100 g (4 oz) shiitake mushrooms, sliced
A little freshly grated nutmeg	8 × 13 cm (5 in) squares of filo pastry
Salt and freshly ground black pepper	1 × 150 g tub fresh soft goats' cheese

To serve
Small-leaved green salad

Pre-heat the oven to 200°c/400°f/gas 6. Grease a baking tray.

If using frozen spinach, empty the bag into a colander then, taking a small handful at a time, squeeze out the water, then tease out the spinach leaves and put them on a plate.

Heat the oil and 25 g (1 oz) of the butter in a frying-pan, then stir in the spinach and cook over a high heat for 3–4 minutes, seasoning it with nutmeg, salt and pepper as it cooks. When the spinach is fairly dry, remove from the pan, transfer to a plate and leave aside until ready to use.

Add 25 g (1 oz) of the butter to the frying-pan, add the lemon juice and garlic. Stir in the mushrooms and continue to cook over a fairly high heat, stirring, until most of the pan juices have evaporated. Season with salt and pepper and remove the pan from the heat.

Lay the filo pastry squares on the work surface. Melt the remaining butter and brush over the squares, then turn and brush the other sides. Now put a small, flat layer of spinach in the centre of each square and top with a slightly flattened pile of mushrooms. Finish the top of each heap with about a teaspoonful of goats' cheese. One at a time, bring the rest of the filo up around the filling, gathering it together just over the filling and pinching the pastry together to enclose the contents in something like a small knapsack or drawstring purse. Arrange on the baking tray and bake for about 10 minutes or until tinged golden brown. Serve hot with a small-leaved green salad.

To prepare ahead: *The filo purses can be made and put on to a baking tray. Covered loosely with clingfilm, they can be kept for up to 8 hours in the fridge before baking. They are best eaten fresh, soon after cooking.*

To freeze: *Not suitable.*

To cook in a fan oven: *Pre-heat the oven to 190°c. Bake for about 8 minutes.*

To cook in the Aga: *Cook on the baking tray on the floor of the roasting oven for about 8 minutes.*

Gravadlax

SERVES 12–16

A classic Scandinavian recipe for pickled fresh salmon, the salmon is served raw with a mustard and dill sauce after the fish has been cured for a couple of days in a mixture of salt, pepper and dill. It has become very popular on many restaurant menus and no wonder. It is simplicity itself to prepare, looks imposing on the plate and tastes wonderful. Scottish farmed salmon is ideal for this recipe and the price is reasonable too. Allowing 4–5 slices per portion, each fillet will serve about 12–16.

*1.75–2.25 kg (4–5 lb) farmed fresh
    salmon*
3 tablespoons dried dill
3 tablespoons coarse sea salt
*1 tablespoon freshly ground black
    pepper*
4 tablespoons caster sugar

For the mustard dill sauce
6 tablespoons Dijon mustard
4 tablespoons caster sugar
2 tablespoons white wine vinegar
2 egg yolks
300 ml (10 fl oz) sunflower oil
*Salt and freshly ground black
    pepper*
*4 tablespoons chopped fresh dill
    or 2 tablespoons dried dill*

Using a strong pair of scissors cut the fins from the fish. To fillet the salmon start by using a large, sharp knife to cut off the head at the point where it joins the soft flesh of the body. Now use a filleting knife to make a long slit down the back of the salmon, slightly above the central bone (see **1**). Working with the knife flat on top of the central bone, slice down the length of the fish then lift off the top fillet (see **2**). At what was the head end use your fingers to pick and free the central bone, then use a small knife to help free this and the small lateral bones, gradually working down to the tail end of the fillet (see **3**). Lay the two fillets skin-side down and run your fingers over the surface so you can detect and pull out any small bones left in the fish.

Sprinkle an equal quantity of dill over each fillet, followed by the salt, then the pepper and finally the sugar. Press these on to the fillets using the flat of your hand, then match the two fillets together, skin-side outside, re-forming the fish. Put it inside a large plastic bag, seal, and put the bag on a tray that will fit in the fridge. Check that the fillets are still in position one on top of the other, then put another baking tray on top and firmly weight it with scale weights or tinned foods (see **4**). Put the fish into the fridge and leave it for about 48 hours until the salt and sugar have dissolved, turning the fish once a day and replacing the weighted tray on top. Quite a lot of syrupy liquid will form over this period. Discard all this liquid before moving to the next stage.

To make slicing easier it is best to partially freeze the fish. Wrap the fillets separately in clingfilm and freeze for 4–6 hours so the fish is firm but still pliable. Remove one fillet, uncover, and using a sharp knife cut thin slices with the knife angled at about 45 degrees (see **5**). This gives the widest possible slices, each with its edge of dill. Arrange the slices on serving plates.

To make the sauce, use a small balloon whisk to beat together the mustard, sugar, vinegar and egg yolks in a bowl. Gradually beat in the oil a drop at a time until the sauce thickens. Season with salt and pepper and stir in the dill. Spoon a little sauce beside the fillets on each plate and serve the rest separately.

To prepare ahead: *Have slices arranged ready on serving plates, covered with clingfilm and chilled. The sauce can be kept in a sealed jar or plastic container in the fridge. Both can be kept for up to 6 hours.*

To freeze: *Wrap each finished gravadlax fillet tightly in clingfilm, seal and label, then freeze for up to 2 months. The sauce is not suitable, as it would curdle on thawing.*

To thaw: *Part-thaw for 1 hour before slicing.*

Three-fish Pâté

SERVES 6

A recipe that looks almost too unassuming and easy but is worth its weight in gold, this pâté is one of those store cupboard recipes that can be put together in no time. Served spooned up in a swirl in individual ramekins it looks as though you have really tried, and tastes like it, too, especially if served with hot Honey-glazed Walnut Bread toast (see page 236). Any left over makes rather superior picnic sandwiches.

1 × 120 g tin sardines in oil
1 × 50 g tin anchovies in oil
1 × 185 g tin tuna in oil
Juice of 1 lemon
175 g (6 oz) soft butter
A small handful of fresh parsley
   sprigs
12 sprigs of fresh dill
Salt and freshly ground black
   pepper

Empty the contents of the tins of sardines and anchovies, including the oil, into a processor. Discard the oil from the tin of tuna then add the fish to the processor, followed by the lemon juice, butter, parsley, half the dill and some pepper. Process until smooth, then taste and add a little salt if need be. Spoon into a serving dish or individual dishes, cover and put in the fridge until about 2 hours before serving. Remove and leave at room temperature to soften to a spreading consistency. Garnish with sprigs of fresh dill before serving.

To prepare ahead: *Prepare the pâté, cover with clingfilm and keep in the fridge for up to 3 days.*

To freeze: *The pâté can be frozen in one large serving dish or individual ones. Cover tightly with foil then seal inside a plastic bag, label, then freeze for up to 1 month.*

To thaw: *Thaw overnight in the fridge.*

CITRUS SENSE
Nowadays I wash oranges and lemons in hot water and detergent before using. This gets rid of any wax coating and helps the fruit give more juice, more freely.

Bruschetta Marinara

SERVES 6

Frozen packs of mixed seafood can be found in several of the large supermarket chains. They are ideal for this recipe, unless you would rather make up the quantity of shellfish according to your own preferences. This dish takes scarcely 25 minutes to make.

For the toasts
6 × 1 cm (½ in) thick slices of French bread cut at an oblique angle
2 tablespoons olive oil
1 garlic clove, crushed
2 tablespoons chopped fresh parsley
Salt and freshly ground black pepper

For the seafood sauce
1 tablespoon olive oil
1 onion, finely chopped
1 large garlic clove, crushed
50 g (2 oz) button mushrooms, coarsely chopped

450 g (1 lb) frozen mixed seafood, such as prawns, scallops, mussels, squid
300 ml (10 fl oz) double cream
2 tablespoons lemon juice
Salt and freshly ground black pepper

To garnish
6 sprigs of fresh parsley
3 paper-thin lemon slices, halved

Pre-heat the oven to 220°C/425°F/gas 7.

First make the toasts. Line a baking tray with foil and arrange the bread slices on top in a single layer. Drizzle with 1 tablespoon of the oil, then turn the slices over, oil-side down. Mix the rest of the oil with the garlic, parsley and some salt and pepper and spread on the other surface of the bread. Bake for about 5–7 minutes or until the bread is browned and crisp. Switch off the oven and put in 6 small plates or a large serving plate to warm, leaving the oven door ajar.

To make the seafood sauce, heat the oil in a medium-sized frying-pan and fry the onion and garlic for about 5–8 minutes over a low to moderate heat until softened and lightly

Bruschetta Marinara (above).

coloured. Add the mushrooms and cook for a further 1–2 minutes. Add the thawed, drained seafood and allow to heat for a further 2 minutes. Stir in the cream, bring to a gentle simmer and continue to cook for 2–3 minutes until everything is tender and the cream has reduced to a nice sauce consistency. Remove the pan from the heat and stir in the lemon juice, then taste and season with salt and pepper.

Arrange the toasts on the serving plate(s) and spoon an equal quantity of seafood mixture on to each one. Quickly garnish with sprigs of parsley and lemon slices and serve hot.

To prepare ahead: *Have the toasts ready made but not spread with garlic and parsley. The seafood mixture can be made, quickly cooled and stored in a covered container in the fridge for up to 6 hours. Then follow the recipe.*

To freeze: *Not suitable.*

To cook in a fan oven: *Pre-heat the oven to 200°c. Bake for about 4 minutes.*

To cook in the Aga: *Bake the toasts on a baking tray on the floor of the roasting oven until brown, about 5 minutes, but keep an eye on them. Keep warm in the simmering oven.*

Spiced Carrot Soup with Gremolata

Makes 2 litres (3½ pints) to serve 6–8

Gremolata is an aromatic mixture of parsley, grated lemon rind and garlic which is excellent for adding to all manner of soups and stews at the last moment to give a really fresh-tasting lift to a dish. This is a warmly spiced soup that combines surprisingly well with a fresh, herb-flavoured gremolata. Taste the soup carefully before serving: the season of the year will affect the flavour of carrots so the quantities of sugar and lemon might need to be adjusted a little.

3 tablespoons sunflower oil	*1 tablespoon plain white flour*
2 onions, coarsely chopped	*900 g (2 lb) carrots, thickly sliced*
2 teaspoons ground coriander	*1.5 litres (2½ pints) Chicken Stock*
1 teaspoon garam masala	*(see page 14)*
¼ teaspoon hot Madras curry powder	*Juice of 1 lemon*
	1 teaspoon sugar
1 teaspoon peeled and grated fresh root ginger	*Salt and freshly ground black pepper*

For the gremolata	*Grated rind of 1 lemon*
A generous handful of fresh parsley	*1 fat garlic clove, crushed*

Measure the oil into a large, deep pan and heat gently. Stir in the onions and cook over a low heat for about 15 minutes or until the onions are softened but not coloured.

While the onions are cooking, measure the dry spices and ginger on to a plate with the flour. When the onions are ready, tip the flour and spices mixture into the pan, stir into the onions and cook for 2 minutes. Stir in the carrots. Now pour in the stock and bring to the boil. Adjust the heat to give a gentle simmer, cover and cook for about 10 minutes. Remove the pan from the heat and leave to cool.

Add the lemon juice and sugar. Pour the soup into a sieve then tip the vegetables into a processor. Process the vegetables until you have a smooth purée. Rinse out the pan. Return both the liquid and the vegetable purée to the rinsed-out pan and re-heat. Taste and season with salt and pepper, adding a little more lemon juice or sugar if you prefer.

To prepare the gremolata, first discard all the parsley stalks, then make sure that the leaves are completely dry. Combine the leaves with the grated lemon rind and garlic and chop very finely. Serve a little of the gremolata sprinkled over each bowl.

To prepare ahead: *The soup can be made, quickly cooled, then stored in a sealed container in the fridge for up to 2 days. Make the gremolata when needed.*

To freeze: *Pour the soup into a large freezer container. Cool, seal and label, then freeze for up to 1 month. Make the gremolata when needed.*

To thaw: *Thaw for about 6 hours in the container at room temperature, or overnight in the fridge.*

To re-heat: *Re-heat in a pan to just below boiling point.*

To cook in the Aga: *Sauté the onions on the boiling plate for 1 minute, then cover and transfer to the simmering oven for about 15 minutes or until tender. Stir in the rest of the ingredients, cover and return to the simmering oven for about 20 minutes or until tender.*

Ⓥ
Crème d'Endives

MAKES 1.5 LITRES (2½ PINTS) TO SERVE 6

A rather sophisticated soup, this is ideal for a dinner party, but not to the taste of most children. Strangely, the flavour is more like asparagus than anything else. It is important to buy very fresh, very pale yellow chicory. If it has a greenish tinge it gives the soup a slightly bitter flavour.

500 g (1 lb 2 oz) heads of chicory
25 g (1 oz) butter
2 medium-sized potatoes, peeled
    and cubed
1.25 litres (2 ¼ pints) light Chicken
    Stock (see page 14) or Vegetable
    Stock (see page 58)

100 ml (3 ½ fl oz) crème fraîche
1 egg yolk
Salt and freshly ground black
    pepper

To serve
150 ml (5 fl oz) single cream
3 tablespoons finely chopped
    fresh parsley

To remove the rather bitter core from the chicory, quarter each bulb lengthways then cut away the visible central core from each piece. Now slice the spears across into about 1 cm (½ in) pieces.

Melt the butter in a large pan, then stir in the chicory and cubed potatoes, turn the vegetables in the butter and cook for 1–2 minutes. Pour in the stock, bring to the boil, then lower the heat to give a bare simmer for 10 minutes or until the vegetables are tender. Pull the pan aside from the heat and leave to cool.

Once cold, process the soup until smooth. Rinse out the pan, then pour the soup through a sieve back into the rinsed-out pan. Re-heat until good and hot, but not boiling.

Beat together the crème fraîche and egg yolk in a small bowl, then beat in a ladleful of hot soup. Stir the mixture into the rest of the soup and re-heat just until hot enough to serve and no more; if the soup is allowed to boil it will curdle. Season to taste with salt and pepper. Serve each portion swirled with a generous amount of single cream and parsley.

To prepare ahead: *Chill after processing and before adding the crème fraîche and egg yolk. The soup can be kept for about 24 hours. Please note that this soup does darken in colour with keeping.*

To freeze: *Pour the soup into a large freezer container after processing but before adding the egg yolk and crème fraîche. Cool, seal and label, then freeze for up to 1 month.*

To thaw: *Leave the container to thaw for 6 hours at room temperature or overnight in the fridge.*

To re-heat: *Re-heat following the recipe above.*

To cook in the Aga: *Once the stock has been added and brought to the boil, transfer the pan to the simmering oven for 25 minutes, then follow the recipe above.*

Clockwise from top: Soupe Grandmère (page 50);
Spiced Carrot Soup with Gremolata (page 44);
Roasted Red Pepper Soup (page 48).

Ⓥ
Roasted Red Pepper Soup

MAKES 1.75 LITRES (3 PINTS) TO SERVE 6−8

Red peppers are so often only associated with summer cooking, but this is a lovely warming soup for the autumn. For anyone who has never grilled peppers before the process can seem a bit extreme, and in this recipe all the blackened skin actually goes into the soup. Let me reassure the nervous: keep going and you will end up with a good, well-rounded flavour. Incidentally, it adapts very happily for vegetarians; simply substitute vegetable stock for the chicken stock.

6 large red peppers	*900 ml (1½ pints) Chicken Stock*
2 tablespoons olive oil	*(see page 14)*
1 large onion, chopped	*4 teaspoons balsamic vinegar*
2 garlic cloves, finely	*4 teaspoons demerara sugar*
* chopped*	*Salt and freshly ground black*
6 tomatoes, quartered	* pepper*

For the garlic croûtons	*Salt and freshly ground black*
350 g (12 oz) sliced white bread	* pepper*
5 tablespoons olive oil	*4 tablespoons freshly grated*
3 fat garlic cloves	* Parmesan*

Pre-heat the grill to maximum and line the grill pan with foil.

Arrange the whole peppers in the grill pan, then toast them under the grill, turning every 3–4 minutes until they are blackened all over. Remove from the grill and transfer the peppers to a large plate to cool.

Meanwhile heat the oil in a large pan, add the onion and garlic, cover and fry gently until softened but not coloured. Add the tomatoes and stock and bring to the boil.

While this is happening, you can tackle the cooled peppers. Working with them on the plate in order to catch all the juices, slit each one and remove and discard the central stalk and seeds, while retaining all the skins and juices. Add the pepper pieces, skin and juice to the pan, bring just back to the boil, then cover and simmer gently for 10 minutes. Leave to cool.

Process the soup until smooth. Rinse out the pan, position a large sieve over the top and pour the processed soup into the sieve. Using a rubber spatula, gently stir the soup around to help it through the sieve, but do not actively rub it through. Discard what is left in the sieve and return the pan to the heat.

While the soup is re-heating, in a separate, small pan combine the vinegar and sugar and warm, stirring until the sugar has dissolved. Turn up the heat and continue to cook until the mixture forms a dark syrup. Do not leave the pan unattended at this stage; the process happens quickly and can burn. Immediately add a ladleful of hot soup to the syrup pan to stop the cooking, mix, then stir into the rest of the soup. Taste and season with salt and pepper. You may like to add a little more sugar to the soup and to thin it with a little additional stock or water.

To make the garlic croûtons, discard the crusts, then cut the bread into small cubes. Put these in a bowl then sprinkle with olive oil and garlic and season well with salt and pepper. Use your hands to toss the bread cubes so they are evenly coated in the oil, garlic and seasoning. Leave aside for 10 minutes.

Meanwhile, brush a baking tray with a little oil and pre-heat the grill to maximum. Sprinkle the bread cubes with Parmesan and toss again. Spread them out in a single layer on the baking tray, then position the tray under the grill. Watch these all the time they are cooking and shake and turn the cubes so they become evenly browned. Cool and serve separately with the hot soup.

To prepare ahead: *The soup can be made, quickly cooled, then stored in a sealed container in the fridge for up to 48 hours. The croûtons can be made up to 2 weeks ahead and stored in an airtight container in the fridge.*

To freeze: *Pour the soup into a large freezer container. Cool, seal and label, then freeze for up to 1 month.*

To thaw: *Thaw in the covered container for about 6 hours at room temperature or overnight in the fridge.*

To re-heat: *Re-heat in a pan to just below boiling point.*

To cook in the Aga: *Roast the peppers in a foil-lined roasting tin on a rack in the roasting oven for about 30 minutes or until blackened. Bake the croûtons in the roasting oven for 10 minutes.*

Use Free Freezer Containers
To freeze stocks and soups, save plastic mineral water bottles and the sturdy cartons that come filled with yoghurt or cream. Wash them thoroughly, then fill to within about 2.5 cm (1 in) of the top. This allows for the expansion of the liquid when freezing.

Soupe Grandmère

MAKES 3.4 LITRES (6 PINTS) TO SERVE 12

A robust, no-nonsense home-made soup, ideal for a main meal served with Parmesan cheese and a warm, grainy, brown bread. It is the sort of soup that is best made in large quantities, so people can have seconds and there is still some left over for the following day.

25 g (1 oz) butter
1 large onion, finely chopped
3 carrots, diced
2 celery sticks, finely chopped
1 leek, thinly sliced
1 tablespoon plain white flour
2.75 litres (5 pints) Chicken Stock
  (see page 14)

4 tablespoons tomato purée
50 g (2 oz) spaghetti, broken into
  short lengths
¼ small head of cabbage, thinly
  sliced
Salt and freshly ground black
  pepper

To serve
Freshly grated Parmesan

Heat the butter in a large, deep pan and fry the onion for about 5–8 minutes over a moderate heat until it begins to soften and colour. Add the carrots, celery and leek and fry gently for 8–10 minutes, stirring frequently. Sprinkle in the flour, then stir it in and cook for 2 minutes. Gradually add the stock and tomato purée, stirring all the while. Bring to the boil then half-cover with a tilted pan lid and continue to simmer gently for 30 minutes or until all the vegetables are tender. Add the spaghetti and cabbage and continue to cook for a further 10 minutes. Taste and season carefully with salt and pepper.

Serve in deep soup bowls accompanied by plenty of freshly grated Parmesan.

To prepare ahead: *The soup can be made, quickly cooled, then stored in the fridge for up to 2 days.*

To freeze: *Pour the soup into a large freezer container. Cool, seal and label, then freeze for up to 1 month.*

To thaw: *Thaw in the container for 4–6 hours at room temperature or overnight in the fridge.*

To re-heat: *Re-heat in a pan to just below boiling point.*

USE FLOUR FOR A WELL-BEHAVED SOUP
I believe in adding a little flour to thicken soups, so all the ingredients remain evenly distributed, even after standing in the fridge.

ⓥ Pea and Pesto Soup

MAKES 1.5 LITRES (2½ PINTS) TO SERVE 6–8

Unbelievably simple, this soup can be served hot or chilled as long as you bear in mind its only drawback: it loses its vibrant green colour if kept much longer than four hours. It might sound an affectation to call for petit pois, but they make a smoother textured soup than frozen garden peas. For a vegetarian version, you can use vegetable stock cubes.

4 chicken stock cubes
6 garlic cloves, finely chopped
1.2 litres (2 pints) water
1 × 900 g packet frozen petit pois
½ × 190 g jar pesto
Salt and freshly ground black
*   pepper*

To serve
Half-fat crème fraîche

Put the stock cubes and garlic in a medium-sized pan and pour in 600 ml (1 pint) of the water. Bring to the boil, then add the peas. Bring back to the boil, cover and simmer gently for 3 minutes. Remove the pan from the heat and transfer only the peas to a processor using a large draining spoon. Process for about 3 minutes so the peas are reduced to as smooth a purée as possible. Leaving the machine running, add the cooking liquor to the purée, then pour the blend through a sieve back into the pan. Press the mixture, but do not rub it, through the sieve.

If serving the soup chilled, add the remaining 600 ml (1 pint) of cold water and stir in the pesto. Taste and season with salt and pepper if necessary, then cover and leave to chill.

If serving the soup hot, return the pan to the heat and stir in the remaining 600 ml (1 pint) of water and the pesto. Re-heat to boiling point. Taste and season with salt and pepper if liked, then serve.

Hot or chilled, the soup can be accompanied by a bowl of crème fraîche so people can help themselves.

To prepare ahead: *Chill after adding the additional water and the pesto but do not keep it more than 4 hours before serving or it loses its bright colour.*

To freeze: *Not suitable.*

(V)
Italian Black Olive and Cheese Rolls

MAKES 12

A lot of people seem frightened of making bread; don't be. These rolls are very simple to make and they are delicious. Once you have made them once or twice you will probably feel brave enough to start adding your own flavouring ingredients. For example, try adding 50 g (2 oz) of sun-dried tomatoes in olive oil, drained and chopped, with 1 teaspoon of dried basil and a chopped, fried onion, instead of the olives and cheese. These tomato rolls are good topped with sunflower seeds. Look out for Pecorino cheese in your supermarket or delicatessen; it is a softer cheese with a salty flavour, often cheaper than Parmesan.

350 g (12 oz) strong plain white flour	*25 g (1 oz) stoned black olives, chopped*
1 teaspoon salt	*25 g (1 oz) strong Cheddar, freshly grated*
½ packet easy-blend dried yeast	
About 250 ml (8 fl oz) warm water	*25 g (1 oz) Parmesan or Pecorino, freshly grated*
1 tablespoon olive oil	*Freshly ground black pepper*

To glaze
1 egg, beaten

You will need a baking tray, greased.

Measure the flour into a large bowl, add the salt and yeast, followed by the water and oil, then mix to a pliable dough. It is far better to be on the wet and sticky side than dry. Turn out on to a lightly floured work surface and knead for about 5 minutes. Alternatively use a stand mixer fitted with a dough hook to do the hard work or use a processor. Once the dough leaves the work surface clean and forms a smooth elastic ball, return it to a greased bowl, cover with clingfilm and leave in a warm place to rise for about 2 hours or until doubled in size.

Again, turn the dough out on to a lightly floured surface and pat out to a flattened shape. Press the olives, half the cheese and a little freshly ground pepper on to the surface, then gather up the dough and knead briefly to distribute the flavouring ingredients evenly.

Divide the mixture into 12 pieces and form into balls. Arrange them on the baking tray, then brush with beaten egg and sprinkle with the remaining cheeses. Seal the tray inside a large plastic bag, trapping a fair amount of air in the bag so it puffs up well above the dough and is not in contact with it. Leave to rise in a warm place for about 30 minutes until the rolls have doubled in size.

Pre-heat the oven to 200°c/400°F/gas 6.

Bake the rolls for 15–20 minutes or until a good crusty, golden brown. Cool on a wire rack and try not to eat them until they are at least warm!

To prepare ahead: *Seal the cooked, cooled rolls inside a plastic bag and keep for up to 24 hours in the fridge. Refresh by sprinkling the rolls with a little water and re-heating in a pre-heated oven at 180°c/350°F/gas 4 for about 5–8 minutes.*

To freeze: *Seal the freshly baked, cooled rolls inside a plastic bag, label and freeze for up to 3 months.*

To thaw: *Leave the unopened plastic bag overnight in the fridge or open the bag, leaving the rolls inside, and thaw at room temperature for 3 hours.*

To re-heat: *Refresh as directed above in 'To prepare ahead'.*

To cook in a fan oven: *Pre-heat the oven to 190°c. Bake for about 12–15 minutes.*

To cook in the Aga: *Bake on the grid shelf on the floor of the roasting oven for about 15 minutes. If the bases of the rolls are not quite brown, place the baking sheet on the floor of the roasting oven for a further 5 minutes.*

The Centre
Attraction

THE CENTRE ATTRACTION

The fish recipes in this section use fish that are commonly available, such as salmon, plaice, cod and tuna. Exotic warm-water fish are expensive, and you would be more likely just to grill them whole – hardly worthy of a recipe. I love salmon, and we're so lucky that they are now farmed; the flavour is good, as is the texture, and they're inexpensive to buy. At one time, if you wanted salmon for Good Friday, say, the price would soar as Easter approached because there weren't many fish about; now farmed fish can be provided to order.

Salmon fits the bill for both family eating and for entertaining, but the Collettes of Plaice is strictly a dinner-party dish – so original in concept, wonderful to look at, and delicious to eat. The Mediterranean Tuna en Croûte is the invention of Luc (short for Lucy), who has cooked with me for six years now. She and her friends, most of them rather hard up, love to entertain. This dish, which is a little like a coulibiac, is full of flavour and has real style, but it costs virtually nothing to make.

Fish cooking is generally a very swift process, as the greatest sin you can commit is to overcook fish. However, at least one element of these fish recipes can be prepared in advance, which saves you time on the day of the meal. The meat and poultry recipes here too, can be prepared and/or cooked well ahead of time, especially the casserole-type dishes.

I have been aware, too, of health considerations when choosing recipes, and have cut down on the use of fat and flour, particularly in some of the beef and lamb dishes. I've even included a classic cottage pie. I wasn't sure whether to put this in, but when I ask my family what they *really* enjoy, it's always this old favourite that they choose. Coming back from a rugby match or a point-to-point, you want

---

PREVIOUS PAGE
Seville Minted Chicken
(page 68).

something hot that all will appreciate, young and old, and you can't beat a really first-rate cottage pie.

I'm not keen on convenience foods in general, but I thoroughly approve of one: the chicken cut up into portions (legs, breasts, thighs, drumsticks, etc) for you by the butcher or supermarket. These cuts are easy to cook in a variety of interesting ways, although I have still included one recipe for a whole, traditional roast chicken. There are also a couple of delicious duck recipes, one a classic which I've included because of my mother's sage and onion stuffing – this really makes the most of the duck.

Pheasants are a great buy, particularly in the country: they are very flavourful and low in fat. The guinea fowl recipe here (the birds taste like slightly gamey chicken) has a wonderful Madeira and tarragon sauce – but do be careful to choose a real French tarragon, the Russian variety tastes like straw!

I have included several pasta dishes, but as I don't like pasta shapes that are difficult to handle or eat, I tend to go for things like penne or quills, or pappardelle. The sauces of many of these pasta dishes can be prepared in advance, while the pasta itself is usually cooked at the last moment (although you'll be pleased to hear that a number of complete pasta dishes can actually be frozen). The pasta meals aren't all Italian either, as I have included some oriental noodle recipes; most or all of these could form part of a buffet selection.

Many of the pasta and other main dishes can be eaten by vegetarians as they are completely meat-free. I'm not vegetarian myself, but our daughter Annabel is, and it's good to have a discerning critic. I'm not a nut-roast sort of person, I'm much more enthusiastic about using fresh vegetables with interesting herbs and spices for flavour, which we can *all* enjoy. I think you'll agree with me when you try some of these recipes, especially the Chestnut Quenelles on Grilled Aubergine Slices, the star of the show!

This sign indicates recipes that are suitable
for vegetarians, but please note that some of them
include dairy products.

Seared Fillet of Salmon with Basil Butter Sauce

Serves 4

Use salmon tail or middle cut fillets and choose a size to suit the appetites of your family or guests. The sauce is made from a concentrated wine and vegetable stock. Sometimes the sauce can separate on standing. If it does, whisk in a tablespoon of double cream.

4 × 100–150 g (4–5 oz) pieces fresh
salmon fillet with skin on
A little oil for brushing
Salt and freshly ground black
pepper

For the vegetable stock
1 small onion
1 leek
3 carrots
2 celery sticks
1 bay leaf

600 ml (1 pint) water
6 sprigs of fresh parsley
6 sprigs of fresh basil
300 ml (10 fl oz) dry white wine
150 g (5 oz) ice cold butter,
diced for sauce

To garnish
2 tomatoes, skinned, seeded and cut
into strips
4 sprigs of fresh basil

Start the recipe the day before, if possible.

To make the vegetable stock, cut the vegetables into roughly 2 cm (¾ in) cubes. Put them in a pan with the bay leaf and water. Bring to the boil, then cover and simmer gently for 10 minutes. Remove the pan from the heat. Add the parsley. Strip about 20 leaves from the basil and keep them aside, then add any remaining leaves and the stalks to the hot liquid with the wine. Cover, leave until cold, then chill overnight if possible.

The following day, strain the stock, discarding the herbs and vegetables, then boil briskly until it is reduced to about 120 ml (4 fl oz). Using a small balloon whisk, gradually beat in the butter cubes one or two at a time until all the butter has been added. Cover and remove the pan somewhere to keep warm.

Pre-heat the grill, or a heavy, cast-iron, ridged stove-top griddle. When thoroughly heated, brush the salmon pieces with oil and season with salt and pepper. Arrange, flesh-side down on the grill pan or griddle and cook for 30–45 seconds. Carefully turn on to the skin side and continue cooking for 4–4½ minutes, according to the thickness of the salmon. Arrange each fillet on a plate and keep warm.

Tear the reserved basil leaves into small pieces and add to the sauce. Taste and season with salt and pepper if necessary. Spoon almost all the sauce over the fish, retaining about 2 spoonfuls in the pan. Add the tomato strips to this and heat briefly before topping each fillet with some tomato. Tuck a sprig of basil on top of each portion and serve.

To prepare ahead: *Have the stock ready, strained. This will keep up to 3 days in a covered container in the fridge ready to make the sauce.*

To freeze: *Not suitable.*

To cook in the Aga: *Pre-heat the Aga grill pan on the floor of the roasting oven for 15 minutes. Using oven gloves, carefully transfer to the boiling plate and cook as in the recipe, using the grill pan lid tilted at a slight angle to cover the fish as it cooks.*

Jansson's Fish Pie

SERVES 10

A very upmarket fish pie!

For the topping	1×50 g tin anchovies, drained and
1.1 kg (2 ½ lb) potatoes	*finely chopped*
A generous knob of butter	*Salt and freshly ground black*
About 250 ml (8 fl oz) milk	*pepper*

For the filling	
50 g (2 oz) butter	*350 g (12 oz) salmon fillet,*
1 large onion, roughly chopped	*skinned and cut in 1 cm (½ in)*
50 g (2 oz) plain white flour	*pieces*
600 ml (1 pint) milk	*4 hard-boiled eggs, coarsely*
2 tablespoons lemon juice	*chopped*
Salt and freshly ground black	*225 g (8 oz) broccoli, broken into*
pepper	*small sprigs*

You will need a shallow 2.25 litre (4 pint) dish, greased.

To make the topping, scrub the potatoes, then cook in boiling salted water in their skins until completely tender when tested with a skewer. Drain the potatoes in a colander. Add the butter and milk to the hot pan and return to the heat until bubbling. Peel the potatoes, then return them to the pan. Remove from the heat, mash, add the anchovies and season to taste with salt and pepper. Cover and put aside until ready to use.

Next, make the sauce for the filling. Melt the butter in a medium-sized pan, stir in the onion and cook over a low heat until softened but not coloured. Sprinkle in the flour and cook for 1 minute, then pull the pan aside from the heat before gradually stirring in the milk. Return the pan to the heat and bring to the boil, stirring. Lower the heat to a gentle simmer and add the lemon juice and salt and pepper, then add the salmon pieces. Remove from the heat and pour the contents of the pan into the greased dish. Sprinkle with the chopped eggs, cover and leave to cool. Heat about 2.5 cm (1 in) of salted water in a medium-sized pan. When boiling, add the broccoli and cook for 4 minutes. Immediately drain in a colander and cool under cold running water. Drain well, dry on kitchen paper then arrange the broccoli in an even layer over the chopped eggs. Using the flat of the hand, press the broccoli down a little into the sauce. Cover and chill for 1–2 hours until firm.

Pre-heat the oven to 180°C/350°F/gas 4.

Spread the mashed potatoes over the surface, smooth with a palette knife, then create a scalloped effect with the rounded end of the palette knife. Bake for 30–35 minutes or until crisp and golden. Serve at once; if kept hot for long the colour of the broccoli will fade.

To prepare ahead: *The pie can be prepared and covered with mashed potato. Cover with clingfilm and keep in the fridge for up to 6 hours before baking, following the recipe.*

To freeze: *Not recommended. Neither the eggs nor the potatoes react well to freezing.*

To cook in a fan oven: *Do not pre-heat the oven. Bake at 190°C for about 25 minutes or until crisp and golden.*

To cook in the Aga: *Cook in the roasting oven on the third set of runners for about 25 minutes.*

Collettes of Plaice

SERVES 4

A way of stuffing fish fillets which I am sure you will not have seen before, the best news is it could not be easier. The recipe calls for plaice fillets, but cheaper dabs could be used.

8 small plaice fillets, skinned
1 × 125 g packet light cream cheese
1 egg yolk
75 g (3 oz) peeled prawns, well
    drained

Salt and freshly ground black
    pepper
1½ tablespoons snipped fresh
    chives
A little melted butter

To garnish
Chopped fresh parsley
4 wedges of lemon

You will need a large, shallow roasting tin or baking tray lined with foil. Grease the foil and season the base with a little freshly ground black pepper.

Pre-heat the oven to 220°C/425°F/gas 7.

Arrange the fillets on the work surface, then match them into 4 pairs according to size. Using a pair of scissors, trim the fillets, cutting away any frilly edges and excess bits so each pair then match neatly (see **1**). Save all the fish trimmings and put them into a food processor with the cream cheese and egg yolk. Reserve about 12 larger prawns for garnishing. Add the remainder to the processor and season well with salt and pepper. Process briefly, no more than about 5 seconds, then tip the mixture into a small bowl, stir in the chives and taste for seasoning.

Have the fillets laid out, skinned-side down. Place 4 of them on the prepared roasting tin or baking tray. Season them with salt and pepper, then place a quarter of the mixture in the centre of each one (see **2** centre). Using a small, sharp knife, cut a slit about 5 cm (2 in) long in the centre of each matching fillet (see **2** right). Position each top fillet over its matching base so the filling just shows through the cut (see **2** left). Arrange 3 of the reserved prawns down the length of the cuts in each of the fillets then press the edges of the fish firmly together. Brush with a little melted butter, season with salt and pepper and bake for 10–12 minutes. Serve hot, sprinkled with chopped parsley accompanied by wedges of lemon.

To prepare ahead: *The stuffed, raw fillets can be kept covered in the fridge for up to 6 hours.*

To freeze: *Wrap the fully prepared, uncooked fish individually, seal in a freezer bag, label, then freeze for up to 3 months.*

To thaw: *Thaw in the freezer wrapping for 6 hours at room temperature or overnight in the fridge.*

To cook: *Cook following the recipe above.*

To cook in a fan oven: *Do not pre-heat the oven. Bake at 200°C for about 10 minutes.*

To cook in the Aga: *Slide the roasting tin or baking tray on to the second set of runners in the roasting oven and cook for 10–12 minutes or until just cooked and still moist.*

The Original and Best Cod Fish Cakes

MAKES 8 LARGE FISH CAKES

Sometimes the old ways are the best because they give the fullest flavour to a recipe. I have found that the slightly more lengthy method of baking the potatoes and fish in the oven makes for delicious fish cakes. Try them and see if I am not right. Smoked cod or haddock fillets are just as delicious as fresh cod in this recipe.

A good 450 g (1 lb) old, floury potatoes such as King Edwards, Golden Wonder, or Desirée	6 tablespoons chopped fresh parsley
450 g (1 lb) fresh cod fillet	3 tablespoons snipped fresh chives
Salt and freshly ground black pepper	Juice of 1 small lemon
175 g (6 oz) breadcrumbs ideally made from 2–3 day old bread	1 egg, beaten
	1 tablespoon milk
	Oil for grilling or frying

To serve
Tomato Passata Sauce (see page 215)

Pre-heat the oven to 200°C/400°F/gas 7.

Scrub the potatoes. Bake for about 1 hour or until the potatoes feel tender when squeezed with an oven-gloved hand.

About 15 minutes before the potatoes finish cooking, season the fish with salt and pepper and wrap in a foil parcel. Bake for about 12–15 minutes or until the fish is opaque and flakes in the centre when tested with a knife. Remove the fish and potatoes and leave to cool. Switch off the oven. Spread out the breadcrumbs on a baking tray and put in the oven to dry. Give them a stir around from time to time so they dry evenly as the oven cools. When cool enough to handle, scoop the potatoes out of their skins with a spoon, discarding the skins. Put the rest into a bowl and mash to a smooth consistency using a potato masher or ricer. Flake the fish, discarding all the skin and bones and add to the potato with the parsley, chives and lemon juice. Taste the mixture and season well with salt and pepper. Divide the mix into 8 and shape into large, round fish cakes, about finger thick.

Have the breadcrumbs ready on a large sheet of greaseproof paper. Beat the egg with the milk and have the mixture ready in a soup plate. Dip the fish cakes first in the egg, then in crumbs, pressing the crumbs on to the fish cakes and neatening the shape with the aid of a palette knife. Cover with clingfilm and chill until ready to cook.

Collettes of Plaice
(page 60).

The fish cakes can be brushed with oil and grilled or shallow-fried in oil. Either method will take about 8 minutes for each side.

Serve with the Tomato Passata Sauce.

To prepare ahead: *The breadcrumbed fish cakes can be covered and kept in the fridge for up to 2 days.*

To freeze: *Put the prepared fish cakes on to a baking tray lined with clingfilm. Freeze until firm, then transfer them to a plastic freezer bag, seal, label and freeze for up to 6 months. If freezing smoked fish cakes, freeze for up to 4 months.*

To thaw: *Remove the fish cakes from the plastic bag and arrange in a single layer on a baking tray. Cover and thaw for 3 hours at room temperature or overnight in the fridge.*

To cook: *Grill or shallow-fry, following the recipe.*

To cook in the Aga: *Bake the potatoes and fish in the roasting oven. Brush the fish cakes with oil, then cook on a baking sheet in the roasting oven for 8 minutes each side or shallow-fry.*

Mediterranean Tuna en Croûte

SERVES 8

This is a good family supper using fairly standard store-cupboard ingredients. Very popular with the young, and inexpensive to make.

2 × 400 g tins tuna chunks in oil	1 tablespoon dried basil
2 garlic cloves, crushed	2 teaspoons sugar
1 medium onion, cut in large chunks	75 g (3 oz) pitted black olives, halved
175 g (6 oz) button mushrooms, quartered	Salt and freshly ground black pepper
1 × 397 g tin chopped tomatoes	1 × 350 g packet frozen puff pastry, thawed
2 tablespoons tomato purée	1 × 50 g tin anchovies, drained and chopped
1 × 350 g jar red peppers, drained and thickly sliced	1 egg, beaten

You will need a baking tray, greased or lined with Lift-Off paper.

Drain the tuna in a sieve set over a bowl. Take 2 tablespoons of the drained oil and heat it in a large frying-pan. Stir in the garlic and onion, then cover and cook over a low heat for about 10–15 minutes or until softened and slightly coloured. Add the mushrooms and continue to cook for a further 5 minutes before adding the tomatoes and tomato purée. Turn up the heat and cook briskly until most of the pan juices have evaporated. Add the drained tuna, the peppers, basil, sugar, olives and salt and pepper. Heat just sufficiently to make sure most of the liquid has evaporated, being careful not to stir too vigorously and break up the peppers and tuna too much. Cover and leave aside to become cold.

Roll out the pastry very thinly on a floured surface to about 38 × 33 cm (15 × 13 in). Trim the edges to make a neat rectangle and reserve the pastry trimmings. Transfer the pastry to the baking tray. Put the cold filling down the centre of the pastry in a band 13–15 cm (5–6 in) wide, leaving a 5 cm (2 in) border free at each short end. Scatter the chopped anchovies over the top of the filling and brush the edges of the pastry with beaten egg. Fold the 2 short ends in over the filling; bring the long sides up to meet down the middle of the filling. Crimp the edges together firmly between thumb and forefinger. Brush the pie all over with beaten egg. Roll out the pastry trimming and cut into long thin strips. Lay the strips diagonally both ways across the surface, making a lattice. Brush the strips with egg then cover with clingfilm and place in the fridge for a few hours to firm up.

Pre-heat the oven to 220°c/425°f/gas 7.

Uncover and bake the pie for about 25–30 minutes or until golden brown.

To prepare ahead: *Once the pie has been made do not glaze but cover with clingfilm and keep in the fridge for up to 12 hours before baking, then glaze and follow the recipe.*

To freeze: *Carefully wrap the unbaked pie in foil, seal and label, then freeze for up to 1 month.*

To thaw: *Thaw for 8 hours at room temperature.*

To cook: *Bake following the recipe.*

To cook in a fan oven: *Pre-heat the oven to 200°c. Bake for about 25 minutes.*

To cook in the Aga: *Bake on the grid shelf on the lowest set of runners in the roasting oven for about 25 minutes until golden brown. Slide the baking tray on to the floor of the oven for a further 10 minutes to crisp the base and, if necessary, slide the cold plain shelf in to prevent the top from getting too brown.*

Stained fingers
Inevitable when cooking, but no problem. Take the shell of a squeezed lemon and scramble your fingers around inside; it is guaranteed to remove all stains and odours!

Pasta Amarilla

SERVES 6–8

A creamy, smoky, fish-flavoured pasta bake. No need to cook the fish separately before it is added to the rest of the ingredients, it cooks beautifully when baked in the mixture.

225 g (8 oz) penne pasta	3 hard-boiled eggs, chopped
1 onion, coarsely chopped	Juice of 1 lemon
350 g (12 oz) smoked haddock fillet, skinned and cut into 2.5 cm (1 in) strips	Salt and freshly ground black pepper

For the béchamel sauce	
900 ml (1½ pints) milk	½ teaspoon black peppercorns
1 bay leaf	50 g (2 oz) butter
	50 g (2 oz) plain white flour

For the topping	
150 ml (5 fl oz) double cream, seasoned	25 g (1 oz) Parmesan, grated
	25 g (1 oz) mozzarella, grated

You will need a shallow baking dish, buttered.

Pre-heat the oven to 220°C/425°F/gas 7.

To make the sauce, pour the measured milk into a pan and add the bay leaf and peppercorns. Bring the milk to just below boiling point, then remove the pan from the heat, cover and leave aside to infuse for about 30 minutes.

Meanwhile bring a large pan of salted water to the boil. Add the pasta and onion and cook according to the packet instructions, or until *al dente* – still with a little bite to it. Drain in a colander.

To finish the béchamel sauce, melt the butter in a medium-sized pan, then pull the pan aside from the heat and stir in the flour. Gradually add the strained, infused milk, stirring quickly. Replace the pan over the heat and bring to the boil, still stirring, then allow to boil for about 2 minutes. Remove the pan from the heat and stir in the strips of smoked haddock. Stir well over the heat for 1 minute, then add the chopped hard-boiled eggs and lemon juice, then the drained pasta and onion. Mix well then taste and season carefully with salt and pepper. Pour the mixture into the baking dish and level the top with the back of a spoon. Pour the cream over the top and sprinkle with the cheeses. Bake for about 25 minutes or until golden brown and piping hot. Serve immediately.

Pasta Amarilla
(above).

PASTA AMARILLA

FOR 4

- 5 ozs PENNE
- 1 ONION
- 9 ozs SMOKED HADDOCK
- 2 HARD BOILED EGGS
- JUICE OF 1 LEMON
- S & P

BECHAMEL SAUCE

- 1 PINT MILK
- 1·2 oz P. FLOUR
- 1·2 oz BUTTER

TOPPING

- 1 oz PARMESON
- 1 oz MOZZERELLA

200°C FOR 20 MINS

To prepare ahead: *The complete dish, minus the cream and cheese topping, can be made, cooled, covered and chilled up to 24 hours ahead. Just before baking, pour over the cream and sprinkle with the cheeses. If cooking ahead or freezing, drain the cooked pasta in a colander and rinse in cold water.*

To freeze: *When making the dish to freeze, add an additional 150 ml (5 fl oz) milk to the béchamel sauce and omit the hard-boiled eggs. Turn into a freezer-proof baking dish without the topping, seal, label and freeze for up to 1 month. Add the chopped, hard-boiled eggs once the dish has thawed.*

To thaw: *Thaw the mixture overnight in the fridge, then stir in the eggs and top with the cream and cheeses just before baking.*

To cook: *Bake in a pre-heated oven at 220°c/425°f/gas 7 for 20 minutes.*

To cook in a fan oven: *Do not pre-heat the oven. Bake at 200°c for about 20 minutes.*

To cook in the Aga: *Cook on the second set of runners in the roasting oven for 20–25 minutes until golden brown and hot right through.*

Seville Minted Chicken

SERVES 6

An unusual but delightful flavour combination. If you have no chicken stock to hand, use a cube. If you have no fresh mint, use a teaspoon of bottled mint sauce.

6 chicken roasting joints	Small bunch of fresh mint, leaves
Salt and freshly ground black	finely chopped
pepper	3 garlic cloves, crushed
4 tablespoons extra thick-cut	Grated rind and juice of 1 orange
marmalade, preferably home-	About 25 g (1 oz) butter,
made, chopped	softened

For the sauce
300 ml (10 fl oz) Chicken Stock
(see page 14)
1 tablespoon plus 1 teaspoon
cornflour
Salt and freshly ground black pepper
(optional)
A dash of sugar (optional)

You will need a roasting tin large enough to hold the chicken joints in a single layer.

Pre-heat the oven to 200°c/400°F/gas 6.

Trim off any excess fatty skin from the joints, then sprinkle the base of the tin with some salt and pepper and arrange the chicken joints on top. Combine the marmalade, chopped mint, garlic, orange rind and butter in a bowl with some additional salt and pepper. Mix well and spread the mixture over the chicken. Roast for 35–45 minutes, basting once or twice with the pan juices.

Test to make sure the chicken is cooked, then remove from the roasting tin to a warmed serving dish. Cover and keep warm while making the sauce.

Skim the surface fat from the pan juices by tilting the pan so the liquid flows to a corner. Use a tablespoon to take off the surface fat. Pour a small amount of the measured stock into a bowl and mix with the cornflour. Pour the remaining stock and the orange juice into the roasting tin, combine together with the juices in the pan, then stir in the cornflour blend. Bring to the boil, stirring briskly and scraping the base and sides of the tin. Simmer gently for 2–3 minutes and taste and season with salt and pepper if needed, perhaps adding a dash of sugar.

Pour the sauce over the chicken joints and serve immediately.

To prepare ahead: *The chicken joints can be spread with the marmalade, mint, garlic, orange rind and butter. Cover closely with foil and keep in the fridge for up to 12 hours. Bring the chicken up to room temperature before cooking.*

To freeze: *Pack the cooked cold chicken into a freezer container just large enough to take it, and store the sauce separately in a clean yoghurt pot. Seal and label, then freeze for up to 3 months.*

To thaw: *Thaw for 4 hours at room temperature.*

To re-heat: *Put the joints into a shallow casserole and re-heat in a pre-heated oven at 200°c/400°F/gas 6 for 20 minutes or until well heated through. Heat the sauce separately in a pan and serve poured over the chicken.*

To cook in a fan oven: *Do not pre-heat the oven. Roast the chicken at 190°c for about 40 minutes.*

To cook in the Aga: *Cook towards the top of the roasting oven for about 30 minutes.*

Garlic Chicken with Oven-roasted British Vegetables

SERVES 6

If you have any lemon shells left over after using their juice for another recipe, use these instead of the fresh half-lemon.

---

1 × 1.75 kg (4 lb) chicken

For the garlic butter
2 fat garlic cloves, finely chopped
½ teaspoon salt
50 g (2 oz) butter, at spreading consistency
Freshly ground black pepper

For the flavouring
1 onion, cut into 6 wedges
½ lemon, cut into 6 wedges
A good sprig of fresh thyme, leaves stripped off
2 bay leaves
Salt and freshly ground black pepper

For the vegetables
250 g (9 oz) shallots
2 turnips
6 small carrots
2 parsnips

For the gravy
1 tablespoon plain white flour
450 ml (15 fl oz) Chicken Stock (see page 14)
Salt and freshly ground black pepper

To garnish
A small handful of fresh parsley sprigs

You will need a small roasting tin for the chicken and a second roasting tin large enough to hold the vegetables in a single layer.

Pre-heat the oven to 200°C/400°F/gas 6.

Sit the chicken breast-side-up on the work surface. Starting from the neck end, use your fingers to free the skin from the flesh over the breast to the legs and down to the wings. Using the flat of a knife, work the garlic into a paste with the salt. Combine this with the butter and some freshly ground black pepper, then use your fingers to spread the mixture between the flesh and skin of the chicken.

Combine the wedges of onion, lemon, the stripped leaves of thyme and the bay leaves in a bowl. Toss together with some salt and pepper, then push the mixture into the cavity of the bird. If you then tie the legs and parson's nose together, none of the flavouring ingredients will escape. Transfer to the snug-fitting roasting tin. Season the bird lightly with salt and pepper and put in the top half of the oven to roast for 30 minutes.

Meanwhile prepare the vegetables. Peel the shallots and leave whole. Peel and quarter the turnips. If the carrots are no more than thumb-thick, simply scrub, top and tail. Top, tail and peel the parsnips, cut in half and quarter the thicker top half, shaving away any woody central core. Pile all the vegetables into a bowl, cover and leave on one side until ready to use.

After 30 minutes, remove the chicken, baste it well with the buttery juices, then spoon off 4 tablespoons into the larger roasting pan that is intended for the vegetables. Over direct heat, briefly sauté the vegetables in the hot fat until starting to brown. Replace the chicken in the lower half of the oven and put the vegetables in the top half. Continue to roast, turning the vegetables and basting the chicken once or twice, for a further 40 minutes. Now check to see if the vegetables are tender by piercing with the sharp point of a knife, then make sure the chicken is cooked by piercing the flesh at the thickest part of the thigh, close to the body; the juices should run clear and not pink. If not quite cooked, continue roasting for a further 10–15 minutes. If cooked, drain the chicken well, tipping the juices from the body cavity back into the roasting tin before transferring the bird to a large, warmed serving dish. Surround with the vegetables and sprinkle with small sprigs of parsley, then cover and leave aside in a warm place while preparing the gravy.

Spoon the excess fat from the gravy, then stir in the flour and cook for 2 minutes. Gradually pour in the stock, stirring quickly. Bring to the boil, stirring, and boil gently for 1–2 minutes. Taste and season carefully with salt and pepper. Strain the gravy if you wish, then serve in a warm jug or gravy boat to accompany the chicken and vegetables.

To prepare ahead: *Pile the prepared vegetables in a bowl, cover and chill. Cover the prepared chicken with clingfilm. These can be kept in the fridge for up to 24 hours. However, remember that the longer the chicken is kept before cooking the more the garlic flavour will develop. Make sure that the chicken is at room temperature before roasting.*

To freeze: *Not suitable.*

To cook in a fan oven: *Pre-heat the oven to 190°C. Roast the chicken for 25 minutes, baste and add the vegetables, replace in the oven and cook for another 30 minutes. Check that the chicken and vegetables are cooked (see recipe). If not, continue roasting for a further 10 minutes before testing again.*

To cook in the Aga: *Follow the recipe using the roasting oven; the timing will be a little shorter.*

Paprika Chicken Suprème

SERVES 6

A quick and easy supper dish for the family, but certainly distinguished enough to serve for a dinner party. If you prefer to cut the calories, substitute chicken stock for half the crème fraîche and thicken the sauce with 1 teaspoon of cornflour. Gently boil the sauce for 2–3 minutes before pouring over the chicken.

50 g (2 oz) butter
1 mild onion, thinly sliced
6 chicken breasts, without skin or
  bone if preferred
Salt and freshly ground black
  pepper
2 tablespoons plus 1 teaspoon mild
  paprika
1 × 200 g carton crème fraîche

To garnish
2 tablespoons chopped fresh parsley

You will need a shallow ovenproof dish large enough to hold the chicken in one layer.

Pre-heat the oven to 200°C/400°F/gas 6.

Heat half the butter in a large frying-pan. As soon as the foam starts to subside, stir in the onion, then cover and cook over a low heat for about 10 minutes or until softened but not coloured. Spread the onion in the base of the ovenproof dish. Melt the remaining butter in the pan. Season the chicken breasts with salt and pepper, then add to the pan, turning each one to coat it in the hot butter. Brown over a moderate heat for 5 minutes before turning the chicken pieces and cooking for a further 5 minutes. Sprinkle with paprika. Remove the chicken with a slotted spoon and arrange on top of the onion in the dish. Now return the frying-pan to the heat and pour in the crème fraîche to de-glaze the pan. Heat until just bubbling, while stirring and scraping the base and sides of the pan. Check and season with salt and pepper. Pour the sauce over the chicken and cover the dish with foil. Transfer to the oven to cook for 15–20 minutes. Sprinkle with chopped parsley and serve.

To prepare ahead: *When the chicken and onions have been pan-fried, the pan deglazed and the sauce poured over, cover with foil, cool quickly and keep in the fridge for up to 24 hours.*

To freeze: *Put the onion in a freezer container and top with the pan-fried chicken and sauce. Cover with foil, cool quickly, seal and label, then store for up to 2 months.*

To thaw: *Thaw in the freezer container for 6 hours at room temperature or overnight in the fridge.*

To re-heat: *Pre-heat the oven as above but bake the foil-covered chicken for about 20 minutes. Expect some fat to come out of the dish when thawed and re-heated; just mop up the fat with kitchen paper.*

To cook in a fan oven: *Pre-heat the oven to 190°C. Bake for about 15 minutes.*

To cook in the Aga: *Cook on the grid shelf on the floor of the roasting oven for about 20 minutes.*

BE AWARE OF THE STRENGTH OF PAPRIKA
Paprika powder is made by grinding dried, aromatic sweet red peppers. Its flavour can range from mild to hot, so take care when buying it and make sure you use the mild variety for this recipe. If you inadvertently use hot (as I have sometimes done), add an additional carton of soured cream to marble the sauce just before serving. Don't breathe a word about your mistake and everyone will love it.

Chicken with Vermouth and Sage

SERVES 4

This recipe serves four, but can be readily expanded to serve six or eight. Very quick, it's a supper dish that can be on the table in a twinkling. Use prosciutto di Parma, Serrano or Black Forest ham, whichever is the best buy.

4 chicken breasts, boned and skinned	1 tablespoon olive oil
10 fresh sage leaves	15 g (½ oz) butter
Salt and freshly ground black pepper	120 ml (4 fl oz) dry vermouth
8 slices prosciutto or other dry cured ham	150 ml (5 fl oz) half-fat crème fraîche

Slice each chicken breast in half lengthways. Snip 2 fresh sage leaves over the chicken then season with a little freshly ground black pepper. Roll up each strip in a slice of prosciutto.

Heat the oil and butter in a pan until the foam from the butter starts to subside. Place the chicken rolls in the pan, seam-side down to prevent them unrolling, then cover and cook over a moderate heat for about 3 minutes. Now turn the rolls and cook for a further 3 minutes or until nicely browned. Spoon off the fat from the pan, then pour in the vermouth. Cover and cook gently for a further 5 minutes. Transfer the chicken to a warmed serving dish; cover and keep warm. Add the cream and remaining snipped sage leaves to the pan and bring to simmering point, stirring and scraping the base and sides of the pan. Taste and season with salt and pepper if necessary, then pour the sauce over the chicken. Serve hot.

To prepare ahead: *This dish is so quick it is hardly worth preparing ahead. However, the rolled up chicken strips can be kept covered in the fridge, ready to cook, for up to 8 hours.*

To freeze: *Not suitable.*

Paprika Chicken Suprème
(page 72).

Guinea Fowl with Madeira and Tarragon Sauce

SERVES 8

Guinea fowl are now being farmed and are widely available in supermarkets. They are a good choice when you are unsure of your guests' tastes as they are flavourful without being too strong or 'gamey'. If you are still in doubt, the recipe works well with both pheasant and chicken.

2 × 1 kg (2¼ lb) oven-ready guinea fowl	225 g (8 oz) shallots, peeled and left whole
40 g (1½ oz) butter	300 ml (10 fl oz) guinea fowl or Chicken Stock (see page 14)
1 tablespoon sunflower oil	120 ml (4 fl oz) Madeira
40 g (1½ oz) plain white flour	1 × 200 g carton crème fraîche
Salt and freshly ground black pepper	1 tablespoon chopped fresh tarragon

To garnish
Sprigs of fresh tarragon

Pre-heat the oven to 180°C/375°F/gas 5.

Take off the thigh/leg joints and the breast/wing joints from the carcase and remove the skin, if liked. Make stock from the bones.

Put the butter and oil in a large, deep, non-stick frying-pan over a moderate to high heat. Meanwhile, combine the flour and some salt and pepper in a plastic bag. Coat half the joints, one at a time, immediately adding them to the pan to brown in the hot fat for about 6–8 minutes. Remove the joints to a casserole, then coat and fry the remaining joints and transfer to the casserole. Fry the shallots for 5 minutes until starting to brown, then add to the casserole. Add the remaining seasoned flour to the pan and stir, then pour in the stock and Madeira. Allow to thicken, stirring. Pour over the guinea fowl in the casserole, cover and transfer to the oven to cook for about 20 minutes or until a thigh is tender when tested with a skewer.

Use a draining spoon to transfer the guinea fowl and shallots to a warmed serving dish, cover and keep warm. Skim the fat from the remaining sauce and stir in the crème fraîche and tarragon. Bring back to simmering point, taste and season with salt and pepper as the sauce heats. Pour the sauce over the guinea fowl and shallots, garnish with sprigs of fresh tarragon and serve hot.

To prepare ahead: *The flavour of this dish improves if prepared ahead. Cook the joints and shallots, but do not add the crème fraîche and tarragon. Cool, cover and keep in the fridge for up to 3 days. Re-heat following the instructions below.*

To freeze: *Cook the joints and onions, but do not add the crème fraîche and tarragon. Cool, then transfer the contents of the pan to a freezer container or 2 plastic bags, 1 inside the other. Seal and label, then freeze for up to 6 months.*

To thaw: *Thaw in the container or bags for 6 hours at room temperature or overnight in the fridge.*

To re-heat: *Re-heat uncovered in a pre-heated oven at 180°c/375°f/gas 5, stirring in the crème fraîche and tarragon when hot.*

To cook in a fan oven: *Do not pre-heat the oven. Cook at 160°c for about 20 minutes; test as directed in the recipe to make sure the guinea fowl is tender, then follow the recipe.*

To cook in the Aga: *Once the joints and shallots have been returned to the pan, bring to simmering point, then cover and transfer to the simmering oven for about 35 minutes or until tender, then follow the recipe.*

Classic Duck with Crisp Sage and Onion

SERVES 5–6

This recipe solves a very common cookery problem: how to roast duck until the skin is crisp without having the meat overcooked and dry. To serve with the bird, here is a very traditional stuffing, but probably made in a way you have not tried. The ingredients are left fairly chunky and baked separately from the duck, so when baked it is very crisp and light. It is my mother's technique and to my mind, unbeatable. She often makes it a day ahead.

SUCCESSFUL SEATING

*If you have a lot of people seated for a formal dinner, I suggest that
when the coffee arrives the men are asked to move two seats to
the left. (This second seat can be noted on the back of a place card.)
It is one of the best ways I know to get guests mingling.*

---

1 × 2.6 kg (5 ½–5 ¾ lb) oven-ready
*   duck*

For the flavouring
1 large onion, cut into
*   6–8 wedges*
1 lemon, cut into 6–8 wedges
1 generous sprig of fresh
*   thyme*
Salt and freshly ground black
*   pepper*

For the stuffing
450 g (1 lb) onions, very coarsely
*   chopped*
300 ml (10 fl oz) water
75 g (3 oz) butter
225 g (8 oz) soft white
*   breadcrumbs*
1 rounded teaspoon
*   dried sage*
Salt and freshly ground black
*   pepper*

You will need a small roasting tin and a wire rack that will fit inside it on which to roast the duck, and a shallow baking dish about 25 × 20 cm (10 × 8 in) in which to bake the stuffing, greased.

Pre-heat the oven to 220°c/425°f/gas 7.

To prepare the duck, remove any giblets and pull away the fat deposits from the interior at the rear end of the bird. These can be discarded or used for cooking if you wish.

Combine the flavouring ingredients in a bowl and toss together with a generous amount of salt and freshly ground black pepper. Put into the cavity of the bird, then use a skewer to close the body opening and prevent the ingredients falling out. Rub the duck skin with salt and pepper and place breast-side down on the roasting rack in the roasting tin. Roast in the top half of the oven for 30 minutes.

During this time, make the stuffing. Put the onions and water together in a pan and bring to the boil. Cook for 10 minutes or until the onions are just tender but not soft. Drain and return the onions to the hot pan with the butter. Once the butter has melted, stir in the remaining stuffing ingredients, seasoning generously with salt and pepper. Lightly toss the ingredients together, then spread lightly in the prepared baking tin without pushing or compressing the mixture.

After the first 30 minutes, remove the duck from the oven, turn it over so it is breast-side up and baste it well. Transfer to the bottom half of the oven and put the stuffing in the top half. Continue to roast for a further 30 minutes.

At this stage, baste the duck again, then lower the oven temperature to 160°C/325°F/gas 3. Continue to cook both the stuffing and the bird for a further 30 minutes or until the duck is thoroughly browned, crisp and cooked. The stuffing should be crisp and browned right through. Serve the duck hot with generous spoonfuls of the stuffing. The flavouring ingredients are not intended to be served.

To prepare ahead: *The duck can be filled with the flavouring ingredients and stored in the fridge, uncovered, for up to 6 hours. (Keeping the duck uncovered helps the skin to stay dry so it will be crisper when roasted.) The stuffing can be made, put in the baking tin, covered and stored in the fridge for up to 6 hours. Make sure the duck is removed 1 hour before roasting to allow it to come up to room temperature.*

To freeze: *Don't freeze the duck. Put the cooked stuffing in a dish inside a plastic freezer bag, seal and label, then freeze for up to 1 month.*

To thaw: *Thaw the stuffing for 4 hours at room temperature.*

To re-heat: *Re-heat the stuffing in a pre-heated oven at 220°C/425°F/gas 7 for 15 minutes. It is unlikely that you would want to re-heat duck, but in that event re-heat with the stuffing.*

To cook in a fan oven: *Pre-heat the oven to 200°C. Roast the duck for 20 minutes, then turn the bird over, put the stuffing in to bake and cook for another 20 minutes or until both are thoroughly browned, crisp and cooked.*

To cook in the Aga: *Roast the duck upside-down in the top section of the roasting oven for 30 minutes. Turn the right way up and roast for a further 25 minutes until golden, then transfer to the simmering oven for about 20 minutes until the legs are tender.*

KEEP KNIVES SHARP

Sharp knives are the first essential in a kitchen, but to sharpen them is not easy. In my experience the problem is usually a well-worn steel. However some knives are difficult to sharpen, so try a local ironmonger to see if they offer a knife-sharpening service, or sometimes a local butcher will help. Having got them sharp, wash them separately by hand, not in the dishwasher unless they have plastic handles.

Crisp Duck Legs with Ginger Sauce

SERVES 6

This method of boiling duck legs then grilling them was something I had never tried before and I was surprised and delighted when it worked so well; they are really moist, tender and crisp.

6 duck legs
Oil for brushing

For the stock
1.75 litres (3 pints) water
50 g (2 oz) fresh root ginger, peeled
    and thinly sliced
5 cm (2 in) cinnamon stick
3 cloves
4 tablespoons dark soy sauce
3 tablespoons clear honey
1 chicken stock cube

For the sauce
3 pieces stem ginger, cut into
    matchsticks
1 tablespoon stem ginger syrup
2–3 teaspoons dark soy sauce
600 ml (1 pint) of the stock

2 tablespoons dry sherry
1½ tablespoons cornflour
3 spring onions, sliced into needle
    slivers
Salt and freshly ground black
    pepper

Start the recipe the day before, if possible.

Put all the stock ingredients in a large pan. Add the duck legs, then bring to the boil. Tilt a lid over the top of the pan and leave to simmer gently for 1 hour until tender. Pull the pan aside from the heat and leave the duck legs to cool in the stock.

Remove the duck legs and keep covered in the fridge. Chill, then skim the fat from the stock. Take 600 ml (1 pint) of the strained duck stock and boil briskly until reduced to 450 ml (15 fl oz). Put on one side until ready to use.

Pre-heat the grill on high for 5 minutes.

Dry the duck legs thoroughly with kitchen paper. Arrange on a grill rack and brush with oil. Grill for about 10 minutes, turning the joints regularly until well browned and crisp.

While the duck legs are grilling, prepare the sauce. Stir the stem ginger, syrup and soy sauce into the reduced stock. Mix together the sherry and cornflour, then whisk into the sauce. Bring to the boil, stirring, then boil gently for about 2 minutes. Sprinkle in the sliced spring onions and swirl in the hot sauce. Check seasoning, add salt and pepper if necessary, and serve immediately with the duck legs.

To prepare ahead: *Have the duck legs boiled, cooled, covered and chilled. The stock can be skimmed, strained and reduced, then chilled in a sealed container. These can be kept in the fridge for up to 2 days.*

To freeze: *Put the boiled, cooled duck legs in a strong plastic bag. Seal and label, then freeze for up to 6 months. The reduced stock can be frozen in clean cream cartons, filling them to within about 2.5 cm (1 in) from the top to allow for expansion of the liquid as it freezes. Seal and label, then freeze for up to 6 months.*

To thaw: *Thaw the unopened bag of duck legs overnight in the fridge; likewise the stock.*

To re-heat: *Grill the duck legs following the recipe and use the stock for the sauce.*

To cook in the Aga: *First cook the duck legs in the simmering oven until tender. Make the sauce on the boiling plate. To finish the duck legs, roast near the top of the roasting oven for about 10 minutes until golden.*

Wild Game Casserole

SERVES 6–8

Some enterprising supermarkets now sell packs of mixed game in which the meat is trimmed of all skin and bone, and ready cut in pieces. Not all of them have caught on to this so you might have to buy a selection of game and do it yourself. I recommend a mixture of pheasant, venison, pigeon and rabbit and, if need be, make up the weight with chicken. Smoked continental sausage, often from Holland or Germany, is pre-cooked and sold by weight or sometimes in a ring, and is widely available. Once cooked and cooled, the mixture can be served as a game pie by covering it with 250 g (9 oz) of puff pastry. However you decide to serve it, the end result has a superb flavour.

> ### KEEP ALL THE FLAVOUR OF DRIED MUSHROOMS
> *Don't throw out the liquid in which you have soaked dried mush-rooms. It is very good for flavouring soups, stews and sauces. Label and freeze it until you are ready to use it.*

*900 g (2 lb) mixed boned and
skinned game, cubed*

For the marinade
*300 ml (10 fl oz) red wine
1 onion, sliced
2 bay leaves
2 sprigs of fresh thyme*

*25 g (1 oz) dried porcini
   mushrooms
1–2 tablespoons oil
8 shallots, peeled and left
   whole
50 g (2 oz) plain white flour
300 ml (10 fl oz) Game or Beef
   Stock (see page 14)*

*1 small, trimmed head of celery,
   sliced on the diagonal
3 tablespoons black treacle
Salt and freshly ground black
   pepper
175 g (6 oz) smoked continental
   sausage
A little gravy browning (optional)*

Start to marinate the dish 1–2 days ahead. You will need a flameproof casserole.

Put 2 plastic bags together, one inside the other. Put the game into the bags with the marinade ingredients and seal well. Chill for about 24 hours.

Pre-heat the oven to 160°c/325°F/gas 3.

Put the dried mushrooms into a small bowl and pour in sufficient boiling water to cover them generously. Cover and leave aside to soak.

Heat the oil in a large frying-pan, add the shallots and cook gently until browned all over. Sprinkle the flour into the pan, then stir and cook for 1–2 minutes before gradually adding the stock. Now add the strained marinade, reserving the other marinade ingredients, stir and bring to the boil. Tip in the meat and marinade flavourings and add about two-thirds of the sliced celery, keeping the remainder to add later. Scoop the soaking mushrooms from their water and squeeze them before adding to the pan followed by the black treacle. Stir, season with salt and pepper and transfer to the flameproof casserole. Bring to simmering point, then transfer to the oven to cook for about 2½ hours or until almost tender. Slice the smoked sausage and add to the casserole with the reserved celery, then return the casserole to the oven for a further 30 minutes. Taste for seasoning and check that the meat is tender. Add a little gravy browning if you like a darker, richer-looking gravy.

Wild Game Casserole
(page 81).

To prepare ahead: *Quickly cool, cover and keep in the fridge for up to 2 days.*

To freeze: *Seal the cooled meat mixture inside a double thickness of plastic bags. Label and freeze for up to 3 months.*

To thaw: *Thaw overnight in the fridge.*

To re-heat: *Re-heat in a pre-heated oven at 180°c/350°f/gas 4 for about 30 minutes.*

To cook in a fan oven: *Do not pre-heat the oven. Cook at 140°c for 2½ hours or until the meat is tender before adding the sausage and celery. Return to the oven for a further 20 minutes.*

To cook in the Aga: *After starting the casserole on the boiling plate, cover and transfer to the simmering oven for about 2–3 hours until tender before adding the sausage and celery. Return to the oven for a further 25–30 minutes.*

Pheasant Normandy-style
SERVES 6–8

A good way of using the less tender leg joints of pheasant if you've used the tender breasts for another recipe such as the Pheasant Breasts with Spiced Cranberry Sauce (see page 86). The legs of older birds could take as long as 3½ hours to cook. Also try the recipe with chicken joints; they'll take less time in the oven.

25 g (1 oz) butter
1 tablespoon oil
8 pheasant leg joints or a brace of
    pheasant, jointed
40 g (1½ oz) plain white flour
450 ml (15 fl oz) dry cider or dry
    white wine
2 onions, cut into thin wedges
4 small dessert apples, peeled, cored
    and cut into eighths
½ teaspoon dried rosemary
1 rounded tablespoon apple or
    redcurrant jelly
5 cm (2 in) cinnamon stick
Salt and freshly ground black
    pepper
150 ml (5 fl oz) half-fat crème
    fraîche

You will need a flameproof casserole large enough to hold the pheasant joints comfortably in a single layer.

Pre-heat the oven to 160°C/325°F/gas 3.

Heat the butter and oil in a large non-stick frying-pan and fry the pheasant joints until evenly browned all over, then remove the joints to a casserole. Pour off all but about 2 tablespoons of fat from the pan, add the flour, then stir in the cider or wine and allow to thicken over the heat for a few minutes. Add the onions, apples, rosemary, apple or redcurrant jelly and cinnamon and season with salt and pepper. Bring to the boil, then pour over the joints in the casserole. Cover and transfer to the oven to cook for at least 1½ hours. Test the joints to make sure they are tender. If not, re-cover and replace in the oven until tender. Use a draining spoon to remove the joints to a serving dish, cover and keep warm.

Boil the remaining sauce, reducing if necessary to a thick sauce consistency. Stir in the crème fraîche. Retrieve and discard the cinnamon, then taste and season with salt and pepper. Bring to simmering point once more, then pour the sauce over the pheasant.

To prepare ahead: *The pheasant can be prepared to the point where it is removed from the oven, quickly cooled, then covered and stored in the fridge for up to 2 days. Re-heat following the instructions below and finish following the recipe.*

To freeze: *Do not add the crème fraîche. Transfer the cooked, cold pheasant to a freezer box or bag. Seal and label, then freeze for up to 2 months.*

To thaw: *Thaw for 6 hours at room temperature or overnight in the fridge.*

To re-heat: *Re-heat in a pre-heated oven at 160°C/325°F/gas 3 for 20–30 minutes or over a low heat on top of the stove, then stir in the crème fraîche.*

To cook in a fan oven: *Do not pre-heat the oven. Bake at 150°C for about 50 minutes. Test to make sure the joints are tender, if not, re-cover and replace in the oven for a further 10 minutes.*

To cook in the Aga: *Once the cider or wine has been added and the pheasant joints replaced in the casserole, bring the mixture to a gentle boil, then cover and transfer to the simmering oven for about 1½ hours or longer until tender.*

TIPS ON PHEASANTS

Hen pheasants make the best buy. They are usually smaller, but more plump and tender than the male bird. If you have no idea of the age of a pheasant, don't risk roasting it, always use it for a casserole.

Pheasant Breasts
with Spiced Cranberry Sauce

SERVES 8

Cranberry sauce is available in almost all supermarkets, and I notice more butchers are now selling this and all manner of pickles and relishes. However, you might prefer to use fresh cranberries when they are available. Substitute the cranberry sauce with 450 g (1 lb) of fresh or frozen cranberries and increase the quantity of redcurrant jelly to four generous tablespoons.

8 pheasant breasts with wings attached	1 rounded tablespoon redcurrant jelly
A little seasoned flour	1 × 200 g jar cranberry sauce
3 tablespoons sunflower oil	3 tablespoons port
½ teaspoon ground coriander	150 ml (5 fl oz) Chicken Stock (see page 14)
½ teaspoon ground cinnamon	
½ teaspoon freshly grated nutmeg	Salt and freshly ground black pepper
900 g (2 lb) red onions, each cut into 8 wedges	

To serve
Mashed celeriac and potatoes

You will need a large, flameproof casserole that will comfortably hold the pheasant breasts in a single layer.

Pre-heat the oven to 200°C/400°F/gas 6.

Toss the pheasant breasts in seasoned flour. Heat 2 tablespoons of oil in the casserole and fry the joints until browned on both sides. Drain and remove the joints to a plate. Add the remaining oil to the pan, heat, then stir in the spices and cook for 1–2 minutes before adding the onions. Stir, then cover and cook over a low heat for 15 minutes, stirring occasionally. Now uncover and stir in the redcurrant jelly, cranberry sauce, port and stock and mix well. Check that the onion is nearly cooked, then replace the pheasant joints in the pan on top of the onion mixture. Season well with salt and pepper. Bring the casserole to simmering point, then transfer to the oven to bake, uncovered, for about 15 minutes or until the pheasant is tender. Serve hot with mashed celeriac and potatoes.

To prepare ahead: *The pheasant can be cooked, quickly cooled, covered and kept in the fridge for up to 2 days.*

To freeze: *Transfer the cooked, cold pheasant to a freezer container. Seal and label, then freeze for up to 2 months.*

To thaw: *Thaw for 6 hours at room temperature or overnight in the fridge.*

To re-heat: *Re-heat in a casserole covered with a lid or foil in a pre-heated oven at 200°C/ 400°F/gas 6 for about 20 minutes, stirring gently half-way through.*

To cook in a fan oven: *Pre-heat the oven to 190°C. When the jelly, cranberry sauce, port and stock have been added, and the onion is almost cooked, replace the pheasant joints and continue as in the recipe, cooking for 10 minutes or until the pheasant is tender.*

To cook in the Aga: *After replacing the browned pheasant joints in the casserole on top of the onion mixture, bring the contents to simmering point, then transfer to the roasting oven for a further 10 minutes or until the sauce is bubbling and the pheasant is tender.*

Spiced Pork Chops with Mango and Avocado

Serves 6

This is inspired by a recipe in a book by Carole Rymer, the wife of one of Britain's greatest pig farmers. Serve it with rice and a tomato and onion salad scattered with a liberal amount of coarsely chopped fresh parsley. You can buy creamed coconut in most supermarkets.

6 loin pork chops, boned	300 ml (10 fl oz) Chicken Stock
3 tablespoons olive oil	(see page 14)
175 g (6 oz) onions, coarsely	50 g (2 oz) creamed coconut, cut in
chopped	small chunks
2 garlic cloves, crushed	1 slightly under-ripe avocado, cut in
1 tablespoon plain white	small chunks
flour	Juice of ½ lemon
1 tablespoon garam masala	3 tablespoons mango chutney

Trim the excess fat from the chops. Heat the oil in a large, deep frying-pan over a moderate heat, then fry the meat for about 4 minutes on each side. Remove the chops to a plate and keep on one side. Stir the onions into the remaining oil in the pan and continue to cook over a fairly high heat until they start to colour. Stir in the garlic and cook for 1–2 minutes. Sprinkle in the flour and garam masala, stir into the onion, then gradually add the stock and coconut. Return the meat to the pan, burying the chops into the sauce mixture. Bring to a simmer, then cover and cook gently for about 20 minutes or until the meat is tender.

Meanwhile prepare the avocado and toss in the lemon juice to prevent it discolouring. As soon as the meat is tender, add the avocado, lemon juice and mango chutney to the pan. Bring back to simmering point, check seasoning and serve.

To prepare ahead: *Prepare the recipe but do not add the avocado, lemon juice and mango. Cool quickly, transfer the mixture to a storage container, cover and keep in the fridge for up to 3 days. Re-heat, covered, in a pan over direct heat until good and hot. Then add the avocado, lemon juice and mango.*

To freeze: *Not suitable.*

To cook in the Aga: *Prepare the first part of the recipe on the boiling plate. When the meat has been returned to the pan, cover and transfer the pan to the simmering oven for 20 minutes. Add the avocado, lemon juice and mango, heat through on the boiling plate and serve.*

Eastern-style Noodles with Spiced Pork and Coriander Meatballs

SERVES 4–6

A most successful supper dish that can be prepared ahead. Passata can now be bought in bottles or cartons in most supermarkets.

For the meatballs
450 g (1 lb) minced pork
3 garlic cloves, crushed
1 fresh chilli, seeded and finely
  chopped
2 teaspoons garam masala
3 tablespoons chopped fresh
  coriander
1 tablespoon dark soy sauce
1 tablespoon vegetable oil

2 tablespoons oil for frying
Plain white flour for coating
1 × 275 g packet medium Chinese
  egg noodles

For the tomato sauce
2 tablespoons vegetable oil
1 onion, very finely chopped
1 fat garlic clove, crushed
600 ml (1 pint) passata
2 teaspoons sugar
Salt and freshly ground black
  pepper
A dash of Tabasco sauce (optional)

To garnish
*4 tablespoons chopped fresh
coriander*

Combine all the ingredients for the meatballs together in a bowl and mix well. Divide the mixture into 12 pieces and form into balls. Heat the 2 tablespoons oil in a large frying-pan. Lightly flour the meatballs, then toss straight into the pan and swirl in the hot oil. Cook over a low to moderate heat for about 7 minutes or until browned. Use a draining spoon to remove to sheets of kitchen paper to drain. Leave aside until ready to use.

To make the tomato sauce, add the further 2 tablespoons of oil to the pan and stir in the onion and garlic. Cover and cook over a low heat for about 15 minutes or until softened and lightly coloured. Add the passata, sugar and salt and pepper and return the meatballs to the pan. Bring to simmering point, then cover and cook for about 15 minutes.

Meanwhile, cook the noodles in boiling salted water according to the instructions on the packet. When ready, drain and put into a warmed serving dish.

Uncover the pan and continue to cook and reduce if the sauce is a little thin. Taste and season with salt and pepper, adding a dash of Tabasco, if liked. Pour the contents of the pan over the noodles and sprinkle thickly with additional coriander. Serve at once.

To prepare ahead: *The meatballs can be cooked in the sauce, quickly cooled, then covered and stored in the fridge for up to 3 days. Re-heat, covered, in a frying-pan whilst the noodles boil.*

To freeze: *Cook the meatballs in the sauce for 15 minutes, then cool quickly and transfer to a freezer container. Seal, label and freeze for up to 4 months.*

To thaw: *Thaw in the freezer container for 4 hours at room temperature or overnight in the fridge.*

To re-heat: *Re-heat as directed in 'To prepare ahead'.*

SMALL ESSENTIALS TO HAVE ON HAND
*There are three items I find very useful in my kitchen and keep close at
hand: a waterproof pen to note the size on bases of tins, the number
of egg whites left in a bowl, details on foods to go in
the freezer, etc; sticky labels; and a retractable tape measure.*

English Fillet of Lamb
Fast-roasted with Lemon and Thyme

SERVES 4

The lamb fillet I use for this recipe is the eye of the best end of neck chops. It is not suitable to use scrag end neck of lamb fillet as this would toughen with this very hot, short method of cooking. The sauce is simple and just enough for the four servings. English lamb is at its best and cheapest in early autumn.

---

2 racks of lamb, about 7 chops in
* each, boned, skin left on*
50 g (2 oz) butter, softened
2 tablespoons mint or redcurrant
* jelly*
Grated rind and juice of
* 2 lemons*
3 fat garlic cloves, crushed
1 tablespoon chopped fresh thyme
* leaves*
1 teaspoon cornflour

To garnish
A sprig of fresh thyme

Start this recipe at least one day ahead.

Trim the meat of fat and membrane, leaving a thin layer of fat on top of the fillet. Cut off all but 2.5 cm (1 in) of the meat flap attached to the fillet. Combine all the remaining ingredients except the cornflour and juice of the lemons and spread over the lean meat surface. Cover and keep in the fridge for up to 2 days to allow the flavours to develop and permeate the meat.

Pre-heat the oven to 220°C/425°F/gas 7.

Bring the lamb up to room temperature. Scrape off the flavoured butter and keep. Heat an empty, medium-weight, non-stick pan over a moderate heat for 1 minute. Place the lamb fillets in the pan and cook for 1 minute on each side or until dark brown. Transfer the fillets to a small roasting tin and roast in the oven for 10 minutes, then remove the tin from the oven and cover with foil. Leave aside in a warm place to allow the meat to rest and 'set'.

Make up the juices in the pan to 250 ml (8 fl oz) with water and blend 2 tablespoons of water with the cornflour. Add the lemon juice to the pan and bring to the boil, then add the blended cornflour and bring to the boil again, stirring continuously.

Carve each fillet fairly thinly on a slight diagonal. Spoon the pan juices over the meat and serve at once, garnished with a sprig of fresh thyme.

To prepare ahead: *The meat can be marinated then browned. At this stage it can be kept covered in a the fridge. Complete the cooking and serve on the same day.*

To freeze: *Not suitable.*

To cook in a fan oven: *Pre-heat the oven to 200°c. Roast the lamb for 8–10 minutes, then follow the recipe.*

To cook in the Aga: *Heat the grill pan on the boiling plate. Cook the fillets for 1 minute on each side until well browned. Put the meat in the small roasting tin, spread with the flavoured butter, then transfer to the top of the roasting oven and cook for 8–10 minutes. Cover the tin with foil and leave to rest on the side of the Aga for 10–15 minutes.*

Manor House Lamb

SERVES 5–6

For this recipe I have tried to add as little fat as possible. Shoulder of lamb is not exactly lean so it seemed sensible to 'dry-fry' the meat. All this method needs is a medium-weight, non-stick frying-pan. The meat is seared in the pan over a fairly high heat with no fat added to the pan whatsoever; a simple way of cutting out a few unnecessary calories. Again, to cut out calories, the stew is thickened with cornflour. It is simple, and delicious served with Watercroft Whipped Potatoes (see page 137).

NO FREEZER CONTAINER? NO PROBLEM
Always having the right size of plastic freezer box to hand is almost impossible. A solution is to freeze the food in any suitable size container, such as bowls, baking dishes or tins – anything that can stand freezing. Once the food has frozen solid, remove it from the container, transfer it to a strong, plastic bag, seal and store in the freezer.

1.5 kg (3 lb) boned shoulder of lamb	*2.5 cm (1 in) cinnamon stick*
	2 cloves
350 g (12 oz) shallots, peeled and quartered	*2 tablespoons redcurrant jelly*
	1 tablespoon cornflour
450 ml (15 fl oz) water	*Salt and freshly ground black pepper*
1 teaspoon Worcestershire sauce	

To garnish
2 tablespoons crème de cassis
A handful of small sprigs of fresh parsley

To serve
Redcurrant jelly

Pre-heat the oven to 160°c/325°f/gas 3. You will need a flameproof casserole.

Cut the meat into approximately 2.5 cm (1 in) cubes, trimming away the excess fat. Heat a non-stick frying pan, empty, over a moderate heat for about 1 minute. Fry the meat, a small batch at a time, until well browned, then drain and remove to a flameproof casserole. When all the meat has been fried, pour the fat from the pan. Add the shallots to the pan and continue to fry over a moderate heat for 2–3 minutes or until browned. Tip the shallots into the casserole, then pour in the water and add the Worcestershire sauce, spices and redcurrant jelly. Bring to simmering point, then cover and transfer to the oven to cook for 1½ hours or until the meat is tender.

Measure the cornflour in a small bowl and blend smoothly with a little water. Stir the blend into the casserole, then bring back to the boil over direct heat. Taste and season with salt and pepper, then drizzle the cassis over the surface of the meat. Scatter with the parsley sprigs and serve hot with redcurrant jelly.

To prepare ahead: *Prepare and cook the casserole but do not add the cassis or parsley. Cool the stew quickly then cover and store in the fridge for up to 3 days. Re-heat on top of the stove and garnish before serving.*

To freeze: *Cool the stew quickly then put in a freezer container or a double thickness of plastic bags. Seal and label, then freeze for up to 6 months.*

To thaw: *Thaw for 4 hours at room temperature or overnight in the fridge.*

To re-heat: *Re-heat on top of the stove, add the cassis and parsley and serve.*

To cook in a fan oven: *Do not pre-heat the oven. Put in the casserole and bake at 150°c for 1½ hours or until the meat is tender. Continue to cook, following the recipe above.*

To cook in the Aga: *When the casserole has been brought to simmering point, cover and transfer to the simmering oven. Cook for about 2 hours until tender.*

Lamb Paysanne with Spinach Stuffing

SERVES 8

Lamb cooked this way is wonderfully moist and really does not need basting during cooking. The bonus is that the meat and vegetables are all ready at the same time. If an unexpected guest turns up for Sunday lunch, add some stir-fried, sliced courgettes to the cooked vegetables before serving to give extra colour and quantity. Incidentally, I do find a meat thermometer very useful, as you will see from this recipe.

1.5–2 kg (3½–4½ lb) boned shoulder or leg of lamb
2 large, mild onions, each cut into 8 wedges
8 whole garlic cloves, skin on
2 medium-sized aubergines, thickly sliced
1 yellow pepper, seeded and cut into 8 sections
2 red peppers, seeded and each cut into 8 sections
Salt and freshly ground black pepper
A sprig of fresh rosemary or a little dried rosemary

For the spinach stuffing
450 g (1 lb) prepared fresh spinach leaves, shredded
1 garlic clove, crushed
125 g (4½ oz) light, cream cheese
25 g (1 oz) fresh white breadcrumbs
Salt and freshly ground black pepper

You will need a large roasting tin, greased with oil.

Pre-heat the oven to 220°C/425°F/gas 7.

Begin by preparing the stuffing and put the spinach and garlic into a large frying-pan. Stir-fry over a high heat until the leaves have wilted and no excess liquid remains. Drain and cool, squeeze any remaining liquid from the spinach and transfer the leaves to a bowl. Beat in the remaining stuffing ingredients and taste and season with salt and freshly ground pepper. Trim off the excess fat from the lamb then stuff with the spinach mixture.

Put the joint in the middle of the roasting tin, surrounded by the onions and garlic. Roast for about 25 minutes until the meat has browned. Add the rest of the vegetables to the tin and turn the meat over. Season well with salt and pepper and sprinkle the lamb with a little rosemary. If using a meat thermometer, put into the thickest part of the joint, then return the tin to the oven for about 1 hour until the lamb is cooked to your taste: the thermometer should read about 80°C (176°F) for well done, 70–75°C (158–167°F) for medium. Carve and serve the meat with the vegetables and any pan juices. You can, if you like, eat the garlic; if you press one end of the clove it will come out like toothpaste at the other and taste mellow and delicious.

To prepare ahead: *The prepared stuffing and vegetables can be kept separately, covered, in the fridge with the meat, for up to 24 hours. Stuff the joint just before roasting, as in the recipe.*

To freeze: *Not suitable.*

To cook in a fan oven: *Pre-heat the oven to 200°C. Roast initially for about 20 minutes, then for about 50 minutes, or according to taste.*

To cook in the Aga: *Slide the roasting tin on to the lowest set of runners in the roasting oven for 25 minutes. Return all the vegetables and meat to the same position in the oven and roast for about 1 hour until done.*

Scrumpy Beef Casserole with Parsley and Horseradish Dumplings

Serves 6–8

Just a little bit different and packed with flavour – the meat and vegetables are marinated in cider then cooked in a casserole. The stew is then thickened and has the dumplings baked on top. The dumplings were an experiment that worked well. I patted out the suet dough to a rectangle, spread it with a mixture of parsley and horseradish, then rolled it up like a Swiss roll, sliced it and put it on top of the stew: a sort of savoury, Chelsea bun, dumpling! All so simple and can be prepared well ahead.

Scrumpy Beef Casserole with Parsley and Horseradish Dumplings (above).

1 kg (2 ¼ lb) chuck steak, cubed
150 g (5 oz) button mushrooms,
    halved
1 ½ tablespoons butter

1 ½ tablespoons plain white
    flour
Salt and freshly ground black
    pepper

For the marinade

450 ml (15 fl oz) strong dry cider
2 celery sticks, cut in 5 mm (¼ in)
    slices
3 medium-sized carrots, obliquely
    cut in 5 mm (¼ in) slices

1 onion, cut in 6–8 wedges
1 bay leaf
2 sprigs of fresh thyme
1 beef stock cube

For the dumplings

175 g (6 oz) self-raising white flour
75 g (3 oz) shredded suet
Salt and freshly ground black pepper

About 10 tablespoons cold water
3 tablespoons very hot horseradish
3 tablespoons chopped fresh parsley

Start the recipe the day before. You will need a large flameproof casserole.

Put the meat and the marinade ingredients in a bowl. Cover with a plate and weight so the ingredients remain covered with the liquid. If you do not have a spare bowl, put the meat and marinade in a strong polythene bag. Keep in the fridge for 24 hours.

Pre-heat the oven to 150°C/300°F/gas 2.

Tip the meat and marinade into a flameproof casserole. It should not be filled more than two-thirds full. Cover, bring to the boil over direct heat, then transfer to the oven and cook for 2 hours or until tender.

Meanwhile, prepare the dumplings. Mix together the flour, suet, ½ teaspoon salt and ¼ teaspoon pepper in a bowl, then stir in enough water to bring them together in a soft but not sticky dough. Turn out on to a lightly floured work surface and pat or roll out to a 15 × 20 cm (6 × 8 in) rectangle. Stir together the horseradish and parsley and a little salt and pepper to form a paste. Spread this evenly over the surface of the dough, right up to the edges. Roll up from one short end, Swiss-roll style. Cover with clingfilm and keep in the fridge until ready to use.

After 2 hours remove the casserole and immediately set the oven temperature to 200°C/400°F/gas 6. Stir in the mushrooms. Combine the butter and flour to form a paste, then stir a small portion at a time into the simmering casserole. Stir and allow to thicken. Taste and season with salt and pepper if necessary.

Remove the suet roll from the fridge and cut evenly into 8 rounds. Arrange these cut-side up on top of the meat, sitting in the juices, 7 around the outside and 1 in the middle. Bring up to simmering point over direct heat, then return to the oven to bake for 30 minutes or until the dumplings start to get a golden crust. Serve immediately.

To prepare ahead: *Prepare and cook the casserole for 2 hours, then cool quickly, cover and put in the fridge. Prepare the dumplings as far as forming the dough into a roll, cover closely with clingfilm and put in the fridge. Both items can be kept for up to 2 days. Re-heat the casserole over direct heat, drop in the dumplings then bake in the oven following the recipe.*

To freeze: *Prepare and cook the casserole for 2 hours, then cool quickly and place in a freezer container or double thickness of plastic bags. Seal, label and freeze for up to 6 months. Make the suet dumplings, slice and freeze uncovered on a foil-lined baking tray. When firm, pack into a plastic bag, seal and label, then freeze for up to 6 months.*

To thaw: *Thaw the stew for 4–5 hours at room temperature or overnight in the fridge. Arrange the frozen dumplings on a foil-lined baking tray, cover and thaw for the same time as the stew.*

To re-heat: *Re-heat as directed in 'To prepare ahead'.*

To cook in a fan oven: *Do not pre-heat the oven. Cook at 140°c for about 1¾ hours or until the meat is tender. Raise the oven temperature to 190°c before the dumplings are baked, then bake for 25–30 minutes.*

To cook in the Aga: *First cook in the simmering oven for 2–3 hours or until tender. Then bring to the boil on the top, add the butter and flour paste and stir until the mixture thickens. Top with the dumplings and transfer to the roasting oven fairly near the top for about 25 minutes or until crisp and done.*

CONCERNING SUET

Do not expect to find suet around kidneys; that went out when the EU came in. When testing this recipe I noticed that the supermarket was offering no less than three different types of prepared suet: the usual beef suet, a vegetable fat suet suitable for vegetarians, and a low-fat version. This last one was completely new to me and I found it worked just as well as usual.

Seared Fillet of Beef

SERVES 6–8

An excellent method of roasting beef, if you follow my cooking times you are guaranteed that the meat will be cooked to perfection.

---

900 g (2 lb) thick end fillet of beef

For the marinade
2 tablespoons olive oil
1–2 tablespoons whole grain
    mustard
2 tablespoons clear honey
4 garlic cloves, quartered

For the sauce
600 ml (1 pint) Beef Stock
    (see page 14)
1 glass red wine, about 150 ml
    (5 fl oz)
40–50 g (1½–2 oz) unsalted butter,
    cubed and chilled

1 teaspoon balsamic vinegar
    (optional)
Salt and freshly ground black
    pepper
A little gravy browning

To garnish
Sprigs of fresh thyme

The meat needs to be marinated 1 or 2 days ahead of cooking.

Mix together the marinade ingredients in a small bowl. Sit the joint inside a snug-fitting plastic bag and pour the marinade over the joint, making sure it runs down into the plastic bag. Seal well and chill for up to 2 days, occasionally turning the bag containing the joint so all parts of the meat are basted with the marinade.

When ready to cook, pre-heat the oven to 220°C/425°F/gas 7.

Keeping the marinade and garlic in the plastic bag, put the meat alone into a small roasting tin. Roast for 25 minutes for rare, 30 minutes for pink, 40 minutes for well done. Then remove from the oven, cover with foil and leave aside for 10 minutes. It will remain hot and be perfectly cooked, but will carve more easily.

Pour the beef stock, red wine and the strained marinade juices, minus the garlic, into a pan, add any juices from the roasting tin and bring to the boil. Continue boiling until the pan juices have reduced to 300 ml (10 fl oz). Using a small whisk, gradually incorporate the cubes of butter, maintaining a gentle heat under the pan. Taste and add the balsamic vinegar, if liked, and season with salt and pepper; add a dash of gravy browning to give a rich brown colour. Carve the beef thinly and serve with the hot sauce. Garnish with fresh thyme.

To prepare ahead: *Leave the roast fillet to cool, then wrap closely in foil. Transfer the sauce to an airtight container. Both can be chilled for up to 2 days.*

To freeze: *Not suitable.*

To re-heat: *Remove the joint from the fridge 1 hour before re-heating. Cook the foil-wrapped joint in a pre-heated oven at 200°C/400°F/gas 6 for 20 minutes. Re-heat the sauce in a small pan over direct heat.*

To cook in a fan oven: *Pre-heat the oven to 200°C. Roast the fillet for 20 minutes for rare, 25 for pink and 35 for well done.*

To cook in the Aga: *Having put the meat into a small roasting tin, slide this on to the top set of runners in the roasting oven and roast for 25 minutes, then follow the recipe.*

First-rate Cottage Pie

SERVES 6

A straightforward, unpretentious cottage pie. If it is cooked carefully and properly it needs no other fancy additions to make it a four-star luxury dish.

2 tablespoons vegetable oil	150 ml (5 fl oz) red wine
1 kg (2 ¼ lb) lean minced raw beef	300 ml (10 fl oz) Beef Stock (see page 14)
2 onions, chopped	1 small head of celery, sliced
2 fat garlic cloves, crushed	2 bay leaves
3 tablespoons plain white flour	Salt and freshly ground black pepper
1 × 397 g tin chopped tomatoes	

For the potato topping

1 kg (2 ¼ lb) old, floury potatoes, peeled	Salt and freshly ground black pepper
200 ml (7 fl oz) milk	100 g (4 oz) mature Cheddar

You will need a flameproof dish measuring 30 × 20 × 6 cm (12 × 8 × 2½ in).

Heat the oil in a large non-stick pan then over a high heat, gradually add the meat, a small handful at a time, allowing each batch to colour before adding the next. When all the meat has been added, continue to cook until the base of the pan starts to brown. Now add the onions and carry on cooking for a further 10 minutes or until they too start to brown. This careful browning process will give the pie a good flavour. Add the garlic, then after 1–2 minutes sprinkle in the flour and stir until browned, then add the remaining ingredients. Turn the heat down low, cover and cook gently for 30 minute, stirring occasionally. Uncover and cook for a further 30 minutes or until the mince has reduced and little free gravy remains. Taste and add more salt and pepper if necessary and check that the mince is tender; cover and keep hot if aiming to serve soon.

Cook the potatoes in boiling, salted water until soft. Leave to drain in a colander. Add the milk to the hot pan and return it to the heat. Season with salt and pepper and bring to the boil. Tip the potatoes back into the pan, remove from the heat and mash to a fluffy consistency with a potato masher or ricer. Stir in all but 25 g (1 oz) of the cheese.

Pre-heat the grill.

Spread the meat mixture in the dish, discarding the bay leaves when you come across them, then gently spread the potato on top. Sprinkle with the reserved cheese and put under the grill to brown for about 5–8 minutes. Serve piping hot.

To prepare ahead: *The pie can be made and kept covered in the fridge for up to 24 hours. Bake the pie in the top half of a pre-heated oven at 200°c/400°f/gas 6 for 40 minutes or until bubbling hot and browned.*

To freeze: *Not ideal as the potato loses texture. However, you could freeze the cooked mince ready to top with freshly made potato when needed.*

To thaw: *Thaw the mince covered overnight in the fridge.*

To re-heat: *Spread the mince with the potato topping and re-heat as directed in 'To prepare ahead'.*

To cook in a fan oven: *Do not pre-heat the oven. Bake at 190°c for about 35 minutes.*

To cook in the Aga: *Cook on a high shelf in the roasting oven for about 20 minutes.*

Ⓥ
Garden Vegetable Cottage Pie
SERVES 6

A good alternative for vegetarians to the usual cottage pie. For an informal buffet or supper it is a good idea to serve one of each type of pie, side by side. Use the vegetables which are to hand or in season: onions, carrots, cauliflowers, leeks, celery would make a good wintery mix. Dice larger vegetables such as carrots, cut cauliflower into small florets, or leave tiny vegetables, such as baby sweetcorn, whole.

2 tablespoons vegetable oil
25 g (1 oz) butter
1 kg (2¼ lb) mixed, prepared
 vegetables (see above)
50 g (2 oz) plain white flour
1 × 397 g tin chopped tomatoes

150 ml (5 fl oz) Vegetable Stock
 (see page 58)
300 ml (10 fl oz) milk
Salt and freshly ground black
 pepper

For the potato topping

*1 kg (2 ¼ lb) old, floury potatoes,
    peeled*
150 ml (5 fl oz) milk
*1 × 125 g tub medium-fat fresh
    goats' cheese*
*Salt and freshly ground black
    pepper*
25 g (1 oz) butter

You will need a flameproof dish about 30 × 20 × 6 cm (12 × 8 × 2½ in).

Heat the oil and butter together in a large pan, then stir in all the vegetables that take the longest to cook, such as carrots, onions and celery. Cook over a fairly high heat, stirring frequently, until the vegetables begin to brown a little. Sprinkle in the flour, stir and cook for 1–2 minutes. Pour in the contents of the can of tomatoes, followed by the stock, then the milk. Bring to the boil, then cover and simmer over a low heat for 30 minutes. Uncover and add the remaining vegetables (cauliflower, leeks, baby sweetcorn and so on) and continue to cook gently, stirring occasionally, for a further 20–30 minutes or until all the vegetables are cooked. Taste and season carefully with salt and pepper; cover and keep hot if aiming to serve soon.

Cook the potatoes in boiling salted water until soft. Leave to drain in a colander. Add the milk and goats' cheese to the pan and return to the heat. Season with salt and pepper and bring to the boil. Tip the potatoes back into the pan, remove from the heat and mash to a fluffy consistency with a potato masher or ricer.

Pre-heat the grill.

Spread the vegetable mixture in the dish then gently spread the potato on top. Dot the top with butter and put under the grill for about 10 minutes or until browned and bubbling. Serve piping hot.

To prepare ahead: *The pie can be made and kept covered in the fridge for up to 24 hours. Bake the pie in the top half of a pre-heated oven at 200°C/400°F/gas 6 for 40 minutes or until bubbling hot and browned.*

To freeze: *Not ideal to freeze as the vegetables lose some of their crispness and the potato some of its texture.*

To cook in a fan oven: *Do not pre-heat the oven. Bake the cold pie for about 30 minutes or until bubbling hot and browned.*

To cook in the Aga: *Cook on a high shelf in the roasting oven for about 20 minutes until golden brown.*

West Country Gratin of Cider, Bacon and Vegetables

SERVES 6

If you have overestimated the vegetables for Sunday lunch, here is the best way to use them up for a supper dish on Monday. Apart from the vegetables I have specified in the recipe, you could add left-overs such as peas, green beans, cauliflower or broccoli. And I have not asked for any particular cut of bacon because it simply does not matter. My choice is anything that is on offer amongst the bacon pieces sold in vacuum packs!

450 g (1 lb) piece of bacon	*225 g (8 oz) cooked, peeled potatoes, cubed*
450 ml (15 fl oz) dry cider	
225 g (8 oz) white of leek, thinly sliced	*Salt and freshly ground black pepper*
50 g (2 oz) butter	*50 g (2 oz) strong Cheddar, coarsely grated*
2 celery sticks, thinly sliced	
50 g (2 oz) plain white flour	*50 g (2 oz) Parmesan, coarsely grated*
300 ml (10 fl oz) warm milk	
225 g (8 oz) cooked carrots, sliced	

You will need a shallow ovenproof dish.

Choose a small pan with a well-fitting lid. Add the bacon and pour in the cider. Bring to the boil, lower to simmering point, then cover and cook gently for about 30 minutes or until cooked and really tender. Remove the bacon from the pan and leave to cool; return the pan to the heat and boil the cider juices, if not too salty, until reduced to 300 ml (10 fl oz). Leave on one side.

Meanwhile wash and thoroughly drain the leek in a colander. Heat the butter in a large pan and stir in the celery. Cover and cook gently for 5 minutes, then stir in the leek. Re-cover and cook for a further 5 minutes. Sprinkle in the flour, stir and take the pan off the heat before gradually stirring in the milk, followed by the cider. Re-heat and bring to the boil, stirring. Simmer for 1–2 minutes then fold in the cooked vegetables.

Pre-heat the grill to medium.

Cut off the rind and excess fat from the bacon and cut the meat into sugar-cube sized pieces. Fold these into the sauce. Taste and season with salt and pepper, then pour the mixture into the ovenproof dish. Sprinkle with the cheeses.

Place under the grill until golden brown and piping hot throughout.

Red Pepper and Fennel Pissaladière
(page 104).

To prepare ahead: *Cover the completed dish with clingfilm, keep in the fridge for up to 2 days. Re-heat in a pre-heated oven at 190°C/375°F/gas 5 for about 40 minutes if cold, or about 30 minutes if at room temperature, until hot and golden.*

To freeze: *Not suitable.*

To cook in a fan oven: *Do not pre-heat the oven. Bake at 180°C for about 25–30 minutes.*

To cook in the Aga: *Bake in the roasting oven on the grid shelf on the second set of runners for about 20 minutes.*

Red Pepper and Fennel Pissaladière

Serves 8

Or, in other words, fennel, peppers and onions on a crisp cheese-pastry base.

For the cheese pastry
175 g (6 oz) plain white flour
75 g (3 oz) chilled butter, cut into cubes
75 g (3 oz) full-flavoured Cheddar, grated
1 heaped teaspoon English mustard powder
A good pinch of cayenne
1–2 tablespoons cold water

For the topping
6 large red peppers
1 tablespoon olive oil
2 Spanish onions, thinly sliced into rings
2 bulbs of fennel, cut lengthways into 6 or 8
2 garlic cloves, crushed
2 tablespoons chopped fresh parsley
1 teaspoon balsamic vinegar
Salt and freshly ground black pepper

To garnish
A few shavings of fresh Parmesan
About 6 fresh basil leaves, torn in pieces

You will need a flat baking tray at least 30 cm (12 in) square.

To make the pastry, put the flour and butter in a processor and process until the mixture resembles breadcrumbs, or put the ingredients in a large bowl and rub together with the fingertips. Add the remaining ingredients and process, or mix together just enough for the pastry to form a ball. Put in the fridge while making the topping.

Pre-heat the grill and line the grill pan with foil.

Arrange the peppers in the foil-lined grill pan and grill, turning regularly, until blackened all over. Remove the peppers to a shallow dish, stacking them on top of each other, then cover with a plate and leave to cool. When ready, grasp the green stalk of each pepper and give it a twist to remove the central core and seeds. Strip off all the skin, then halve the peppers over the dish to catch the juices, then cut each pepper into 6 strips. Heat the olive oil in a large frying-pan, then stir in the onions and fennel. Fry until beginning to soften and colour, then cover and cook gently for about 30 minutes or until tender. Add the garlic and any pepper juices, then turn up the heat and cook until the excess liquid has evaporated. Add the peppers, parsley and vinegar, then taste and season with salt and pepper. Re-cover and leave aside until cold.

Put the dough in the centre of the baking tray and roll out to a 30 cm (12 in) circle. Pinch the edge between thumb and forefinger to create a rim. Return the tray to the fridge for 30 minutes.

Pre-heat the oven to 400°F/200°C/gas 6.

About 20 minutes before serving, spread the vegetable mixture over the pastry up to the raised edge. Bake for 20 minutes or until the edge of the pastry is golden. Top with shavings of Parmesan and torn basil leaves and serve.

To prepare ahead: *The filling can be prepared, closely covered with clingfilm and kept in the fridge with the rolled-out pastry on the baking tray.*

To freeze: *The dish is best not frozen, although if some is left over, freeze the remaining wedges and re-heat in a hot oven.*

To cook in a fan oven: *Pre-heat the oven to 190°c. Bake for about 15 minutes.*

To cook in the Aga: *The onion and fennel can be cooked in a pan on the floor of the simmering oven for 30–35 minutes. Bake the pissaladière on the floor of the roasting oven for 20 minutes.*

Pappardelle with Tomato and Vodka Sauce

SERVES 4–6

Rather an adult sauce! Ideal for serving when tempers are a little ruffled or your guests seem a little shy or even rather stiff and formal. This recipe is the formula for relaxing everyone and getting a party going with a swing. Try it if you don't believe me. It is not always easy to get pappardelle, a broad ribbon pasta, so go for tagliatelle or fettucine instead.

25 g (1 oz) butter
1 onion, chopped
2 garlic cloves, crushed
1 teaspoon dried oregano
1 × 397 g tin chopped tomatoes
100 g (4 oz) Parma, Black Forest
*   or Serrano ham, chopped*
150 ml (5 fl oz) vodka
1 × 200 g carton half-fat crème
*   fraîche*
A small handful of fresh basil
*   leaves*
40 g (1½ oz) Parmesan, grated
Salt and freshly ground black
*   pepper*
400–450 g (14–16 oz) pappardelle

To garnish
A good handful of small sprigs of
*   fresh parsley*
Freshly grated Parmesan

GRATE YOUR GARLIC
A quick way to finely chop a large quantity of garlic – about 8 cloves –
is to grate the peeled cloves on the coarse side of the grater.

Melt the butter in a medium-sized deep frying-pan and fry the onion, garlic and oregano over a medium to high heat for about 5 minutes until the onion is quite brown. Pour in the contents of the tin of tomatoes and stir in the ham. Leave the mixture to simmer gently, uncovered, for about 10 minutes. Pour in the vodka and simmer, uncovered, for a further 5 minutes. Add the crème fraîche and basil leaves and carry on simmering for about 5–10 minutes or until the mixture is a good consistency for coating pasta. Remove the sauce from the heat and add the Parmesan. Taste and season with salt and pepper if needed.

Meanwhile cook the pasta until *al dente* in boiling salted water, then drain. Quickly toss the pasta with the sauce and sprinkle with parsley sprigs. Serve immediately with additional Parmesan.

To prepare ahead: *The sauce can be made ahead, quickly cooled, covered and kept in the fridge for up to 1 week.*

To freeze: *Place the cooked sauce in a freezer container. Cool, seal and label, then freeze for up to 2 months.*

To thaw: *Thaw in the freezer container for about 6 hours at room temperature or overnight in the fridge.*

To re-heat: *Re-heat and bring to the boil in a pan before serving with the freshly boiled pasta.*

To cook in the Aga: *Toss the onion and herbs in a large non-stick frying-pan on the boiling plate for a few minutes. Cover and transfer to the simmering oven for about 10–15 minutes or until tender. Then follow the recipe, cooking on simmering plate.*

(V)

Mega Pasta Shells Stuffed with Spinach and Italian Cheeses with a Garlic and Tomato Sauce

SERVES 4

A rather different style of pasta dish that makes a change from cannelloni or lasagne. You could use a 1.25 kg bag of frozen leaf spinach, thawed, if fresh is not available. You should find the large pasta shells in delicatessens and some supermarkets; if not, the smaller ones are readily available.

*12 large pasta shells (conchiglie),
or 24 smaller ones*

For the filling
*25 g (1 oz) butter
225 g (8 oz) fresh young spinach,
coarsely chopped
225 g (8 oz) mascarpone
50 g (2 oz) Parmesan, freshly
grated
1 egg, lightly beaten
1 tablespoon chopped fresh basil
Salt and freshly ground black
pepper
A little freshly grated nutmeg*

For the sauce
*1 tablespoon olive oil
1 onion, chopped
2–3 garlic cloves, crushed
1 rounded tablespoon plain white
flour
1 × 400 g tin chopped tomatoes
2 tablespoons tomato purée
450 ml (15 fl oz) Vegetable Stock
(see page 58) or light Chicken
Stock (see page 14)
2 teaspoons sugar
Salt and freshly ground black
pepper*

To garnish
*A few shavings of fresh Parmesan
About 6 fresh basil leaves*

You will need a shallow baking dish measuring about 30 × 20 cm (12 × 8 in).

Pre-heat the oven to 200°c/400°f/gas 6.

Melt the butter in a frying-pan, then stir in the spinach and cook over a high heat for 3–4 minutes. When it is fairly dry, remove the pan from the heat, stir in the remaining filling ingredients and leave to cool.

To make the sauce, heat the oil in a pan, stir in the onion and garlic and cook over a low heat for about 10 minutes or until softened but not coloured. Remove the pan from the heat and stir in the flour, followed by the tomatoes, tomato purée and stock. Season with sugar, salt and pepper, then return to the heat and bring to the boil, stirring. Reduce the heat to a bare simmer, then cook, stirring occasionally to make a thickish sauce. Taste and season with salt and pepper. Leave on one side until ready to use.

Check the cooking instructions for the pasta; the shells will probably need cooking in boiling salted water for 7–10 minutes. Be careful not to overcook them as it makes them difficult to fill. When cooked, drain well, then leave in cold water. Divide the filling into equal portions and fill the shells.

Spread the base of the dish with half the sauce and arrange the pasta shells in a single layer in the sauce. Coat each one with the remaining sauce. Bake for about 20 minutes until piping hot and bubbling. Scatter with a few shavings of fresh Parmesan and torn fresh basil leaves, then serve.

To prepare ahead: *The dish can be fully prepared and kept covered in the fridge for up to 24 hours.*

To freeze: *The stuffed shells are best frozen if put into a shallow freezer container just the right size to contain them in a single layer. Cover with freezer tissue then the lid. Label and freeze for up to 4 months. Freeze the sauce separately in clean cream or yoghurt pots, seal and label, then freeze for up to 3 months.*

To thaw: *Thaw in the freezer container overnight in the fridge. Treat the container of sauce the same way.*

To re-heat: *Bake for about 25 minutes following the recipe.*

To cook in a fan oven: *Do not pre-heat the oven. Bake at 190°c for about 25 minutes.*

To cook in the Aga: *Bake the completed pasta shells in the roasting oven on the grid shelf on the floor for 25–30 minutes.*

ⓥ
Pasta with Fresh Tomatoes and Asparagus

SERVES 6 AS A STARTER OR 4 AS A MAIN COURSE

The cheaper, thinner stalks of asparagus, sometimes called 'sprue', are good in this pasta dish. It is a very light, fresh, summery sort of sauce, made a little like a Carbonara and it is one of my all-time favourites. Pecorino is a mature sheeps' cheese with an excellent sharp flavour. Keep a lookout for it as it is often cheaper than Parmesan.

750 g (1½ lb) ripe tomatoes
750 g (1½ lb) asparagus spears
2 eggs
1 egg yolk
50 g (2 oz) Parmesan or Pecorino,
    freshly grated
450 g (1 lb) penne

15 g (½ oz) butter
1 tablespoon oil
1 garlic clove, crushed
2 tablespoons chopped fresh
    basil
Salt and freshly ground black
    pepper

To garnish
*A handful of small fresh basil
leaves*

Bring a large pan of salted water to the boil. To save a little time and effort you can skin the tomatoes by dipping them in the boiling water for about 1 minute, then scooping them out and immediately cooling under cold running water. Then skin, discard the seeds and chop the flesh. Leave the water on the boil.

Discard the tough ends of the asparagus, then cut the rest into 4 cm (1½ in) lengths). Drop these into the boiling water and cook for about 4 minutes or until just tender but still with plenty of bite. Scoop from the water and refresh under cold running water. Drain on kitchen paper and leave aside until ready to use. Leave the water on the boil.

Break the eggs and egg yolk into a bowl and, using a fork, beat together with the cheese.

Put the pasta into the boiling water and cook until *al dente* or according to the instructions on the packet.

While the pasta is cooking, heat the butter and oil in a medium-sized frying-pan. Add the garlic and cook for about 1 minute, then tip in the tomatoes and toss together for another minute. Add the asparagus and basil. Taste and season well with salt and pepper. Cover and take the pan off the heat.

Drain the pasta and quickly return it to the hot pan. Swiftly add the egg mixture and swirl the pan to coat the pasta. Now add the tomatoes and asparagus. Season with more salt and pepper if necessary, toss and serve immediately strewn with torn fresh basil leaves.

To prepare ahead: *Skin, seed and chop the tomatoes and cook the asparagus spears.*

To freeze: *Not suitable.*

Chestnut Quenelles
on Grilled Aubergine Slices
(page 113).

Chinese Noodles with Asparagus

SERVES 6

This is ideal for a family supper or interesting lunch. The colour is wonderful and it is a complete meal that needs no extras.

1 × 275 g packet Chinese medium egg noodles	1 small red chilli, seeded and thinly sliced
3–4 tablespoons sesame or sunflower oil	275 g (10 oz) asparagus spears
350–450 g (12 oz – 1 lb) boneless chicken breast or pork fillet strips	5 spring onions, diagonally sliced
1 large, mild onion, thinly sliced	2 small red peppers, seeded and thinly sliced
2 fat garlic cloves, crushed	250 ml (8 fl oz) Chicken Stock (see page 14)
2.5 cm (1 in) fresh root ginger, peeled and cut into fine shreds	2 teaspoons cornflour
1 tablespoon finely chopped fresh lemon grass (about 3 bulbs)	2 tablespoons water
	2 tablespoons soy sauce
	Freshly ground black pepper

To garnish
A small bunch of fresh coriander, chopped

You will need a generous-sized serving bowl ready warming.

Bring a large pan of well-salted water to the boil. Check the cooking instructions on the noodle packet. If the noodles need 10 minutes to cook, pop them into the boiling water and time their cooking. If you work quickly, the noodles will be ready at almost the same time as the remaining ingredients.

Measure about 2 tablespoons of the oil into a large frying-pan. Stir-fry the chicken or meat strips over a moderately high heat for 2–3 minutes until browned but a little under-done. Lift from the pan with a draining spoon on to a plate and keep on one side. Add a further tablespoon of oil to the pan and stir in the onion, garlic, ginger, lemon grass and chilli. Stir-fry over a moderately high heat for about 5 minutes. Trim the cut ends of the asparagus spears, then cut the rest into 2.5 cm (1 in) lengths and add to the pan with the spring onions and peppers. Continue to stir-fry for a further 5 minutes, adding more oil if needed. Now pour in the stock and bring to the boil.

In a small bowl, stir together the cornflour and water, then add to the pan, stirring briskly. Bring to the boil and simmer as you return the chicken or meat to the pan to heat. Add the drained noodles, then taste and season with soy sauce and pepper. Turn into the warmed serving bowl and sprinkle generously with the chopped coriander.

To prepare ahead: *The recipe is so quick to prepare it is hardly worth preparing ahead, but the vegetables could be prepared to the point before adding the stock and cornflour. The noodles can be ready boiled and kept in cold water. Vegetables and noodles can be kept in this manner for up to 4 hours, then follow the recipe.*

To freeze: *Not suitable.*

Ⓥ
Chestnut Quenelles
on Grilled Aubergine Slices

MAKES 18 TO SERVE 6–8

Frozen chestnuts are easiest and best for this recipe, but if not available use dried, which you can buy from good delicatessens or health food shops. Dried chestnuts need soaking overnight and they swell to double the dried weight. So for this recipe you will need just 150 g (5 oz).

4 tablespoons olive oil	75 g (3 oz) sunflower seeds, coarsely chopped
1 large onion, finely chopped	1 egg, beaten
2 celery sticks, finely chopped	150 ml (5 fl oz) Vegetable Stock (see page 58)
275 g (10 oz) frozen chestnuts, thawed	Salt and freshly ground black pepper
1 teaspoon mixed spice	2 medium-sized aubergines, the long, slim type
½ teaspoon ground allspice	4 tablespoons melted butter
½ teaspoon ground cinnamon	
75 g (3 oz) fresh wholemeal breadcrumbs	
2 rounded tablespoons chopped fresh parsley	

To decorate
A little chopped fresh parsley

You will need 2 baking trays, greased.

Pre-heat the oven to 190°C/375°F/gas 5.

Heat 2 tablespoons of the oil in a large frying-pan. Stir in the onion and celery, then cover and cook over a low to moderate heat for 10 minutes. Meanwhile chop or process the chestnuts to the size of large salt crystals taking care not to chop them too finely. Stir these into the pan, then cover and cook for a further 10 minutes, stirring occasionally. Sprinkle in the spices and continue to cook, stirring frequently, for a further 5 minutes. Transfer the contents of the pan to a large mixing bowl and add the breadcrumbs, parsley and sunflower seeds. Mix the egg and stock together and pour into the bowl; thoroughly mix the ingredients, then season with salt and pepper.

Trim both ends of the aubergines before cutting across into 18 round slices slightly less than 1 cm (½ in) thick. Brush with some of the remaining oil and season with salt and pepper on both sides.

Using 2 dessertspoons, mould the chestnut mixture into 18 rounded, oval shapes and arrange on the baking trays. Gently brush the quenelles with melted butter, then bake in the pre-heated oven for 20 minutes until pale golden and crisp.

While they bake, the aubergine slices can be either grilled or cooked on a heavy, ridged, oven-top grill pan until browned and softened. Arrange the cooked slices on a warmed serving platter and top with the baked quenelles. Sprinkle with chopped parsley and serve hot.

To prepare ahead: *Prepare the quenelle mix, put into a bowl, cover and keep in the fridge for up to 24 hours.*

To freeze: *The uncooked nut roast freezes very well either in a container or well-covered as individual quenelles. Seal and label, then freeze for up to 2 months. It is not worthwhile freezing the aubergine.*

To thaw: *Thaw the mix for about 2 hours at room temperature, then shape into quenelles. Quenelles that are already shaped need not be thawed before cooking.*

To cook: *Follow the recipe. Frozen, shaped quenelles will need a slightly longer cooking time.*

To cook in a fan oven: *Pre-heat the oven to 180°c. Bake for about 15 minutes or until the quenelles are pale golden and crisp.*

To cook in the Aga: *Roast the aubergine slices on a ridged, grill pan. Roast the quenelles in the roasting oven for about 15–20 minutes.*

FRESH EGGS
Ever since the 'egg scare' I store eggs in the fridge, in their boxes, and use them in strict rotation. I have found no problem in using eggs for cooking straight from the fridge.

Ⓥ Peppers Stuffed with Spinach and Three Cheeses

SERVES 4–6

A vegetable dish that is a meal in its own right, ideal for a family supper. Bake the peppers alongside the Leek and Potato Gratin (made without the cheese) on page 139 and serve with a crisp green leaf salad for a satisfying meal.

4 medium-sized red or yellow peppers	75 g (3 oz) mature Cheddar, grated
About 1 tablespoon sunflower oil	75 g (3 oz) Gruyère or Emmental, grated
Salt and freshly ground black pepper	1 × 125 g packet light cream cheese
1 × 500 g packet frozen leaf spinach, thawed	2 eggs, beaten

You will need a roasting tin large enough to accommodate 8 pepper halves.

Pre-heat the oven to 190°C/375°F/gas 5.

Cut each pepper in half through the stem and down to the base. Use a small knife to cut away the central core and ribs but leave the stalk on. Arrange the peppers in the roasting tin cut-side up, drizzle with a little oil and season with salt and pepper.

Use your hands to squeeze every last drop of water from the spinach, then put the leaves in a large mixing bowl with the remaining ingredients. Beat well to mix thoroughly then taste and season with salt and pepper. Spoon the mixture into the pepper halves, then cover the roasting tin with greased foil. Bake for 30 minutes. Remove the foil and bake for a further 15 minutes or until the peppers are tender when tested with the sharp point of a knife and the filling is puffed and browned. Serve hot.

To prepare ahead: *The uncooked, stuffed peppers can be covered and kept in the fridge for up to 24 hours.*

To freeze: *Not suitable.*

To cook in a fan oven: *Do not pre-heat the oven. Bake at 180°C for about 25 minutes until puffed and brown.*

To cook in the Aga: *Cook on the grid shelf on the floor of the roasting oven for about 35–40 minutes, keeping covered for the first 20 minutes.*

Onion, Olive and Goats' Cheese Tart

SERVES 8

The carton of soured cream is divided between the pastry and filling. It is an unusual ingredient in pastry but it makes one that handles well and tastes wonderful. You may prefer to cook the onions in the oil drained from the jar of olives – the extra olive flavour is too good to lose.

For the soured cream pastry
225 g (8 oz) plain white flour
175 g (6 oz) chilled block margarine,
    cubed
1 tablespoon fresh thyme leaves
Freshly ground black pepper
1 × 284 ml carton soured cream

For the filling
4 large, mild Spanish onions
3 tablespoons olive oil
4 eggs
1 teaspoon clear honey
½ teaspoon freshly grated
    nutmeg

1 × 230 g jar mixed olives in olive
    oil, pitted and coarsely chopped
1 × 150 g tub fresh soft goats'
    cheese
Salt and freshly ground black
    pepper

You will need a 28 cm (11 in) flan tin and a heavy baking tray.

Pre-heat the oven to 200°c/400°f/gas 6. Put the baking tray in the oven to heat.

Measure the flour, margarine, thyme and some pepper into a food processor or bowl. Process or rub together with the fingertips until the mixture resembles breadcrumbs. Spoon in 5 level tablespoons of the soured cream then process or mix again just as long as it takes for the ingredients to come together. Turn out on to a lightly floured work surface and roll out to a circle about 5 cm (2 in) larger than the top diameter of the tin. Line the tin with the pastry then put it in the freezer.

Slice the onions; if available you can use the thick slicing blade on a processor. Heat the oil in a large sauté pan, then stir in the onions. Cook over a moderate heat, stirring frequently, for about 15 minutes, then turn the heat down low and continue to cook for a further 10–15 minutes or until softened and slightly coloured. Remove the pan from the heat and leave aside to become cold.

Line the pastry with silicone paper and weight with baking beans. Put on the baking tray and bake for 10 minutes, then remove the paper and baking beans and continue to bake for a further 10 minutes. Remove the flan tin, leaving the baking tray in the oven. Turn the oven temperature down to 180°C/350°F/gas 4.

Combine the remaining soured cream with the eggs, honey and nutmeg in a bowl. Beat with a balloon whisk until smooth. Pour into the pan containing the onions and stir in two-thirds of the chopped olives and half the goats's cheese, crumbled in soft lumps. Taste and season with salt and pepper, then pour into the pastry shell. Sprinkle with the remaining olives and crumbled goats' cheese, then return to the oven to bake on the baking tray for a further 35–40 minutes. When baked the tart should be gently puffed up and browned. Serve warm.

To prepare ahead: *Have the pastry baked blind for 20 minutes and the filling ready to pour into it. The filling can be kept covered in the fridge for up to 8 hours.*

To freeze: *If you can bear being parted from the flan tin base, the freshly baked and cooled flan can be sealed inside a double thickness of plastic bags, all the air removed and sealed. To avoid damage to the flan in the rough and tumble of the freezer it is best to put it in a snug-fitting freezer container. Seal and label, then freeze for up to 4 months.*

To thaw: *Thaw in the sealed bags for 3–4 hours at room temperature or overnight in the fridge.*

To re-heat: *Cover with foil and put in a cool oven at 150°C/300°F/gas 2 for 15 minutes just to warm through.*

To cook in a fan oven: *Pre-heat the oven to 190°C. Bake the pastry for 10 minutes. Remove the paper and baking beans and return to the oven for about 5 minutes. Reduce the oven temperature to 170°C and bake the filled tart for 30 minutes.*

To cook in the Aga: *No need to bake blind; bake the complete tart on the floor of the roasting oven for about 30 minutes.*

Salads and Vegetables

SALADS AND VEGETABLES

This is not a large section, but there are a lot of new ideas here for vegetables and salads. Some of the salads would make interesting first courses as well, and they could also happily appear on a buffet table.

I think accompanying vegetables should always look attractive, and should be freshly and lightly cooked, perhaps with just a little butter on top, and a sprinkling of salt and pepper. You don't need full recipes for this, but I have given here something I've often demonstrated at my Aga classes: a Platter of Fresh Vegetables. It uses the chef's technique of blanching the vegetables in advance, then cooking and refreshing them in cold water before a fast re-heat to serve. If you arrange the blanched and well-drained vegetables attractively on a large platter and cover them with buttered foil, you can leave them in the fridge until the next day. Then all you have to do is blast them with heat in a very hot oven which leaves them thoroughly heated through, steaming hot, crisp to the bite, and still very bright in colour. It's a brilliant technique, and the vegetables look wonderful on a dinner or buffet table.

The celeriac dish is unusual. This knobbly, celery-flavoured root vegetable is usually puréed with an equal quantity of potato. I've peeled and sliced it, blanched the slices, then baked them with some stock, topped with cheese and breadcrumbs. Another favourite is baked potato slices layered with leeks, cream and cheese, for a savoury gratin. Because a gratin like this can often be dry, I've made it in two stages. The potatoes and leeks are cooked first until they are still wonderfully juicy; this could be done in the morning. Then, when you want to serve, you add the cream and sprinkle the cheese on top. The cream augments the juiciness and the

PREVIOUS PAGE
Platter of Fresh Vegetables
(page 135).

flavour, and the cheese topping looks glossy and fresh, just right. Pommes Anna is layered slices as well, but the unusual thing here is that they are little individual dishes, not the more usual large dish. And, finally, I've included my recipe for Watercroft Whipped Potatoes simply as a reminder of how to make the very best mashed potatoes.

Rice goes well with many main courses and the Aromatic Rice here would be particularly good with a curry, or a plain grilled piece of chicken or pork, or a steak. The cous cous salad is a wonderful bright green in colour. The other standbys for salads are pulses and pasta, and the recipes for these are quite special: the beans in the pulse salad are lightly spiced, full of flavour, and the pasta salad, unlike most, is heavy on other flavourings and ingredients, light on the actual pasta content.

The cucumber and the onion salads are rather unusual, but very good to eat, and can be prepared a while in advance, not normally one of the benefits of most salads. However, even the green salad can be prepared several hours ahead. I put all the things that could take marination – spring onion, celery and fennel – in the bottom of my salad bowl with the dressing, then I put the other salad ingredients on top, the flimsy lettuce leaves separated from the dressing by cucumber slices and the sturdier rocket leaves. In this way, the salad is ready to go, just having to be tossed – no last-minute washing, drying and chopping – and yet the tender leaves aren't dressed too far in advance, when they become soggy.

Don't forget either that a couple of first-course recipes could be served as a vegetable – the mushrooms, for instance – giving you even more ideas.

This sign indicates recipes that are suitable
for vegetarians, but please note that some of them
include dairy products.

Warm Salad of Cauliflower, Parsley and Crisp Bacon

SERVES 5–6

The sort of vegetable I would cheerfully eat instead of a main course with good bread, cauliflower is delicious hot with grilled or fried meat or fish, or served at room temperature with other salads. If you don't have balsamic vinegar, use white wine vinegar.

1 large cauliflower	1 tablespoon balsamic vinegar
175 g (6 oz) smoked streaky bacon, rinded	Salt and freshly ground black pepper
2 tablespoons olive oil	2 tablespoons chopped fresh parsley

Separate the cauliflower into sprigs about 2.5 cm (1 in) across. Cut the bacon across into thin strips about 5 mm (¼ in) wide. Heat an empty, non-stick frying-pan for about 1 minute before adding the bacon strips to the pan. Fry until crisp and then take the pan off the heat.

Cook the cauliflower in boiling salted water or steam it over boiling water until just tender but still with bite. Remove the cauliflower from the heat and drain if necessary.

Re-heat the pan containing the bacon, adding the olive oil and vinegar. Tip the cauliflower into the pan and turn gently in the bacon and pan juices until thoroughly hot. Taste and season if necessary, then tip the contents of the pan into a heated serving dish, sprinkle lavishly with parsley and serve.

To prepare ahead: *Have the cauliflower sprigs ready, slightly undercooked, in a covered bowl in the fridge. The bacon can be ready fried and kept aside in the pan. Finish cooking the same day, following the recipe above.*

To freeze: *Not suitable.*

COOKING PASTA
Here is a useful guide when cooking pasta. Don't use less than 2 litres (3½ pints) of water, and the proportions should be 1 litre (1¾ pints) water to every 100 g (4 oz) pasta with 10 g (1½ teaspoons) salt – so 2 litres (3½ pints) would need 1 tablespoon. This amount of salt often surprises people.

$\widehat{V}$
Quite the Best Pasta Salad

SERVES 6–8

Cold pasta dishes have never been a favourite of mine, but this recipe is an exception. It is a combination of tuna, hard-boiled eggs and avocado mixed with a comparatively small amount of cooked pasta shells, and the ratio seems exactly right. It is simplicity itself to make and it looks good on a buffet table if you follow the instructions for the garnish.

150 g (5 oz) pasta shells	3 hard-boiled eggs
Salt	1 firm but just ripe avocado
3 × 185 g tins tuna in oil	Juice of 1 lemon
150 ml (5 fl oz) light mayonnaise	3 tablespoons snipped fresh
Freshly ground black pepper	chives

To garnish
Long chives
About 6 black olives in oil, pitted
  and halved

Cook the pasta shells in plenty of boiling salted water until just cooked *al dente*. Drain in a colander, then rinse under cold running water to cool quickly. Turn the well-drained pasta into a large bowl.

Empty the cans of tuna into a sieve standing over a bowl and leave to drain for 5 minutes. Flake the tuna into the bowl that contains the pasta. Measure the mayonnaise in a jug, then stir in 2 tablespoons of the drained juices from the tuna. Taste and season the mayonnaise with salt and pepper. Peel and chop the cold, hard-boiled eggs in largish pieces and add to the pasta and tuna, followed by the mayonnaise. Turn the mixture gently together to mix, then cover the bowl with clingfilm and chill until ready to serve.

Just before serving, peel and dice the avocado and toss in lemon juice. Add the avocado, lemon juice and chives to the salad, toss lightly together, then taste and add more seasoning if necessary. Serve the salad in a large, shallow serving dish. Create a diamond pattern on its surface with the long chives and put a halved olive in the centre of each diamond. Serve lightly chilled.

To prepare ahead: *Prepare the pasta, tuna, egg and mayonnaise, cover with clingfilm and keep for up to 24 hours; then add the avocado, not before or it will discolour.*

To freeze: *Not suitable.*

Ⓥ Salad of Red and Yellow Tomatoes with Oranges

SERVES 5–6

An unusual, refreshing salad. You may not have tried this method of preparing oranges before. All I would say, first and last, is to use a sharp knife, then with a little patience you will soon be proficient at skinning and segmenting oranges. It is a surprisingly useful technique to master. If you cannot buy yellow tomatoes, use sliced medium tomatoes instead and arrange them in a circle at the edge of the dish.

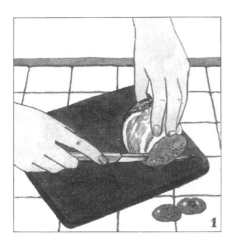
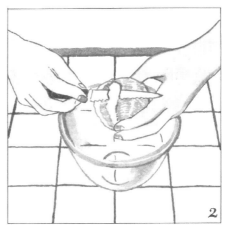

For the salad
*225 g (9 oz) red cherry tomatoes,
    halved*
*225 g (8 oz) yellow cherry
    tomatoes, halved*
2 small, thin-skinned oranges

For the dressing
4 tablespoons olive oil
2 teaspoons whole grain mustard
1 tablespoon lemon juice
1 teaspoon sugar
Salt
*1 teaspoon cracked black
    peppercorns*

To garnish
*A handful of torn fresh basil or
    mint leaves*

Place the tomatoes in a serving bowl or dish.

Prepare the oranges. Using a sharp knife, slice off the top and bottom of an orange, exposing the coloured flesh. Standing the fruit on one cut end, remove a strip of peel and pith, working from the top to the base of the fruit, following the curve of the fruit as you cut (see **1**). You should then be able to see a clean strip of exposed orange flesh. In the same manner, work your way around the fruit until all the pith and peel has been removed. If any stray bits of pith still remain on the orange, shave these off with a knife (see **2**). With the bowl of tomatoes beneath to catch the juice, hold the fruit in one hand and slip the knife alongside the membrane that divides each segment, cutting in towards the centre (see **3**). This will release the segments of orange completely free of pith, peel and membrane. Let them drop into the bowl beneath. Work your way around the fruit until all the segments are free, then squeeze the juice from the orange left in your hand. Also, squeeze the juice from the peel strips into the bowl. Repeat with the second orange.

In a separate bowl, whisk together all the ingredients for the dressing, pour over the salad and toss together to mix. Chill lightly until ready to serve. Just before serving, sprinkle the salad with the torn basil or mint leaves.

To prepare ahead: *The salad can be prepared without the herbs, covered with clingfilm and kept in the fridge for up to 6 hours. Add the fresh leaves just before serving.*

To freeze: *Not suitable.*

Ⓥ
Scandinavian Cucumber Salad

A well-behaved salad that can wait around until you are ready to serve, this is one of those basic salads that goes with just about everything and always has a place on a buffet table. One of my all-time favourites is cucumber salad served with hot or cold poached salmon.

2 large cucumbers	*4 tablespoons white wine vinegar*
2 tablespoons salt	*2 tablespoons snipped fresh chives*
4 tablespoons caster sugar	*2 tablespoons chopped fresh dill*

To garnish
A few sprigs of fresh dill

Top, tail and peel the cucumbers, then slice thinly into a bowl. Add the salt, sugar and vinegar, then use your hands to turn the cucumber slices evenly in the mixture. Cover and chill for a minimum of 1 hour.

Turn the contents of the bowl into a colander and leave for about 10 minutes to drain thoroughly. Sprinkle with the chives and dill and turn the slices again with your hands to mix. Transfer the cucumber to a serving dish and garnish with extra sprigs of dill.

To prepare ahead: *The salad can be prepared without the herbs, covered and kept in the fridge for up to 24 hours. Add the herbs just before serving.*

To freeze: *Not suitable.*

Ⓥ
Green Cous Cous Salad

Cous cous has to be the best of all the 'instant' foods. It is semolina that has been rolled in flour, which means the grains stay separate when cooked. Nowadays it is sold already pre-treated to cook very quickly and easily. Here is a very simple but exotic type of salad that would appeal to vegetarians. As it stands, the recipe is ideal as an accompaniment to grilled kebabs, chicken or fish. To make it into more of a main course you could add crumbled goats' or feta cheese. Many supermarkets now sell small trays of fresh asparagus tips in the vegetable section.

Green Cous Cous Salad
(above).

250 g (9 oz) cous cous
400 ml (14 fl oz) Vegetable Stock
    (see page 58)
150 g (5 oz) fresh asparagus tips
1 teaspoon salt
Freshly ground black pepper
6 spring onions with 7.5 cm (3 in)
    green tops

150 g (5 oz) sugar snap peas or
    mangetout
Juice of 1 lemon
4 tablespoons olive oil
50 g (2 oz) pine nuts, toasted
6 tablespoons chopped fresh flatleaf
    parsley
3 tablespoons chopped fresh mint

To garnish
Lemon slices
Sprigs of fresh parsley

Have the cous cous ready in a large bowl. Heat the vegetable stock. Cut the asparagus spears into 2.5 cm (1½ in) lengths and toss them into the boiling stock. Cover and cook for about 3 minutes or until just tender but still with plenty of bite, then remove the pan from the heat. Position a colander over the bowl of cous cous, then pour the contents of the pan into it. Add the salt and some pepper to the cous cous, give it a stir then cover and leave aside to cool. Refresh the asparagus under cold running water, drain, then pat dry on kitchen paper; leave aside until needed.

Chop the spring onions and obliquely slice the sugar snap peas or mangetout. By this time the cous cous should have absorbed all the stock. Add the lemon juice and olive oil and toss with 2 forks to mix. Now add the spring onions, sugar snap peas or mangetout, pine nuts, parsley and mint. Toss again, then taste and flavour with more salt, pepper or lemon juice if preferred. Serve at room temperature, garnished with slices of lemon and sprigs of mint and parsley.

To prepare ahead: *The salad can be prepared without the garnish, cooled, covered and stored in the fridge for up to 6 hours.*

To freeze: *Not suitable.*

Ⓥ
Mixed Leaf and Herb Salad
SERVES 6–8

Vary green salads by adding different types of lettuces; seasonal leaves; young spinach leaves; lambs' lettuce (also known as corn salad); radicchio; some home-grown purslane; chicory; endive; and fresh, leafy herbs. I particularly like adding torn leaves of mint and chopped garlic chives.

For the French dressing
1 tablespoon lemon juice
1 tablespoon white wine vinegar
1 teaspoon mustard powder
Salt and freshly ground black
  pepper
1 garlic clove, crushed
1 tablespoon caster sugar
2 tablespoons sunflower oil
1 tablespoon olive oil

For the salad
4 spring onions, shredded
4 celery sticks, diagonally cut in
  5 mm (¼ in) slices
1 small bulb of fennel, thinly sliced
½ small Webb's or iceberg lettuce
2 Little Gem lettuces
½ cucumber
A few rocket leaves
Sea salt and freshly ground black
  pepper

Take a screw-topped jam jar and fill with the dressing ingredients. Replace the lid firmly and shake well until mixed. Pour into the base of a large salad bowl. Add the spring onions, celery and fennel and toss well to coat the vegetables.

To prepare the salad, break the lettuces into manageable pieces. Halve the cucumber lengthways, then cut across into fairly thick slices. Have the rocket ready. Gently lay half this mixture on the dressing. Sprinkle with a little salt and pepper before adding the remaining salad. Season again then cover with clingfilm and keep in the fridge for up to 4 hours. Toss just before serving.

To prepare ahead: *You can prepare the salad several hours in advance, say on the morning of a dinner party. Put the bowl with the dressing, spring onions, celery and fennel in the fridge, covered. Put the prepared salad leaves and cucumber in a large plastic bag in the fridge. When it is time to serve, empty the contents of the bag into the bowl, season and toss in the dressing.*

To freeze: *Not suitable.*

ⓥ
Spicy Mexican Bean Salad

SERVES 6 AS A SIDE SALAD

This recipe is even better if prepared in advance as far as adding the Tabasco sauce so that the flavours have time to develop. If preferred, make a mixed bean salad using a tin of kidney beans and a tin of haricot or flageolet beans.

2 × 420 g tins kidney beans in water	1 red pepper, seeded and diced
2 garlic cloves	2 celery sticks, diced
2.5 cm (1 in) fresh root ginger, peeled	2 tablespoons tomato purée
3 tablespoons sunflower oil	Juice of 1 lemon
1 large onion, finely chopped	1 teaspoon sugar
1 teaspoon ground cumin	A few drops of Tabasco sauce (optional)
1 teaspoon ground coriander	Salt and freshly ground black pepper
½ teaspoon chilli powder	
1 teaspoon salt	

To garnish
2 tablespoons chopped fresh mint
2 tablespoons chopped fresh coriander

Drain the beans in a colander, then dry them on kitchen paper and transfer them to a large bowl. Chop the garlic and ginger together very finely.

Heat the oil in a medium-sized frying-pan and fry the onion for about 5 minutes over a low to moderate heat. Stir in the garlic and ginger and continue cooking for a further 5 minutes or until the onion is softened and golden. Sprinkle in the cumin, coriander and chilli powder and continue to cook for 1–2 minutes, stirring. Scrape the contents of the pan into the bowl containing the beans. Add the remaining ingredients, stir well, then taste and season carefully with salt and pepper. If you would prefer it more chilli-hot, add a few drops of Tabasco sauce. Spoon the salad into a serving bowl. Sprinkle thickly with the chopped mint and coriander and loosely fork the herbs into the bean mixture. Serve at room temperature.

To prepare ahead: *Prepare the salad without the herbs, cover with clingfilm and chill for up to 2 days. Toss with the herbs before serving.*

To freeze: *Not suitable.*

Ⓥ
Onion and Soured Cream Salad

SERVES 4–6

Simple, delicious and unusual. Serve this salad with cold meats, grilled and poached fish.

---

2 very large, mild Spanish onions,
*   cut in 5 mm (¼ in) slices*
1 × 250 g carton crème fraîche
2 tablespoons snipped fresh chives
½ teaspoon sugar
Salt and freshly ground black
*   pepper*

To garnish
About 8 whole chive stems, and
*   chive flowers if available*

Put the sliced onions in a bowl and cover generously with boiling water. Cover and leave aside for 30 minutes.

Drain the onions in a colander, then pat dry on kitchen paper. Mix the crème fraîche, chives and sugar, add the onions, then taste and season with salt and pepper. Turn into a shallow, rectangular serving dish, cover with clingfilm, then chill until ready to serve. Lay the chive stems obliquely down the length of the dish, scatter with chive flowers and serve.

To prepare ahead: *The prepared salad can be kept covered in the fridge for up to 2 days.*

To freeze: *Not suitable.*

KEEPING HERBS AND SPICES
The quality of herbs and spices used in cooking makes a great
difference to the taste of the finished dish so it makes sense to look
after them. They should really be stored away from the light, and try
to buy small quantities that can be used up quickly while they
retain the maximum taste and fragrance. Where possible
buy the whole spices and grind them yourself when needed.

Ⓥ
Pak Choi and Shiitake Stir-fry

SERVES 4

Also known as bok choy, this Chinese cabbage has broad, white, succulent stems and mildly mustard-flavoured green leaves. It looks something like Swiss chard and I cook it in a similar way, slicing off the leaves and cooking the stem end separately. In this recipe there is the option to cook the stems and add the sliced leaves 2 or 3 minutes before the end of cooking; or keep the leaves, cook them like spinach and serve with a later meal. A special note: be careful with the chilli. Handle it as little as possible and wash your hands thoroughly after preparing it, or wear rubber gloves if you prefer.

450 g (1 lb) pak choi	*1 small fresh red chilli, seeded and*
2 tablespoons sesame or	*thinly sliced*
sunflower oil	*2 fat garlic cloves, crushed*
1 small red pepper, seeded and	*2.5 cm (1 in) fresh root ginger,*
sliced (optional)	*peeled and cut in slivers*
12 small spring onions,	*175 g (6 oz) shiitake mushrooms,*
trimmed	*sliced*
2 sticks lemon grass, bulb section	*2 tablespoons oyster sauce*
only, finely chopped	*A dash of dark soy sauce*

Discard any damaged outer leaves or stalks of the pak choi. In a similar fashion to the way celery is trimmed, cut straight across the stem where the leaves start. Leaving the stems attached at the base, wash them and the leaves and drain. If you intend adding the leaves, roll them into cigar-like bundles and slice across into thin strips; keep on one side. Halve each thick bundle of stems lengthways.

Heat the oil until smoking in a large wok or frying-pan. When hot, add the pepper, if liked, spring onions, lemon grass, chilli, garlic and ginger and toss constantly over a fairly high heat for about 1 minute. Add the stem halves and mushrooms and continue to fry, briskly tossing the vegetables for a further minute. Now reduce the heat, cover and cook for 2–3 minutes or until the stems are barely tender. Stir in the oyster sauce and leaves, if using. Add a dash of soy sauce to season. Toss and cook only for as long as it takes to get everything piping hot, then if cooked and seasoned to your taste, serve immediately.

To prepare ahead: *Have all the raw ingredients prepared and ready to cook; keep chilled for up to 6 hours before cooking.*

To freeze: *Not suitable.*

Pak Choi and Shiitake Stir-fry (above).

Ⓥ
Shiitake Mushroom Stir-fry

SERVES 6

Stir-frying is one of the best ways of cooking vegetables: short and sharp so they arrive on the plate still having plenty of texture, colour and food value. For everything to work smoothly and quickly all the ingredients need to be prepared before you start to cook.

3 tablespoons vegetable oil	150 g (5 oz) fresh bean
2.5 cm (1 in) fresh root ginger, cut	sprouts
into julienne strips	150 g (5 oz) shiitake mushrooms,
2 garlic cloves, crushed	thinly sliced
4 spring onions, diagonally sliced	150 g (5 oz) white cabbage,
1 small, trimmed head of celery,	shredded
sliced	1 tablespoon dark soy sauce
100 g (4 oz) mangetout, trimmed	1 tablespoon oyster sauce
1 red pepper, seeded and cut in	Salt and freshly ground black
strips lengthways	pepper

Use a large wok if available, or a large frying-pan. Heat the oil in the pan until really hot. A simple method to test the heat of the oil is to put the point of a wooden chopstick in it. When the oil is hot enough it will immediately bubble around it. Throw in the ginger and garlic and cook for about 10 seconds before adding the spring onions, celery, mangetout and red pepper. Cook for about 2 minutes, briskly turning the vegetables over and over in the oil. Add the bean sprouts, mushrooms and cabbage. Cook for a further 2 minutes. Add the soy and oyster sauces to the pan. Season with salt and pepper and serve immediately.

To prepare ahead: *Have all the vegetables prepared ready to fry: the garlic and ginger on one plate, spring onions, celery, mangetout and red pepper in a bowl. Have the bean sprouts, mushrooms and cabbage in a separate bowl. Cover all the ingredients. They can be kept in the fridge for up to 6 hours before cooking.*

To freeze: *Not suitable.*

To cook on the Aga: *Use a large flat non-stick frying-pan.*

Ⓥ
Platter of Fresh Vegetables

SERVES 6–8

Here is a way to serve a variety of vegetables all at the same time, all perfectly cooked, with no last-minute, frantic rattling of pots and pans. The quantities can be varied to your taste. The washing up can all be done ahead too.

25 g (1 oz) butter, melted
225 g (8 oz) fresh green French
    haricot beans or runner beans,
    sliced
450 g (1 lb) tiny new potatoes
225 g (8 oz) leeks, thinly
    sliced
225 g (8 oz) small carrots, quartered
    lengthways
225 g (8 oz) broccoli sprigs
Salt and freshly ground black
    pepper

To garnish
Chopped fresh parsley

You will need a flat ovenproof serving plate about 35 × 30 cm (14 × 12 in) brushed liberally with some of the melted butter.

Pre-heat the oven to 220°c/425°f/gas 7.

Par-boil the vegetables separately in boiling salted water, then drain in a colander and refresh under cold running water. Cook the beans for 2 minutes; the potatoes for about 10–15 minutes or until tender when tested with the fine point of a knife; the leeks for about 1 minute; the carrots for about 2 minutes or until cooked but with plenty of bite; the broccoli for 2–3 minutes until just tender.

Arrange the vegetables on the prepared dish. Season with salt and pepper. Brush a sheet of foil with the remaining melted butter and cover the vegetables (butter-side down). Seal tightly around the edges and cook in the oven for about 25–30 minutes until the vegetables are piping hot. Just before serving, garnish the potatoes and carrots with chopped parsley.

To prepare ahead: *Have all the part-cooked vegetables arranged ready on the serving dish, brushed with butter and covered closely with foil. Keep for up to 8 hours, then follow the recipe.*

To freeze: *Not suitable.*

To cook in a fan oven: *Do not pre-heat the oven. Bake at 190°c for about 20 minutes.*

To cook in the Aga: *Place the foil-covered baking dish flat on the floor of the roasting oven and bake for about 20 minutes.*

Glazed Onions

SERVES 6–8

A good, homely dish. Large Spanish onions can be used for a supper dish, or double the number of medium onions for a side vegetable, say with the Sunday roast.

50 g (2 oz) butter, melted	1 tablespoon white wine vinegar
Salt and freshly ground black pepper	½ teaspoon salt
	½ teaspoon mustard powder
3 large, mild Spanish onions, halved	2 tablespoons soft brown sugar
	1 teaspoon mild paprika

You will need a baking dish or tin the right size to take 6 onion halves.

Pre-heat the oven to 180°c/350°f/gas 4.

Brush the base of the dish with a little of the melted butter and season with salt and pepper. Arrange the halved onions in the prepared dish, cut-side down. Combine the remaining ingredients together in a bowl and spoon over the onions. Cover and roast for 45–50 minutes or until the onions are tender when pierced with a skewer.

To prepare ahead: *Have the onions ready to roast. They can be kept, covered, in the fridge for up to 8 hours before roasting.*

To freeze: *Not suitable.*

To cook in a fan oven: *Do not pre-heat the oven. Roast at 140°c for about 40 minutes or until the onions are tender when pierced with a skewer.*

To cook in the Aga: *Roast on the grid shelf on the floor of the roasting oven for about 35 minutes. If the onions are getting too brown and are not yet tender, slide the cold plain shelf above the onions.*

Ⓥ
Watercroft Whipped Potatoes

SERVES 6–8

You may wonder why I am giving a recipe for something as simple as mashed potatoes. Maybe it is because it is so simple that mashed potato is often cooked so badly. And yet when properly cooked, it is the most delicious and satisfying vegetable of all. It is important to start with the right sort of potatoes that mash well, such as King Edwards, Golden Wonder, Desirée or Wilja. These all have a mealy, floury texture that holds the air, butter and milk that are beaten into them in a light, fluffy consistency. Never attempt to mash new potatoes or anything that is described as a salad potato. These will have a compact, waxy texture that will only ever produce a nasty, gluey, lumpish mess. By the way, do consider buying a potato ricer – a bit like a huge garlic crusher – you won't regret it.

1.25 kg (2½ lb) old, floury
*   potatoes*
Salt
About 250 ml (8 fl oz) milk
100 g (4 oz) butter
Freshly ground black pepper

Because they are to be boiled in their skins, scrub the potatoes and, if large, halve or quarter them. Try to keep the pieces an even size so they cook in the same time. Put into a pan, cover with cold water and add about 2 teaspoons of salt. Bring to the boil, then boil gently for about 30 minutes or until the potatoes feel absolutely tender when tested with a skewer. Drain, cool a little, then quickly remove the skins. Add most of the milk and the butter to the pan and heat until bubbling. Now either press the potatoes through a sieve or a potato ricer into the pan. Beat the potatoes, adding more milk if necessary, until you have the ideal consistency to accompany the main course. Taste and season with salt and pepper. Spoon a soft drift of potatoes into a warmed serving dish and serve immediately topped with an extra knob of butter.

To prepare ahead: *Prepare the potatoes and spoon into a warmed serving dish. Cover with a butter paper then seal with foil and place in a cool oven at 140°c/275°f/gas 1 for up to 1 hour. If oven space is not available, do as the chefs do and keep the potatoes hot in the top half of a double pan over hot water. Serve as described above.*

To freeze: *Not suitable.*

ⓥ
Pommes Anna

One of the great, classic potato dishes, this is usually made in one large potato cake of interleaved layers of thinly sliced potatoes sprinkled with clarified butter, all baked in a special, lidded copper pan. When turned out the cake has a glorious deep golden-brown top. Here is a way to make individual potato cakes, like the classic version, but much less work. The long Charlotte new potatoes are best for this recipe if you can get them. For a dinner party, the recipe will easily double up to serve 8 but don't forget you will need an extra Yorkshire pudding tray.

75 g (3 oz) butter
Salt and freshly ground black
  pepper
450 g (1 lb) new potatoes, small egg
  size

You will need 1 × 4-hole non-stick Yorkshire pudding tray or 4 individual non-stick patty tins measuring 10 × 2 cm (4 × ¾ in), greased, and 1 heavy baking tray.

Pre-heat the oven to 230°C/450°F/gas 8. Put the baking tray in the oven to heat.

Melt the butter in a medium-sized pan and add some salt and pepper before taking the pan off the heat.

Wash the potatoes and remove the skins if you prefer. Thinly slice them into rounds using a mandolin cutter, a food processor fitted with a thin cutting disc, or a sharp knife. Don't rinse the potato slices or dry them on kitchen paper as their starch helps the potato cake bind together. Immediately turn the sliced potatoes in the seasoned butter, then arrange the potatoes in overlapping slices in the Yorkshire pudding tray or tins. This may seem a bit fiddly but again, the overlapping of the slices helps the potato cakes hold together when turned out of the tin. Build each potato cake up above the rims using all the sliced potatoes, then press each one down firmly with the palm of your hand. Cover with buttered foil then place on the baking tray in the oven. Bake for 15 minutes then uncover, lower the heat to 200°C/400°F/gas 6 and bake for a further 15 minutes or until the surface potatoes are beginning to turn golden brown and crisp. Test to see if the potato cakes are tender by piercing them with the point of a knife. When you are sure they are cooked, remove them from the oven, re-cover with foil and leave aside in a warm place for up to 10 minutes. Loosen the edges of the potato cakes with a knife.

Put a warm baking tray on top of the Yorkshire pudding tray then flip over so that it is on top. Holding on to both trays give them a sharp rap on the work surface to turn the potato cakes out on to the warmed baking tray. If you are using individual tins each one will have to be turned out separately. Use a fish slice to transfer each cake to a warmed serving plate. Serve hot.

To prepare ahead: *Cook completely, turn out on to a flat baking tray, cool, cover and keep in the fridge for up to 12 hours.*

To re-heat: *Re-heat uncovered in a pre-heated oven at 200°c/400°F/gas 6 for about 15–20 minutes.*

To freeze: *Not suitable.*

To cook in a fan oven: *Pre-heat the oven to 220°c, putting a baking tray in the oven to heat. Bake for 8–10 minutes, then reduce the temperature to 190°c. Uncover and bake for a further 10 minutes or until the surface potatoes are tender and beginning to turn golden brown and crisp.*

To cook in the Aga: *No need to stand the tin(s) on a pre-heated baking tray; cook them directly on the floor of the roasting oven for 15 minutes covered and about 15 minutes uncovered until the potatoes are done. Turn out on to a baking tray or serving dish and keep hot in the simmering oven for up to 30 minutes before serving.*

Leek and Potato Gratin

SERVES 6

The great advantage of this potato dish is that the main part of the cooking can be done several hours ahead. This can be useful sometimes if only to free the oven for other things. After the topping is added the dish has a final short bake and emerges a melting, golden mass of creamy potatoes and cheese.

GIVE CHILLED FOODS A CHANCE
When food is taken straight from the fridge to be cooked, remember to allow extra time for it to heat through. With meats it is preferable to allow them to come up to room temperature before cooking.

225 g (8 oz) leeks, trimmed
900 g (2 lb) potatoes
40 g (1½ oz) butter
1 teaspoon salt
Freshly ground black pepper
Freshly grated nutmeg

300 ml (10 fl oz) light Chicken Stock
(see page 14) or Vegetable Stock
(see page 58)
4 tablespoons double cream
40 g (1½ oz) Gruyère,
grated

You will need a shallow oven dish about 20 × 28 cm (8 × 11 in), buttered.

Pre-heat the oven to 200°C/400°F/gas 6.

Finely slice the leeks, wash well and drain. Peel the potatoes and slice thinly using a mandolin, in a food processor fitted with the thin cutting disc, or with a sharp knife.

Melt the butter in a large, deep frying-pan and stir in the prepared leeks. Cook over a moderate heat for about 2 minutes. Add the sliced potatoes and sprinkle with the salt, a generous amount of pepper and a liberal amount of grated nutmeg. Stir well to mix then turn into the prepared dish. Spread the potato mixture evenly, then pour in the stock. Bake for 45 minutes or until the potatoes are cooked, then remove the dish from the oven.

Re-set the oven temperature to 220°C/425°F/gas 7.

Pour the cream over the potatoes then sprinkle with the cheese. Replace the dish near the top of the oven to re-heat and brown. This will take about 20 minutes if the potatoes are hot, about 30 minutes if the dish was cold.

To prepare ahead: *Bake the potatoes until cooked, then remove from the oven and cover. They can be kept at room temperature for up to 4 hours. When ready add the cream and cheese, then follow the recipe above.*

To freeze: *Not suitable.*

To cook in a fan oven: *Do not pre-heat the oven. Bake the potatoes at 190°C for about 40 minutes or until cooked. Cover with the cream and cheese and bake at 200°C for about 15 minutes if the potatoes are hot, about 20–25 minutes if the dish is cold.*

To cook in the Aga: *Bake on the grid shelf on the floor of the roasting oven for about 45 minutes. The potatoes should be just tender and most of the stock absorbed. After adding the cream and cheese, raise the shelf to the highest position and bake for a further 20 minutes or until golden brown. Add an extra 10 minutes or so if the gratin was cold when returned to the oven.*

Leek and Potato Gratin
(page 139).

Ⓥ
Celeriac au Gratin

SERVES 5–6

Celeriac is the Cinderella of the vegetable world. Although it made its appearance in Britain at the same time as broccoli, it has never caught on to the same extent. Its mild celery flavour goes particularly well with potatoes. Usually the two vegetables are mashed together and served with game stews, but just for a change I decided to do a gratin and the result was as good as, if not better.

---

1 tablespoon lemon juice
2 medium celeriac roots
300 ml (10 fl oz) light Chicken Stock
(see page 14) or Vegetable Stock
(see page 58)
Salt and freshly ground black
pepper
40 g (1½ oz) fresh white
breadcrumbs
40 g (1½ oz) Parmesan, freshly
grated

You will need a shallow, oval gratin dish, about 28 cm (11 in) long. Butter the dish and sprinkle with some salt and pepper.

Pre-heat the oven to 220°C/425°F/gas 7.

Have ready a pan of cold salted water mixed with the lemon juice. Peel the celeriac thickly, then cut in quarters. Slice each quarter about 3 mm (⅛ in) thick. Immediately drop the slices into the cold water to prevent the vegetable discolouring. Bring the water to the boil, then simmer for 6–7 minutes. Drain and arrange the celeriac in the prepared gratin dish. Pour in the stock and season with salt and pepper. Combine the breadcrumbs and cheese and sprinkle evenly over the celeriac. Bake for about 25–30 minutes or until the celeriac is tender when tested with a skewer. The top should be toasted golden and crisp. Serve hot.

To prepare ahead: *Have the par-boiled celeriac ready in the dish, minus the cheese and breadcrumb topping. Cover and keep in the fridge for up to 6 hours. Add the topping just before baking, then follow the recipe above.*

To freeze: *Not suitable.*

To cook in a fan oven: *Do not pre-heat the oven. Bake at 200°C for about 20 minutes or until the celeriac is tender and the top is golden and crisp.*

To cook in the Aga: *Bake on the second set of runners in the roasting oven for 20 minutes or until brown on top and the celeriac is tender.*

Ⓥ
Aromatic Rice

SERVES 6

A softly spiced rice that will complement and not dominate what it is served with. If you follow the method for cooking the rice you will have no problems in obtaining non-sticky, separate rice grains.

350 g (12 oz) basmati rice	*2 bay leaves, crumbled*
3 tablespoons vegetable oil	*½ teaspoon cumin seeds*
1 onion, finely chopped	*½ teaspoon cracked black*
2 cloves	*peppercorns*
6 green cardamoms,	*Freshly grated nutmeg*
cracked open	*600 ml (1 pint) water*
2.5 cm (1 in) cinnamon stick	*1 teaspoon salt*

Put the rice in a large sieve, then stand it in a bowl of cold water and soak for 30 minutes if time allows, then rinse until the water runs clear. Leave aside in the sieve to drain thoroughly.

Heat the oil in a large pan, then fry the onion over a moderate heat for about 5 minutes or until softened and coloured. Stir in the spices and heat for 1–2 minutes to release the flavours. Add the rice, then pour in the water and add the salt. Bring to the boil, cover, then turn the heat down as low as possible and leave without disturbing for 10 minutes. At this stage, remove the lid and gently stir the rice a couple of times with a large wooden fork. Remove the pan from the heat and cover with a clean, folded tea towel and then the lid to seal it completely. Leave aside for a further 5–10 minutes until the grains are separate, dry and cooked. Serve hot.

To prepare ahead: *As soon as the rice is cooked to your liking, turn into a bowl. Once cold, put the covered pan in the fridge and keep for up to 6 hours.*

To freeze: *Not suitable.*

To re-heat: *Place the rice on a large sheet of foil and sprinkle with a little water. Wrap in a neat, tightly sealed parcel and bake in a pre-heated oven at 150°C/300°F/gas 2 for 25–30 minutes.*

To re-heat in a fan oven: *Do not pre-heat the oven. Wrap in foil, as described above, and bake at 140°C for about 20 minutes.*

To cook in the Aga: *Follow the recipe as far as adding the water. Bring to a full, rolling boil, cover and put in the simmering oven for about 20 minutes or until the water has been absorbed and the rice is cooked. Re-heat as above in a foil parcel in the simmering oven for about 30 minutes. Open up the foil if not really hot by then.*

Hot Puddings and Chilled Desserts

HOT PUDDINGS AND CHILLED DESSERTS

At this stage of a meal, you can offer a choice. What I usually do, whether I'm cooking for a dinner party for six or a buffet party for twelve or more, is have two puddings, one rich, sinful, and probably calorie-laden; the other a wonderful fruit salad. In this way, most tastes are catered for: those who hanker after sweet, luscious textures are satisfied, while those who are weight-watching can feel they are being careful while still indulging in something delicious to eat. Many people – from experience, *most* of my guests – will have a little of both!

The puddings I give you here are just what I say they are in the title of the chapter – hot *and* chilled. Some are hot for wonderful winter fare, and some are chilled, perfect for a summer party. But many of the puddings can be served hot or cold, and a few of them taste nicest when they are warm. I have also given plenty of alternatives in terms of ingredients: using apricots with the apples (or rhubarb instead of them) in Bramley Caramel, for instance, and three variations on the basic Red Plum Ice-cream. So you have yet more choices, which make all the recipes very versatile indeed. And most of them can be prepared at least a day ahead, which can further help your party organization; they usually require no more than a few minutes' re-heating in the oven, or an hour or so coming to room temperature out of the fridge.

I've also selected recipes that are fairly easy to achieve, because sometimes desserts can be rather complicated. It's always been part of my philosophy of cooking to think up short cuts, and to find easier equivalents or techniques. You'll find a few of those here – amply announced by the recipe titles which include a

PREVIOUS PAGE
Bramley Caramel
(page 149).

number of words like 'foolproof' (floating islands), 'quick' (lime mousse) and 'cheats' (lemon meringue pie). In each of these I introduce you to a new way of doing something, which means it's quicker and simpler to prepare, but just as delicious to eat! The brandysnap baskets are a case in point. Brandysnaps are ghastly to make, as they require perfect timing, and also break very easily. But the answer is simple. Just go into your local supermarket and buy a packet of their brandysnaps. Bring them home. Put them on a baking sheet in a warm oven for a few minutes, and they will soften and unroll. Quickly put them over cups to shape them, and they will harden in a minute or two. A cheat, yes, but *so* much easier than making your own!

Some of the recipes are a little more complicated, though. I'm thinking particularly of Bombe Marie, an invention of mine which makes an ideal replacement for a traditional pudding on Christmas Day. Basically it's an ice-cream pudding with a heart of vanilla ice-cream, a layer of grated chocolate in the middle, and an outside casing of brandy and coffee ice-cream, topped again with grated chocolate. However, you don't need a physics degree to work out how to do it – I'm sure you'll be able to follow our very detailed instructions. (It's actually easy when you know how.) My Velvet Chocolate Torte is absolutely straightforward, with a luscious taste and texture; the melting of the chocolate is foolproof, too. I know you'll *enjoy* all these recipes!

This sign indicates recipes that are suitable
for vegetarians, but please note that some of them
include dairy products.

Ⓥ My Mother's Bread and Butter Pudding

SERVES 6–8

A great family favourite as a pudding to follow a weekend lunch, this is far more exciting than it sounds because, I have to admit, the recipe is not economical – just delicious! Ideally use a rectangular dish simply because the bread fits it better.

---

100 g (4 oz) butter, melted
75–175 g (3–6 oz) mixed dried fruit
75 g (3 oz) sugar
Grated rind of 1 lemon
½ teaspoon mixed spice
12 thin slices white bread, crusts
*   removed*
3 eggs
600 ml (1 pint) milk
2 tablespoons demerara sugar

You will need an ovenproof dish about 18 × 23 × 5 cm (7 × 9 × 2 in). Use some of the melted butter to grease the dish.

Pre-heat the oven to 180°C/350°F/gas 4.

Combine the dried fruit, sugar, lemon rind and spice together in a bowl and toss to mix well. Cut each bread slice into 3 strips. Take sufficient slices to cover the base of the dish and dip one side of each one in melted butter. Lay them in the dish, buttered-side down. Sprinkle with half the dried fruit mixture. Repeat the layering, laying the bread strips buttered-side up. Lay the third and final layer of bread strips on top, buttered-side up.

Beat together the eggs and milk in a bowl and pour over the pudding. Sprinkle with demerara sugar, then leave to stand for about 1 hour if time allows.

Bake for about 40 minutes or until the top is golden brown and crisp and the pudding slightly puffed up. Serve hot, or there are some who insist that it is delicious cold!

To prepare ahead: *Have the pudding prepared but without the demerara topping. Keep covered in the fridge for up to 6 hours before baking.*

To freeze: *Not suitable.*

To cook in a fan oven: *Do not pre-heat the oven. Bake at 170°C for about 30 minutes.*

To cook in the Aga: *Bake on the grid shelf on the floor of the roasting oven. Cook for about 20–25 minutes or until golden brown and crisp.*

ⓥ Bramley Caramel

SERVES 6–8

This is a very adaptable recipe. Use dessert or cooking apples, whichever you have to hand, or rhubarb works well. Adding about nine halved, easy-cook apricots to the apples is also a favourite.

175 g (6 oz) self-raising white flour	Grated rind of 1 lemon
1 teaspoon baking powder	150 ml (5 fl oz) milk
50 g (2 oz) caster sugar	A generous 450 g (1 lb) apples,
50 g (2 oz) soft baking margarine	peeled and cut in
1 egg	5 mm (¼ in) slices

For the topping
50 g (2 oz) butter, melted
About 175 g (6 oz) demerara sugar

To serve
Crème fraîche

You will need a shallow ovenproof baking dish about 28 cm (11 in) diameter, well greased.

Pre-heat the oven to 230°C/450°F/gas 8.

Measure the flour, baking powder, caster sugar, margarine, egg, lemon rind and milk into a bowl. Beat together until the mixture forms a soft, cake-like consistency. Spread this in the base of the prepared dish and arrange the apple slices on top. Brush or drizzle the butter over the apple, then sprinkle with the demerara sugar. Bake for about 35 minutes or until the top has caramelized to a deep golden brown. Serve warm with crème fraîche.

SUCCESS WITH CARAMEL

If you are making caramel, do not attempt this in a pan that is non-stick or has a dark interior. You cannot see clearly when the caramel is dark enough, and I have found it impossible to make a caramel in a non-stick saucepan. The syrup crystallizes and will not caramelize. Heavy gauge aluminium or stainless steel pans are better for this.

To prepare ahead: *Have the sponge made and spread in the dish. Cover with clingfilm and keep in the fridge for up to 8 hours. Prepare the apples and finish the topping while the oven is heating.*

To freeze: *Wrap the baked, cooled pudding and dish, if freezer-proof, in clingfilm and slip inside a large plastic bag. Exclude all the air, seal and label, then store for up to 3 days.*

To thaw: *Remove from the plastic bag. Leave to thaw for 4 hours in the fridge.*

To re-heat: *Remove the clingfilm and cover loosely with foil. Re-heat in a pre-heated oven at 180°c/350°f/gas 4 for 20 minutes. On the whole this recipe is not ideal to re-heat as the appearance is not quite as good.*

To cook in a fan oven: *Pre-heat the oven to 220°c. Bake for about 20 minutes.*

To cook in the Aga: 2-DOOR: *Place on the grid shelf on the floor of the roasting oven and bake for about 25 minutes until the apples are pale golden and the sponge is cooked. If the top is getting too brown before the sponge is cooked, slide the cold plain shelf above on the second set of runners.*

4-DOOR: *Place on the grid shelf on the floor of the baking oven and cook as in recipe.*

Ⓥ Baked Apple Lemon Sponge

SERVES 6

Something like the old-fashioned Eve's pudding, but this one makes its own creamy, lemon sauce. If buying lemon curd, check that it contains butter, sugar and lemons. It may be labelled lemon cheese or luxury lemon curd.

For the base	2 tablespoons caster sugar
300 ml (10 fl oz) single cream	*1 heaped teaspoon plain white flour*
6 tablespoons real lemon curd	*750 g (1¾ lb) cooking apples*

For the topping	*100 g (4 oz) soft baking margarine*
2 eggs	*1 teaspoon baking powder*
175 g (6 oz) self-raising white flour	*2 tablespoons milk*
100 g (4 oz) caster sugar	*1–1½ tablespoons demerara sugar*

You will need an ovenproof dish about 27 × 18 × 4.5 cm (10½ × 7 × 2 in).

Pre-heat the oven to 160°c/325°f/gas 3. Put a heavy baking tray to heat in the oven.

To prepare the base, combine the cream, lemon curd, sugar and flour in a bowl and whisk until smooth. Peel, core and very thinly slice the apples. I find it easiest to use a mandolin cutter or the thin slicing disc in the processor. Mix the sliced apples into the cream mixture, spoon into the base of the baking dish and level with the back of a spoon.

To make the topping, combine all the ingredients except the demerara sugar in a mixing bowl. Beat until smooth, then spread gently over the fruit in the baking dish. Sprinkle with demerara sugar then transfer to the oven to bake on the baking tray for 30 minutes or until it is a perfect golden brown. At this stage, cover the pudding with foil, then continue to bake for a further 45 minutes or until the sponge springs back when lightly pressed in the centre with a fingertip. Serve warm.

To prepare ahead: *The unbaked pudding can be kept covered in the fridge for up to 6 hours. Bring up to room temperature before baking on the pre-heated baking tray.*

To freeze: *Not suitable.*

To cook in a fan oven: *Do not pre-heat the oven. Bake on the baking tray at 150°C for about 25 minutes. Cover with foil, tucking the ends firmly underneath the dish to anchor them so the foil cannot be dislodged by the fan action of the oven. Bake for a further 35 minutes or until the sponge springs back when pressed with a fingertip in the centre of the pudding.*

To cook in the Aga: 2-DOOR: *Cook on the grid shelf on the floor of the roasting oven with the cold plain shelf on the second set of runners above. Cook for about 40 minutes until the sponge is cooked through. If getting a little too dark, cover with foil for the last 10 minutes.*
4-DOOR: *Bake on the grid shelf on the floor of the baking oven without the cold plain shelf. Cook as above.*

Ⓥ Canterbury Tart

SERVES 10

This is quite the best apple tart I know. A deep tart shell of crisp, buttery pastry filled with a magical mixture that is like *tarte au citron* combined with grated apples. It freezes well, too! To get a really crisp base to the tart put a thick baking tray in the oven whilst it pre-heats, then when the tart bakes on top of it the base will be golden and crisp.

THE USES OF BOTTLED LEMON JUICE
Just recently I have come round to using bottled lemon juice. It is handy to sprinkle over sliced apples and pears as it will prevent them from browning before cooking, and it will keep vegetables such as celeriac and mushrooms white. But for cooking where the flavour counts, such as lemon meringue pie or lemon curd, I use the real thing.

For the pastry
100 g (4 oz) chilled butter, cubed
225 g (8 oz) plain white flour
25 g (1 oz) icing sugar, sifted
1 egg, beaten

For the filling
4 eggs
225 g (8 oz) caster sugar
Grated rind and juice of 2 lemons
100 g (4 oz) butter, melted

4 large cooking apples, peeled, cored
 and quartered
2 dessert apples, peeled, cored,
 quartered and thinly sliced
25 g (1 oz) demerara sugar

To serve
Cream

You will need a 27 cm (10½ in) flan tin about 4 cm (1½ in) deep.

If making the pastry by hand, rub the butter into the flour and icing sugar until the mixture resembles breadcrumbs, then stir in the beaten egg and bring together to form a dough. If made in a processor, combine the flour, butter and icing sugar in the bowl, then process until the mixture resembles ground almonds. Pour in the beaten egg and pulse the blade until the dough starts to form a ball around the central stem. Form the pastry into a smooth ball, put inside a plastic bag and chill for 30 minutes. Roll out the pastry on a lightly floured work surface until slightly larger than the tin, then use a rolling pin to lift the pastry into the tin. Trim the edges and prick the base all over with a fork. Chill for a further 30 minutes.

Pre-heat the oven to 200°C/400°F/gas 6. Put a heavy metal baking tray to heat in the oven.

To prepare the filling, beat the eggs, sugar, lemon rind and juice together in a large mixing bowl. Stir in the warm melted butter, then coarsely grate the cooking apples directly into the mixture and mix well. Have ready the thinly sliced dessert apples.

Remove the tart tin from the fridge and spread the lemon mixture in the base. Level the surface with the back of a spoon and arrange the dessert apple slices around the outside edge, neatly overlapping. Sprinkle the apple slices with demerara sugar. Put the tart on to the heated baking tray in the oven and bake for about 40–50 minutes or until the centre feels firm to the touch and the apple slices are tinged brown. Serve warm with cream.

Canterbury Tart
(page 151).

To prepare ahead: *The pastry-lined tart tin can be kept in the fridge for up to 8 hours. The filling can be prepared and kept covered at room temperature for up to 4 hours.*

To freeze: *The tart tin base should be lined with a circle of silicone paper before the pastry goes in. Remove the metal collar from the cooled baked tart. Wrap the tart carefully in clingfilm and seal inside a plastic bag. Label and freeze for up to 1 month, if you are prepared to do without the flan tin base for this length of time. Lining the base with silicone or Lift-Off will guard against any acid from the filling reacting with the metal.*

To thaw: *Thaw for about 8 hours at room temperature.*

To re-heat: *Bake following the recipe for about 20 minutes or until piping hot.*

To cook in a fan oven: *Pre-heat the oven to 200°c and put the baking tray in to heat. Put the tart in the oven, lower the temperature to 190°c and bake for 30–35 minutes.*

To cook in the Aga: *Bake on the floor of the roasting oven for 25–30 minutes. If necessary, after 10 minutes slide the cold plain shelf on the second set of runners to prevent the pastry browning further. Transfer to the simmering oven to set the filling for about a further 10 minutes.*

Ⓥ
Mincemeat and Apricot Streusel

MAKES ABOUT 16 SLICES

Making a large pie and cutting it into serving pieces is a lot easier than making individual mince pies, and this version makes a welcome change to the usual mince pies around Christmas. Any other time of the year it can be made with Bramley apples instead of apricots, reserving the brandy for high days and holidays. If you regard yourself as a below-average pastry maker, be reassured; this pastry, although rolled out thinly, just needs pushing around with your fingers to repair it. The streusel topping is made by coarsely grating a dough, so no problem there either. The extra bonus is that it freezes well.

For the pastry base
175 g (6 oz) plain white flour
1½ tablespoons icing sugar, sifted
100 g (4 oz) butter
A little cold water

For the filling
100 g (4 oz) ready-to-eat dried
   apricots, chopped
1 tablespoon brandy
About 750 g (1½ lb) mincemeat

For the topping
75 g (3 oz) butter
75 g (3 oz) self-raising white flour
40 g (1½ oz) semolina
40 g (1½ oz) caster sugar

To serve
A little icing sugar, sifted
Cream

You will need a 23 × 33 cm (9 × 13 in) Swiss roll tin, lightly greased.

Pre-heat the oven to 200°C/400°F/gas 6.

Combine the apricots and brandy for the filling in a bowl so they can soak while the pastry is made.

Measure the flour and icing sugar into a mixing bowl and rub in the butter until the mixture resembles coarse breadcrumbs. Add just sufficient water to mix to a firm dough that leaves the sides of the bowl clean. Or if you prefer, make the pastry in a processor. If time allows, wrap the dough in clingfilm and chill for about 30 minutes. Roll out to a rectangle slightly larger than the tin, then line the base and sides of the tin with pastry. Do not worry if the pastry breaks or falls short in some places. Trim the pastry level with the top edges of the tin and use the off-cut pieces to patch and fill wherever necessary. Mix the mincemeat with the apricots and brandy then spread over the pastry base.

To make the topping, melt the butter in a small pan. Leave aside to cool while you measure the remaining ingredients into a bowl. Pour in the cooled butter and stir to form a soft dough. Using the coarse side of a grater, grate the dough evenly over the mincemeat. If the dough is too soft to grate, it means the butter was too hot when it was mixed into the dough, but this is easily put right: simply chill the dough for about 15 minutes and it will behave beautifully. Bake for about 20–25 minutes until pale golden brown. Check the streusel after about 10–12 minutes and, if necessary, turn the tin so the mixture cooks evenly. Leave to cool in the tin until just warm. Before serving, dust with icing sugar and divide into slices. Delicious with cream, unfortunately!

PERFECT PASTRY

For perfect pastry, cold hands, chilled fat, cold water and a cold rolling-out surface are best. The air trapped in the making of the dough will expand more if it is cold, making the pastry rise well. For this reason, too, chill pastry dough for about 30 minutes before baking.

To prepare ahead: *Cool and cut the streusel into slices and store in an airtight container in a cool place. Warm and dust with icing sugar just before serving.*

To freeze: *Store the slices in a plastic freezer container. Seal and label, then freeze for up to 3 months.*

To thaw: *Thaw in the freezer box for 4 hours at room temperature or overnight with the box lid resting on top.*

To re-heat: *Warm in a pre-heated oven 150°C/300°F/gas 2 for about 20 minutes. Dust with icing sugar before serving.*

To cook in a fan oven: *Pre-heat the oven to 180°C. Bake for 15–20 minutes.*

To cook in the Aga: *2-DOOR: Bake on the grid shelf in the roasting oven and position the cold plain shelf on the second set of runners. Bake the streusel for 15–20 minutes, then transfer to the floor of the roasting oven and bake for a further 10 minutes or until the streusel is a light golden brown.*
4-DOOR: Bake as above in the baking oven without the cold plain shelf.

Ⓥ
Austrian Apricot and Almond Tart

SERVES 8

This tart looks wonderful when it has cooked because the top layer of pastry moulds itself around the shape of the apricot halves that fill it. It has become known in our family as 'bums and tums tart'. You might prefer to use fresh apricots, but I have found some of them rather expensive and flavourless; tinned apricots make a much more reliable and readily obtainable alternative.

The pastry is a bit fragile to handle but this turns out to be no problem in the end. Wherever breaks occur just patch them with small pieces of pastry and they will be invisible when the tart has baked.

Mincemeat and Apricot
Streusel
(page 154).

For the pastry

150 g (5 oz) chilled butter, cubed
275 g (10 oz) plain white flour

150 g (5 oz) icing sugar, sifted
1 egg, beaten

For the filling

175 g (6 oz) almond paste or golden
marzipan, grated

2 × 400 g tins apricot halves in
natural juice, drained

You will need a 25–28 cm (10–11 in) fluted flan tin or dish and a heavy baking tray.

First make the pastry. If you are making it by hand, rub the butter into the flour and icing sugar until the mixture resembles breadcrumbs, then stir in the beaten egg and bring together to form a dough. If made in a processor, combine the butter, flour and icing sugar in the bowl, then process until the mixture resembles ground almonds. Pour in the beaten egg and pulse the blade until the dough starts to form a ball around the central stem. Form the pastry into a smooth ball, put inside a plastic bag and chill for 30 minutes.

Pre-heat the oven to 180°C/350°F/gas 4. Put the baking tray in the oven to heat.

Cut off a little less than half the pastry, wrap it in clingfilm and return it to the fridge until ready to use. Take the larger piece and roll out to a circle about 5 cm (2 in) bigger than the flan tin or dish. Line the base and sides with the pastry, then trim the excess from the top edge with a knife. Use the trimmings to patch the pastry if necessary. Spread the grated almond paste evenly over the pastry base. Dry the apricots on kitchen paper, then evenly space the apricots on top of the almond paste, rounded side up.

Roll out any left-over trimmings with the remaining pastry to a circle large enough to fit the top of the flan tin. Use a little water to dampen the rim of the pastry in the flan tin then, with the aid of the rolling pin, lift the top circle of pastry into position. Trim off any excess pastry then press the edges together so no juices can escape. Again, use the pastry trimmings to patch if necessary. Transfer to the oven to bake on the heated baking sheet for about 30–35 minutes or until pale golden. Watch this pastry carefully. Because it is a rich, sweet pastry it browns quickly and mostly around the edge. If it looks to be browning too quickly, protect the edge with crumpled strips of foil. If the tart is baked in a flan dish it will take a little longer to cook.

To prepare ahead: *The made tart can be covered in clingfilm and kept in the fridge for up to 24 hours before baking. Remove the tart from the fridge and leave at room temperature for about 20 minutes before baking.*

To freeze: *Not suitable.*

To cook in a fan oven: *Pre-heat the oven and a heavy baking tray to 160°C. Bake on the baking tray for about 25–30 minutes or until pale golden brown.*

To cook in the Aga: *Bake on the floor of the roasting oven for about 20 minutes or until pale golden. Protect the edge of the tart with foil if necessary, following the recipe.*

Ⓥ
Strawberry Dessert Cake

SERVES 6

Delicious served warm with cream, when it tends to be more of a dessert. Served cold, it is more of a cake. Either way, it is home cooking at its best, restaurants and supermarkets can offer nothing like it. It is also adaptable: fresh, sliced peaches can be used, and then you might like to add almond essence instead of vanilla. It is also an excellent way of using up windfall apples, but with these I add grated lemon rind rather than vanilla.

225 g (8 oz) self-raising white flour	*1 teaspoon vanilla extract*
1½ teaspoons baking powder	*150 g (5 oz) margarine, melted*
225 g (8 oz) caster sugar	*350 g (12 oz) fresh strawberries, sliced*
2 eggs	*25 g (1 oz) flaked almonds*

To serve
Cream

You will need either a fluted flan tin with a removable base 20 cm (8in) diameter and 5 cm (2 in) deep, or a 20 cm (8 in) cake tin, 4 cm (1½ in) deep, with a removable base. Line the base with greaseproof paper, then liberally grease the base and sides of the tin.

Pre-heat the oven to 160°C/325°F/gas 3.

Put the flour, baking powder and sugar into a bowl. In a separate bowl, beat the eggs and vanilla extract together, then stir them into the dry ingredients together with the melted margarine. Stir until thoroughly mixed, then spread half the mixture in the prepared tin. Arrange the strawberries on top to within 1 cm (½ in) of the edge. Spoon the remaining mixture in blobs on top of the strawberries, then spread to cover the surface. It does not matter if there are a few gaps; the mixture will melt and spread to fill them with the heat of the oven. Sprinkle with almonds. Bake for 1½ hours or until the cake is golden brown and shows signs of shrinking from the side of the tin. Leave to cool for about 15 minutes before removing the cake from the tin. Serve warm with cream.

To prepare ahead: *The unbaked cake can be covered and kept in the fridge for up to 24 hours, but it will need time to come back up to room temperature before baking, following the recipe above.*

To freeze: *Not suitable.*

To cook in a fan oven: *Do not pre-heat the oven. Bake at 150°C for about 1½ hours.*

To cook in the Aga: 2-DOOR: *Bake in the roasting oven on the grid shelf with the cold plain shelf on the second set of runners above, for about 25 minutes, until a perfect pale golden brown. Then carefully transfer to the simmering oven to cook for a further 1 hour.* 4-DOOR: *Bake in the baking oven for about 1 hour. When the top is golden brown after about 30 minutes, slide the cold plain shelf above on the second set of runners to prevent further browning.*

Ⓥ Gooey Almond and Apricot Dessert Cake

SERVES 8–10

The almond paste melts and blends with the sponge so this is a spoon and fork recipe, especially if served warm. In fact, the hotter the almond paste, the gooier the cake. Expect the almond paste to sink in the middle.

4 eggs	*½ teaspoon almond extract*
225 g (8 oz) caster sugar	*225 g (8 oz) ripe apricots, chopped*
225 g (8 oz) soft margarine	*or 400 g tin apricot halves,*
50 g (2 oz) self-raising white flour	*drained and chopped*
1 teaspoon baking powder	*225 g (8 oz) almond paste or golden*
175 g (6 oz) ground almonds	*marzipan*

To decorate
A little icing sugar, sifted

You will need a 20 cm (8 in) spring-form pan or loose-bottomed cake tin, 4 cm (1½ in) deep. Line the base and sides with greaseproof paper then grease the paper.

Pre-heat the oven to 160°C/325°F/gas 3.

Place the eggs, sugar, margarine, flour, baking powder, ground almonds and almond extract into a large bowl and beat until smooth. Stir in the chopped apricots. Spread half this mixture into the tin. Roll out the almond paste to a diameter slightly smaller than that of the tin, then drop the circle of paste on top of the mixture in the tin. Cover the almond paste with the remaining mixture. Bake for 30 minutes, then cover with a sheet of foil and bake for a further 45 minutes or until the mixture springs back when lightly pressed in the centre. Leave to cool in the tin for about 10 minutes, then remove from the tin and transfer to a wire rack until warm. Dust with icing sugar and serve warm.

To prepare ahead: *The unbaked pudding can be covered and kept in the fridge for up to 24 hours, but it will need to come up to room temperature before baking.*

To freeze: *Remove the cooled pudding from the tin, wrap closely in clingfilm and seal in a plastic bag. Label and freeze for up to 3 months.*

To thaw: *Remove from the plastic bag and thaw for 5 hours at room temperature or overnight in the fridge.*

To re-heat: *Wrap the pudding in foil and warm in a pre-heated oven at 180°C/350°F/ gas 4 for 20 minutes.*

To cook in a fan oven: *Do not pre-heat the oven. Bake at 150°C for about 1½ hours.*

To cook in the Aga: 2-DOOR: *Bake on the grid shelf on the floor of the roasting oven with the cold plain shelf above on the second set of runners for about 25–30 minutes until a perfect golden colour. Then transfer carefully to the simmering oven for a further hour.* 4-DOOR: *Bake on the grid shelf on the floor of the baking oven for about 1 hour, loosely covered with foil after 30 minutes.*

Ⓥ

Foolproof Floating Islands

SERVES 8

Serve this on its own or with Red Fruit Salad with Cassis (see page 185). To be honest I have always found poaching meringues to be a tricky business so I have devised an easier method to cook the meringues.

3 eggs, separated	1 heaped teaspoon
200 g (7 oz) caster sugar	cornflour
600 ml (1 pint) milk	½ teaspoon vanilla extract

You will need a shallow round ovenproof dish about 23–25 cm (9–10 in) in diameter.

Pre-heat the oven to 160°C/325°F/gas 3.

Put the egg whites in a large, grease-free bowl. Preferably using an electric hand mixer – but a balloon whisk and plenty of energy is fine – whisk the whites at full speed until the mass looks like a cloud. Reserving 25 g (1 oz) of sugar for the custard, gradually whisk the rest into the meringue a teaspoon at a time. This will take about 8 minutes (2–3 minutes with one of the newest mixers), and when finished the meringue will be very stiff and shiny and hold sharp peaks. Leave aside whilst preparing the custard.

Bring the milk to just below boiling point. Meanwhile, in a separate bowl, whisk together the remaining sugar, the egg yolks, cornflour and vanilla extract. Pour in the milk in a thin stream, whisking all the while. Immediately return the custard to the pan over a low heat and stir gently until the froth disappears and the custard is lightly thickened. Pour it into the dish; it will form only a thin layer but this is as it should be.

Now form 10 rounded ovals of meringue, each using 2 tablespoons of the meringue mixture, and place them in a circle on top of the custard. Bake for about 20 minutes or until the meringues are set and no longer sticky when lightly pressed with a finger. Serve warm or chilled.

To prepare ahead: *The pudding can be made, cooled, covered and kept in the fridge for up to 2 days. It is usual for the meringues to shrink slightly during this time.*

To freeze: *Not suitable.*

To cook in a fan oven: *Do not pre-heat the oven. Bake at 150°c for about 15 minutes.*

To cook in the Aga: *Put the custard and meringues in the simmering oven to bake for 15–20 minutes.*

Ⓥ Cheats' Lemon Meringue Pie

SERVES 6

What's the cheat? Well this recipe does away with the usual pastry base and instead has an easier, quicker crumb crust. The filling does not have to be cooked before pouring into the pie; you have only to stir a few ingredients together and it is ready. If you prefer to trim away a few calories, skimmed condensed milk can be used in the filling which, incidentally, is not sweet or sticky despite the condensed milk. In fact it is a really good, fresh, lemony flavour that balances well with the meringue topping.

> ### CHEESE BEFORE DESSERT
> *A meal seems to flow along more easily if the red wine served with the main course continues with a cheese course to follow, before the dessert, in the French style. When serving cheeses there is no need to have more than three: one hard cheese, one soft, one strong, tasty cheese – and remember that British cheeses are amongst the best!*

Velvet Chocolate Torte
(page 165).

For the base
75 g (3 oz) butter
175 g (6 oz) digestive biscuits,
crushed

For the filling
1 × 397 g tin sweetened condensed
milk
3 egg yolks
Finely grated rind and juice of
3 lemons

For the topping
3 egg whites
175 g (6 oz) caster sugar

You will need a 20 cm (8 in) fluted flan dish, 4 cm (1½ in) deep.

Pre-heat the oven to 190°C/375°F/gas 5.

Melt the butter in a medium-sized pan. Remove the pan from the heat and stir in the biscuit crumbs. Press the mixture into the flan dish using the back of a spoon to bring the crumbs up around the edge of the dish and smooth the base evenly.

Pour the condensed milk into a bowl, then beat in the egg yolks, lemon rind and strained juice. The mixture will seem to thicken on standing, then loosen again as soon as it is stirred. This is caused by the combination of condensed milk and lemon juice and is nothing to worry about. Pour the mixture into the biscuit-lined dish.

Put the egg whites into a large, grease-free bowl and, preferably using an electric hand beater, or otherwise using a balloon whisk, whisk the egg whites until stiff but not dry. Now start adding the measured sugar slowly, a teaspoon at a time, whisking well between each addition at full speed. When about two-thirds of the sugar has been added, the process can be speeded up; in total it should take about 8 minutes (2–3 minutes with one of the newest mixers). Pile separate spoons of meringue over the surface of the filling, then spread gently to cover the filling to the biscuit edge. Lightly swirl the meringue, then bake for 15–20 minutes or until the meringue is pinkish-brown. Leave aside for about 30 minutes before serving warm.

To prepare ahead: *The flan dish can be lined with the biscuit crumb mix, covered and kept in the fridge for up to 3 days. The filling can be mixed, covered and kept in the fridge for up to 8 hours before baking. Once baked, the pie can be eaten warm or cold but the meringue shrinks a little on standing.*

To freeze: *Not suitable.*

To cook in a fan oven: *Pre-heat the oven to 170°C. Bake for about 10–15 minutes.*

To cook in the Aga: 2-DOOR: *Slide a small roasting tin on to the lowest set of runners in the roasting oven and position the cold plain shelf on the second set of runners. Bake the pie for 3–4 minutes, then transfer to the floor of the simmering oven for a further 10–15 minutes or until the meringue is crisp.*

4-DOOR: *Bake as above in the baking oven but without the cold plain shelf for 3–4 minutes, then transfer to the simmering oven for 10–15 minutes.*

Ⓥ
Velvet Chocolate Torte

SERVES 12

Yes it really does serve twelve, it is so rich! If you do not have a spring-form tin, spoon the mixture into a freezer-safe bowl, cover with clingfilm, then freeze. After thawing for 20 minutes the chocolate will be ready to spoon on to serving plates and be decorated with strawberries. You can make half the quantity if you prefer, or simply cut off and thaw the amount you wish to serve and leave the rest in the freezer.

200 g (7 oz) plain good chocolate	4 egg yolks
100 g (4 oz) caster sugar	2 tablespoons brandy
6 tablespoons water	600 ml (1 pint) double cream

To decorate
A little icing sugar, sifted
12 large strawberries, sliced
A little single cream

You will need a 20 cm (8 in) loose-bottomed or spring-form tin, oiled and lined with clingfilm.

Break the chocolate into sections and drop into a processor. Process for 1 minute or until just a few pieces remain in the otherwise powdery chocolate. Alternatively finely grate the chocolate.

Measure the sugar and water into a small pan and heat gently until the sugar has dissolved, stirring occasionally. Now turn up the heat and boil briskly for 3–4 minutes to obtain a thin syrup. Set the processor running and pour in the hot syrup through the funnel on to the chocolate so it melts and becomes liquid. Add just a little more boiling water if some unmelted chocolate remains. Next add the egg yolks and process for a few seconds before adding the brandy. If you are not using a processor, beat the ingredients together.

In a separate bowl beat the cream to a soft, floppy consistency then fold in the chocolate mixture. Spread in the prepared tin, levelling the top with the back of a spoon, then cover with clingfilm and transfer to the freezer for a minimum of 4 hours to freeze.

Take the torte from the freezer 20 minutes before serving. Remove from the tin, strip away the clingfilm, put on a plate and leave to thaw; it should still be slightly frozen when it is cut in wedges for serving. Sift a little icing sugar over the surface of each plate, place a wedge of chocolate torte in the centre and arrange a sliced strawberry around each serving. Drizzle a little cream over each portion and serve immediately.

To prepare ahead: *The torte can be ready in the freezer.*

To freeze: *The torte can be frozen in the tin for up to 3 days. For longer freezing, once the torte is firmly frozen remove it from the tin, wrap in more clingfilm and seal in a plastic bag. Label and freeze for up to 3 months.*

To thaw: *Follow the recipe.*

Lime and Ginger Cheesecake

SERVES 8

I have an upside-down method of making a cheesecake: the mixture is set in the tin with the biscuit crumb on top. Dip the tin in very hot water for a moment, put a serving plate over the top of the tin, then turn so the cheesecake is delivered on to the plate, crumb layer on the base. This method can be easily done with a standard cake tin and guarantees a crisp crumb base. The recipe does not pander to those people with a sweet tooth – it is sharp, rich and moderately creamy.

4 tablespoons boiling water
1 sachet or 1 tablespoon powdered gelatine
225 g (8 oz) full-fat soft cream cheese
225 g (8 oz) curd cheese
Grated rind and juice of 4 limes
75 g (3 oz) caster sugar
300 ml (10 fl oz) whipping cream

For the base crust
100 g (4 oz) ginger biscuits
50 g (2 oz) butter
25 g (1 oz) demerara sugar

To decorate
1 egg white
A little caster sugar
A small bunch of 3–4 grapes
Several small sprigs of fresh
  mint leaves

You will need a 20 cm (8 in) cake tin, lightly oiled and base-lined with greaseproof paper. To frost the grapes and mint leaves you will need a paint brush and a wire rack.

Measure the boiling water into a small heatproof jug and sprinkle over the gelatine, stirring well. Leave it for 2–3 minutes, stirring once or twice, until the mixture is liquid and clear. Allow to cool for 5–10 minutes.

Combine the cheeses in a large mixing bowl and beat together until well mixed and softened. Gradually beat in the lime rind and juice and caster sugar. Stir in the cooled gelatine. Whisk the cream until it becomes a soft, floppy consistency, then fold into the cheesecake mixture. Spoon the mixture into the prepared tin and level the top with the back of a spoon. Transfer to the fridge to set for about 2 hours.

Crush the biscuits finely, either by putting them in a bag and crushing with a rolling pin, or in a processor. Melt the butter in a pan and stir in the biscuit crumbs and demerara sugar. Mix well and leave to cool, then gently press the mixture over the surface of the cheesecake. Return the cheesecake to the fridge and leave for a further 2 hours.

While the cheesecake is firming up in the fridge, frost the grapes and mint leaves. Whisk the egg white to a foam, then paint the grapes with the egg white. Sprinkle with caster sugar, then gently shake off the excess and lay the grapes on the wire rack. Do the same with the mint leaves, laying them on the rack. Put the rack in a warm dry place: the top of a boiler or the back of an Aga is ideal. After an hour or so, the egg white will dry and the sugar coating become crisp.

Turn the cheesecake out on to a serving plate and decorate with the frosted grape and mint leaves so it looks as fresh and pretty as possible.

FAST CRUMBS
My way of crushing biscuits is simple and effective. Put the biscuits
in a strong plastic bag and seal; then put the bag on the floor
and stamp on it!

To prepare ahead: *The prepared cheesecake can be kept covered in the fridge for up to 8 hours.*

To freeze: *If you intend to freeze the cheesecake, line the tin closely with clingfilm. This prevents the rather acid mixture reacting with the metal. When the cheesecake has been made, cover the top of the tin with foil and seal it inside a plastic bag. Label and freeze for up to 2 weeks.*

To thaw: *Remove the tin from the plastic bag and thaw overnight in the fridge. Unmould and decorate, following the recipe.*

Quick Lime Mousse

SERVES 6–8

This recipe relies on egg whites alone to give a light, airy and refreshing mousse. I have suggested whipped cream to decorate, but a half-fat crème fraîche, or a virtually no-fat fromage frais could be used instead if every calorie counts.

4 tablespoons boiling water
1 sachet or 1 tablespoon powdered
*   gelatine*
4 eggs, separated
100 g (4 oz) caster sugar
Finely grated rind and juice of
*   3 limes*

To decorate
Whipped cream
Thin strips of lime zest

A QUICK DE-FROST
A job that needs to be done quickly so the foodstuffs can be returned to the freezer. Switch off the freezer, unpack it and store the foods in freezer bags or boxes, surrounded with frozen gel blocks if you can. Heat a large pan of water and put in the freezer on a thick wad of newspapers. Leave until the ice thaws, then wipe the inside of the freezer with a solution of bicarbonate of soda (1 teaspoon bicarb to 600 ml/1 pint), or the fluid used for sterilizing baby bottles.

Measure the boiling water into a small heatproof jug and sprinkle over the gelatine, stirring well. Leave it for 2–3 minutes, stirring once or twice, until the mixture is liquid and clear. Allow to cool for 5–10 minutes.

Put the egg yolks in a small bowl with the sugar, and the whites in a large, grease-free bowl. Preferably using an electric hand beater, or with a balloon whisk, whisk the egg yolks and sugar until thick and creamy. Add the grated rind and strained juice of the limes and beat into the yolks. Stir in the gelatine and leave the mixture until cool and syrupy but not quite set.

With a clean, dry beater or balloon whisk, whisk the egg whites until stiff but not dry, then fold into the egg yolk mixture. Spoon into 6–8 individual glasses and put in the fridge for a minimum of 2 hours to set.

When ready, decorate with whipped cream and strips of lime zest and serve lightly chilled.

To prepare ahead: *The mousse can be made, covered in clingfilm and kept in the fridge for up to 8 hours. At this stage it will have a fairly firm set. Decorate as above before serving.*

To freeze: *Not suitable.*

Victorian Trifle

SERVES 10

One of the surest signs of the success of a recipe is when people come back for more, and most of them eat embarrassing amounts of this trifle. It is truly luscious without being unduly rich, which is exactly what most people want nowadays. The trifle benefits from being made a day ahead; it sets and serves well and the sherry can gently permeate throughout. Since it is usually a dessert made for special occasions, I have given a larger quantity for the recipe. If time is short use a tin of custard, then fold in 300 ml (10 fl oz) of whipped cream to cheer it up.

LUXURY CUSTARD
*Chill 600 ml (1 pint) of thickish custard made with custard powder.
Put it in a processor and whizz for 2 minutes until pale and light,
then serve; you can add a little single cream if you like. This
saves on calories and is also good on top of trifles instead
of home-made custard.*

For the custard
3 egg yolks
25 g (1 oz) cornflour
50 g (2 oz) caster sugar
600 ml (1 pint) milk
300 ml (10 fl oz) single cream

For the filling
16 trifle sponges
Strawberry jam
2 bought macaroons or
20 ratafias

1 × 810 g tin pear halves in natural
juice or light syrup
250 ml (8 fl oz) medium-dry sherry
175 g (6 oz) red seedless grapes,
halved

To decorate
150 ml (5 fl oz) whipping cream, or
more if liked
50 g (2 oz) flaked almonds, toasted

You will need a shallow 2.25 litre (4 pint) glass bowl.

Put the egg yolks, cornflour and sugar into a large bowl and stir together with a whisk. Heat the milk and cream together in a pan until hot but not boiling. Gradually whisk into the yolks, then return the mixture to the pan. Stir over a high heat until the mixture just comes to the boil and the custard thickens. Take off the heat, cover and allow to cool.

Split the sponges and spread generously with strawberry jam. Sandwich together and arrange in the base of the dish, close together, cutting to fit if necessary. Crumble the macaroons or ratafias over the top. Combine 150 ml (5 fl oz) of pear juice drained from the tin with the sherry and sprinkle over the sponge and crumbled biscuits. Level the surface by pressing down with a spoon.

Drain the pears, discarding the remaining juice. Cut each half in 3 lengthways and arrange over the sponges. Scatter the grapes on top. Spread the custard over the fruit. Cover and leave until cold before transferring to the fridge to chill and set.

Beat the whipping cream until just stiff enough to hold a soft, floppy shape. Gently spread over the surface of the set custard and scatter with the almonds. Cover and chill until ready to serve.

To prepare ahead: *The made trifle can be covered with clingfilm and kept in the fridge for up to 2 days before serving.*

To freeze: *Not suitable.*

Victorian Trifle
(page 169).

ⓥ
Almond Florentine Dessert

This is very thin discs of toffee-almond, a bit like large, flat, nutty brandysnaps, layered with cream, pears and ginger. If ginger is not to your taste, sandwich with fresh raspberries and whipping cream. It is quite a tricky recipe to make and it is essential to measure or weigh the ingredients carefully since even a minor variation can make a considerable difference to the result. It is also a recipe where good quality bakeware really pays off. You *must* use good, solid baking trays that will not bend in the oven, or this mixture will simply flow off the bent baking trays and on to the bottom of the oven.

For the almond florentines
150 g (5 oz) butter
120 g (4½ oz) caster sugar
1½ tablespoons plain white flour
3 tablespoons milk
165 g (5½ oz) flaked almonds

For the filling
1 × 810 g tin pear halves in fruit juice
300 ml (10 fl oz) whipping cream
3 pieces stem ginger, finely chopped
2 tablespoons ginger syrup
2 tablespoons Poire Williams pear liqueur

To decorate
A little icing sugar, sifted

You will need 3 × 25 cm (10 in) circles drawn on separate sheets of silicone paper. Turn over and place on 3 separate, good quality baking trays. Or mark circles in chalk on Lift-Off paper.

Pre-heat the oven to 180°c/350°F/gas 4.

Melt the butter and sugar in a pan over a low heat.

Meanwhile, combine the flour and milk in a small bowl and stir to form a smooth paste. As soon as the butter has melted, stir in the paste, followed by the almonds. Bring to the boil and boil for 30 seconds. Divide the mixture equally between the 3 trays and spread out very thinly to the edges of the circles. Bake, in rotation if necessary, for 9–11 minutes until a toffee-golden all over. Until you get the timing just right for your oven, watch carefully towards the end of the baking time as the mixture can over-brown very quickly. Remove from the oven. If the mixture has flowed a little outside the marked circles simply bring it back into line with a small palette knife, then leave to cool and set.

Drain the pears and discard the juice. Dry them well on kitchen paper, then coarsely chop. Pour the cream into a bowl and whisk until stiff enough to hold a shape. Fold in the pears, ginger, ginger syrup and liqueur. Select the best almond florentine round for the top and reserve. Carefully strip the baking papers off the other 2 and put one round on a serving plate. Spread with half the filling and place the second round on top. Spread very gently with the remaining filling and put the last and best round in position. Ideally chill for 4 hours before serving. At this stage, the toffee-almond biscuits cut and eat well.

To prepare ahead: *The made pudding will keep for up to 24 hours. The filling can be made, covered and stored for up to 2 days in the fridge.*

To freeze: *The almond florentines can be baked, cooled, left on their baking papers and stacked. Carefully put them inside a plastic bag, seal and label, then store for up to 1 month. The dessert cannot be frozen when layered with filling.*

To thaw: *No thawing needed; the almond florentines can be used straight from the freezer. Spread with the filling and assemble as in the recipe.*

To cook in a fan oven: *Pre-heat the oven to 170°c. Bake for about 8 minutes.*

To cook in the Aga: 2-DOOR: *Bake in the roasting oven a tray at a time on the grid shelf on the floor with the cold plain shelf on the second set of runners above for about 7 minutes. Watch very carefully during the last minutes of cooking.*
4-DOOR: *Bake in the baking oven as above but without the cold plain shelf.*

SIMPLE MEAL ENDINGS
It is not necessary always to offer a pudding. In fact, a lot of people prefer to be offered a choice of fruit and cheese. This can be made to look very attractive with little effort. Put grapes, cherries or perhaps Worcester apples on a board or flat basket that has the base covered with vine or blackcurrant leaves. Group the fruits at the back of the board and the cheeses at the front, then sit back and let people help themselves.

Ⓥ
Frozen Pineapple Parfait

SERVES 8

This is a delicious individual ice-cream dessert flavoured with pineapple and served with fresh pineapple sweetened with caramel syrup. Fruits vary in quality so if the pineapple has a slightly woody stem it is better to discard it rather than have it adversely affect the ice-cream.

For the parfait
1 medium-sized, ripe pineapple
Rind and juice of 1 lemon
3 egg yolks

175 g (6 oz) caster sugar
300 ml (10 fl oz) double cream, chilled

For the caramel
100 g (4 oz) caster sugar
4 tablespoons water

To decorate
1 small, ripe pineapple
Sprigs of fresh mint

You will need 8 × 7.5 cm (3 in) ramekins, lightly oiled and closely lined with clingfilm, and a baking tray, lightly oiled.

Top and tail the pineapple, then cut in quarters. Remove the core from each quarter, then blend the cores to a purée in a processor with the lemon rind and juice. Now cut the rind from the pineapple and add the flesh to the processor. Blend again until smooth. Add the egg yolks and sugar and blend once more until thick. Beat the cream until it is just thick enough to hold a shape. Fold the pineapple mixture into the cream, then spoon into the prepared ramekins. Cover with clingfilm and freeze for 4 hours or until firm.

HASSLE-FREE ICE-CREAM
Serving ice-cream quickly to a number of people need not be a problem. Ahead of time, scoop the ice-cream into balls, put on lined baking trays and re-freeze. If it is something a little more formal, pile the balls in a pyramid in a suitable serving dish and have ready, frozen. Put in the fridge about 10 minutes before serving, to soften.

Meanwhile, prepare the caramel for the topping. Put the sugar and water into a pan and stir over a low heat until the sugar has dissolved. Bring to the boil and continue to boil steadily until the syrup has become a shade darker than golden syrup. Immediately remove the pan from the heat and pour the syrup on to the prepared baking tray. Leave until cold and set, then break the caramel into small chips by tapping with the handle of a knife.

Peel, quarter, core and thinly slice the second pineapple. Put in a dish and sprinkle with the caramel chips. Cover and chill in the fridge for about 4 hours.

About 15 minutes before serving, remove the parfaits from the freezer. Turn out on to individual plates and leave in the fridge to soften a little. Serve each with some sliced pineapple and caramel juices. Decorate with sprigs of mint and serve immediately.

To prepare ahead: *The parfaits can be kept in the freezer until ready to serve. The caramel and pineapple can be covered and kept in the fridge for up to 1 day.*

To freeze: *The individual parfaits can be covered and stored on a tray sealed inside a plastic bag. Label and freeze for up to 2 months. The pineapple and caramel should be prepared fresh when needed and not frozen.*

Ⓥ
Bombe Marie
with Brandy and Raisin Sauce

MAKES 16–20 WEDGES

This is an ice-cream pudding lined with rum and coffee-flavoured ice-cream with an inner layer of grated chocolate and a vanilla centre. An inspired alternative to the usual Christmas pudding, and a very clever recipe – even if I say so myself! It freezes happily, cuts beautifully, and is an easy dessert to serve to a crowd if you follow my technique.

MAKING THE MOST OF VANILLA PODS
Vanilla pods are an expensive ingredient so I make sure I get the maximum use out of mine. Rinse and dry the pods when they have been used, for example, to flavour a custard. Put into a jar of caster sugar to impart flavour. When the amount of vanilla pods in the sugar gets too much, chop the pods into short lengths and put them into small bottles. Top these up with vodka and within a month you will have an excellent vanilla extract!

---

2 teaspoons instant coffee
2 teaspoons boiling water
7 eggs
450 ml (15 fl oz) double cream,
    chilled
200 g (7 oz) caster sugar
1 teaspoon vanilla extract
2 tablespoons brandy
175 g (6 oz) plain chocolate,
    grated

You will need 1 × 2.25 litres (4 pint) and 2 × 900 ml (1½ pint) freezer-proof bowls to make the bombe. Before starting the recipe, put the bowls into the freezer. You will also need an old, clean, standard-size cotton reel or something of a similar size.

Measure the instant coffee into a cup and mix with the boiling water. Leave on one side to cool.

Separate the eggs, putting the whites in a large, grease-free bowl and the egg yolks in a small basin. Pour the chilled cream into a separate bowl. The next stage involves a lot of whisking so use an electric hand whisk it you have one. Start by whisking the egg whites until they stand in firm peaks, then gradually whisk in the measured sugar, a teaspoon at a time. When all the sugar has been added and the mixture has formed a stiff, shiny meringue, briefly whisk the egg yolks, then whisk the cream just enough for it to thicken to a soft, floppy consistency. Combine the yolks, cream and vanilla into the egg whites so it is evenly mixed – this is easily done using a balloon whisk. Fill 1 × 900 ml (1½ pint) chilled bowl to the top with some of the mixture. Cover with clingfilm and replace in the freezer.

Mix the cooled coffee and the brandy into the remaining vanilla-cream mix and pour it into a large measuring jug. Remove the remaining bowls from the freezer. Position the cotton reel centrally in the base of the large bowl and stand the smaller bowl on top of the cotton reel. Check that the smaller bowl is centred and carefully pour the coffee-brandy mixture into the gap between the two bowls (see **1**) until the mix reaches the rim. Holding the bowls firmly in place, carefully replace them in the freezer. Freeze all the ice-cream for a minimum of 4 hours.

Remove the small bowl of vanilla ice-cream from the freezer and leave at room temperature for 15 minutes. Meanwhile take the large bowl from the freezer. Rinse out a clean cloth in hot water and put it in the smaller, central bowl. Repeat, rinsing the cloth once or twice more until the inner bowl has warmed sufficiently for you to twist it, then remove it. Tease out the cotton reel and use the bowl of a spoon to fill and smooth over the hole (see **2**). Leave for several minutes so that the ice-cream melts slightly, then use half the grated chocolate to evenly coat the hollow left by removing the smaller bowl. It helps if you use a large spoon to spread, then gently press the chocolate on to the sides of the hollow (see **3**).

Take the small bowl of vanilla ice-cream and dip it, for a count of 15–20, in a bowl of hot water. Cover one hand with a sheet of clingfilm and turn the ice-cream out on to it (see **4**). Immediately turn the ice-cream into the matching chocolate-lined cavity in the coffee-brandy ice-cream and press it in firmly to bond all the layers together. Spread the top flat with a palette knife, cover with the clingfilm and replace in the freezer. Freeze again for at least 8 hours.

Dip the bowl in hot water for a count of 10. Then invert on to a serving dish. Quickly sprinkle the ice-cream with the remaining grated chocolate, cover with clingfilm and return to the freezer.

To serve: *Thaw for 15 minutes in the fridge, cut in wedges like a cake, and serve with Brandy and Raisin Sauce. It helps to use a hot, wet knife for cutting.*

To freeze: *Freeze completely covered with grated chocolate for up to 1 month.*

Brandy and Raisin Sauce

This is a store-cupboard sauce which will keep indefinitely. After being made it can be kept in a screw-topped jar in a cupboard and dipped into for serving with all manner of ice-creams, pancakes, waffles and baked sponge puddings. Or try it spooned over natural yoghurt. It is such a delicious, useful sauce I guarantee it will become a permanent standby. Just one word of reassurance; it will take time – a surprising amount of time – to dissolve the sugar in the water. You could use rum instead of brandy if you prefer.

225 g (8 oz) caster sugar
6 tablespoons water
225 g (8 oz) raisins
75 ml (2½ fl oz) brandy

You will need a clean screw-topped or preserving jar. Combine the water and sugar in a medium-sized pan and leave over a low heat until the sugar has completely dissolved, stirring gently. When the syrup is completely clear, stir in the raisins. Remove the pan from the heat and add the brandy. Cool and pour into the storage jar. Serve cold.

The sauce will keep indefinitely. If the syrup crystallizes, add a little more water and re-heat with the raisins till the crystals disappear.

Brandysnap Baskets of Ice-cream, Bananas and Toffee Sauce

SERVES 8

This is a dessert that can be ready to go up to a week ahead of time. Don't be frightened away by the brandysnap baskets in the title because these are an enormous cheat. You buy the brandysnaps, soften them for a moment in the oven then mould them, so within 5 minutes of opening the packet, the little baskets are ready to use! The toffee sauce is brilliant with ice-cream too.

Bombe Marie with
Brandy and Raisin Sauce
(page 175).

1 × 100 g box of brandysnaps
1–2 bananas, sliced
A little lemon juice
Vanilla ice-cream

For the toffee sauce
50 g (2 oz) butter
150 g (5 oz) soft brown sugar
150 g (5 oz) golden syrup
1 × 170 g tin evaporated milk

You will need 2 baking trays lined with silicone paper.

Pre-heat the oven to 180°c/350°F/gas 4.

Have ready 4 spice jars or upturned tea cups. Arrange 4 brandysnaps on each of the 2 lined baking trays, then put one tray into the oven for about 1 minute. This is all the time the brandy snaps need to soften and unfold. Carefully lift the soft brandysnaps from the tray and lay them over the jars or cups. As soon as they are cool enough, mould each one into a ruffle-edged basket. Leave until cool and set before proceeding with the second batch.

To make the sauce, put the butter, sugar and syrup in a pan and heat gently until melted and liquid. Turn up the heat so the mixture boils gently for 5 minutes. Remove the pan from the heat and gradually stir in the evaporated milk. The sauce is now ready and can be served hot, warm or cold.

Just before serving, assemble the dessert. Slice the bananas then, if there is to be any delay, toss them in a little lemon juice to prevent them browning and drain before using. Arrange about 3 slices in the base of each basket, spoon in the ice-cream then spoon over the toffee sauce. Serve immediately.

To prepare ahead: *The brandysnap baskets can be formed and stored in an airtight container for up to 2 weeks. The toffee sauce can be made and stored in a sealed container in the fridge for up to 3 weeks. If tossed in lemon juice the bananas can be kept for up to 3 hours at room temperature before draining and using. Soft scoop ice-cream can be used straight from the freezer.*

To freeze: *Not suitable.*

To cook in a fan oven: *Pre-heat the oven to 170°c. Warm the brandysnaps in the oven just long enough for them to soften and unfold, then follow the recipe above.*

To cook in the Aga: *Soften the brandysnaps in the simmering oven until flattened. This will take 1–5 minutes depending on the heat of the Aga.*

(V)
Iced Coffee Flummery

SERVES 10

It may seem odd to use both instant coffee and coffee beans to flavour this 'iced cream' but each one serves a slightly different purpose. The beans give a fragrant flavour and the instant coffee gives it strength. An easy, iced dessert that, once made, can be kept in the freezer.

50 g (2 oz) coffee beans
600 ml (1 pint) milk
100 g (4 oz) golden
    sugar
1 tablespoon instant coffee
300 ml (10 fl oz) double
    cream

To decorate
Whipped cream
12–18 chocolate-covered
    coffee beans

You will need 6 × 7.5 cm (3 in) ramekins or small dishes, lightly oiled.

Put the beans, milk, sugar and instant coffee into a pan and heat until the milk steams. Stir, cover and remove the pan from the heat. Leave aside until cold. Strain and discard the beans.

Put the cream into a bowl, then whisk in the flavoured milk. Pour the mixture into a plastic freezer container, cover with a lid and freeze for at least 6 hours or until frozen firm.

Remove the container from the fridge and leave at room temperature for about 10 minutes or until slightly softened. Break the iced mix in pieces and process in a food processor until it is smooth. Alternatively beat well until smooth. Turn the mixture into the dishes, cover with clingfilm and return them to the freezer overnight.

About 15 minutes before serving, pipe or decorate each dish with a blob of cream and top with a few chocolate-covered coffee beans.

To freeze: *Cover each dish with foil, seal, label and freeze for up to 1 month.*

To thaw: *Leave in the fridge for about 20 minutes before decorating and serving.*

ⓥ Red Plum Ice-cream

SERVES 8

If you would like a rather sweeter ice-cream or the plums are rather sharp, add an additional 25 g (1 oz) of caster sugar. Whisk on full speed when whisking the egg whites.

1 tablespoon water	*A little lemon juice, to taste*
175 g (6 oz) caster sugar	*4 eggs, separated*
8 oz (225 g) red plums	*300 ml (10 fl oz) double cream*

Start the recipe the day before it is to be served.

Measure the water and 50 g (2 oz) of the caster sugar into a pan. Add the plums and adjust the heat to give a very gentle simmer. Cover and cook until tender. Cool.

Have a plastic sieve positioned over a bowl. Empty the contents of the pan into the bowl, then rub the fruit through the sieve. Discard any skin and stones left behind, then taste and flavour the purée with lemon juice, if liked. Cover and chill in the fridge.

Put the egg whites in a large, grease-free bowl, then, preferably using an electric hand beater, or using a balloon whisk and a large bowl, whisk the whites at full speed until the mass looks like a cloud. Gradually whisk in the remaining sugar, a teaspoon at a time. When all the sugar has been added the meringue should be stiff and form sharp, glossy peaks. Fold in the beaten egg yolks. Quickly whisk the cream until thick and fold into the meringue mixture, followed by the plum purée. Pour the mixture into a shallow plastic freezer container and freeze overnight or for at least 12 hours.

To prepare ahead: *Pile scoopfuls of ice-cream into a chilled dish to form a pyramid. Cover with clingfilm and return to the freezer. Ice-cream frozen in this manner can be served almost straight from the freezer.*

To freeze: *Seal and label, then freeze for up to 3 months.*

To thaw: *Transfer the freezer container to the fridge about 20 minutes before scooping.*

ⓥ Blackcurrant Ice-cream

Following the recipe for Red Plum Ice-cream, use 5 tablespoons Ribena in place of the plums. Whisk the egg whites with 100 g (4 oz) caster sugar, then fold in the egg yolks and Ribena. Freeze as directed in the recipe above.

Red Fruit Salad with Cassis
(page 185).

Lemon and Lime Ice-Cream

Following the recipe for Red Plum Ice-cream, use the strained juice of 1 large lemon and 1 large lime in place of the plums. Whisk the egg whites with 100 g (4 oz) caster sugar, then fold in the egg yolks and juices. Taste; you may prefer to add a little more sugar.

Coffee Ice-cream

Follow the recipe for Red Plum Ice-cream, adding 4 tablespoons liquid coffee essence or 2 teaspoons instant coffee dissolved in 2 tablespoons hot water in place of the plums. Whisk the egg whites with 100 g (4 oz) caster sugar, then fold in the egg yolks and coffee. Serve with Brandy and Raisin Sauce (see page 179).

Charentais Melon Sorbet

MAKES ABOUT 1 LITRE (1¾ PINTS)

I have opted for this type of melon because it gives a gorgeous orange-coloured sorbet with an excellent flavour, best when the melon is fully ripe.

1 × 900 g (2 lb) ripe Charentais melon	Juice of 2 lemons, strained
285 g (10½ oz) sugar	3 tablespoons white port or dry sherry

Halve the melon and scoop out the seeds with a soup spoon. Remove the rind. Put the flesh in a processor with the sugar, lemon juice and port or sherry and blend until smooth.

If you are going to use an ice-cream machine to churn the sorbet, transfer the purée to a jug, cover and chill in the fridge. When ready, pour the purée into the machine and churn for 10–15 minutes or until the sorbet is firm enough to serve.

If freezing without an ice-cream machine, pour the purée into a shallow freezer container and place in the freezer for about 30 minutes until ice crystals start to form around the edges. Remove and beat, preferably with an electric hand whisk, then cover and replace in the freezer for a further 30 minutes. Repeat the process once or twice more until no free liquid remains. Leave for a minimum of 1 hour in the freezer to harden before serving.

To prepare ahead: *The sorbet can be stored in the freezer. Quickly scrape the freshly made sorbet into plastic freezer containers and cover with greaseproof paper to prevent ice crystals forming. Seal and label, then freeze for up to 4 weeks.*

To thaw: *Transfer to the fridge about 20 minutes before serving in scoopfuls.*

ⓥ Red Fruit Salad with Cassis

SERVES 6–8

A fruit salad that can be served hot or chilled. I love to serve it warm because of the intoxicating aromas of all the different fruits that come wafting up from the plate. This very deep, dark red salad looks very pretty if served in a glass bowl on a plate lined with fresh blackcurrant or raspberry leaves. It is a good way of using frozen currants.

A generous 450 g (1 lb) redcurrants, stalks removed	225 g (8 oz) fresh strawberries, halved if large
A generous 450 g (1 lb) blackcurrants, stalks removed	150 g (5 oz) fresh blueberries
75 g (3 oz) caster sugar	450 g (1 lb) fresh raspberries
4 ripe nectarines, sliced	3 tablespoons crème de cassis

The salad is very simple to make. Put the redcurrants and blackcurrants in a pan with the sugar and warm gently, covered. As they begin to cook, the berries will release some of their juice and dissolve the sugar so no additional water is needed. When the fruits are warm remove the pan from the heat and add the nectarines, strawberries and blueberries. If you are intending to serve the salad warm, add the raspberries and cassis now. If the salad is to be served cold, pour the fruits into a serving dish and cool before putting in the fridge to chill. Just before serving, gently stir in the raspberries and cassis.

To prepare ahead: *The salad can be made without the raspberries and kept covered in the fridge for up to 24 hours. Reheat and add the raspberries just before serving.*

To freeze: *Cool. Put in a plastic freezer container, seal and label, then freeze for up to 3 months.*

To thaw: *Thaw overnight in the fridge.*

ⓥ Quite the Best Fruit Salad

SERVES AT LEAST 10–12

It's quite the best because it can be made ahead, can be frozen, leaving only a couple of soft fruits to add just before serving, and the other fruits are all in generous-size pieces. The ones I have used are only suggestions. Your choice will be governed by season and what is available. Just make sure the fruits make an attractive salad, and avoid ones that discolour once cut – peaches and nectarines – unless you can add them at the last minute. It is quite easy to halve the quantities.

For the basic fruit salad   *6 thin-skinned oranges*
1 Charentais melon   *1 pink grapefruit*
1 Galia or Honeydew melon   *1 ripe pineapple*
100 g (4 oz) caster sugar   *1 ripe mango*

Later additions
225 g (8 oz) seedless red or green
  grapes or strawberries or
  raspberries

You will need a very sharp knife and a large container that will store the fruit salad in the fridge.

To prepare the melons, halve, scoop out the seeds with a spoon, then cut each one into a total of 6–8 wedges. Remove the rind and cut the flesh into chunks. Transfer the prepared fruit and any juices to the container and sprinkle with a little of the measured sugar.

Peel the oranges as described in Salad of Red and Yellow Tomatoes with Oranges (see pages 124–5), then slice the fruit into thin rounds not segments. Prepare the grapefruit in the same manner, but cut into segments. Transfer the citrus fruit and any juices to the container and sprinkle with a little more of the sugar.

Top and tail the pineapple. Sit it on its cut base, then cut away a strip of rind, working from the top to the base of the fruit and following the shape. Work your way around the fruit in this fashion until all the rind has been removed. Quarter the fruit lengthways then trim away the central, woody core. Slice the strips of pineapple across into chunks. Add the fruit and juices to the container and sprinkle with the last of the sugar.

To prepare the mango, cut off thick slices above and below the stone (see **1**). Trim away the band of flesh around the stone (see **2**) and remove the skin. Strip away the flesh from the slices, or scoop it out using a tablespoon (see **3**). Add all the skinned, chopped mango to the container. Cover and chill for about 2 hours.

Just before serving, add the grapes, strawberries or raspberries. Transfer the fruit salad to a serving bowl and take to the table.

To prepare ahead: *The basic fruit salad can be kept covered in the fridge for up to 24 hours. Add the grapes or soft fruit just before serving.*

To freeze: *Select a suitably sized lidded freezer container that will take the quantity of fruit salad and fit into your freezer. Place the basic fruit salad in a freezer container, seal and label, then freeze for up to 1 month.*

To thaw: *Thaw overnight in the fridge. Add the grapes or soft fruit just before serving.*

Ⓥ
Hazelnut Meringue Torte Filled with Raspberries and Cream

SERVES 10

I am particularly fond of this meringue. If you have difficulty buying flaked hazelnuts, slice whole hazelnuts on a fine slicing disc in a processor. These, folded into the meringue, give it a delightful flavour and crisp texture.

> ### KEEP NUTS AT THEIR BEST
> *To keep nuts fresh, store in plastic bags in the freezer, rather than keeping them in jars in warm kitchen cupboards.*

For the meringue

6 egg whites
375 g (13 oz) caster sugar
1 teaspoon white wine vinegar

1 teaspoon cornflour
175 g (6 oz) flaked hazelnuts, with
  skin if possible

For the filling

300 ml (10 fl oz) whipping cream

225 g (8 oz) raspberries, fresh; or
  frozen, thawed and drained

To decorate

A little icing sugar, sifted

Draw 2 circles 1 × 25 cm (10 in) diameter, 1 × 28 cm (11 in) diameter on separate sheets of silicone paper. Turn over and place on 2 separate baking trays. Or mark the circles with chalk on Lift-Off.

Pre-heat the oven to 160°C/325°F/gas 3.

Preferably using an electric hand beater, whisk the egg whites in a large, grease-free bowl until stiff but not dry. Now, whisking at full speed, gradually add the sugar, a teaspoon at a time. The process may take about 8 minutes depending on the power of the machine. When all the sugar has been added the mixture will be shiny and very stiff. Mix the vinegar and cornflour to a smooth paste, then fold the mixture into the meringue with 150 g (5 oz) of the nuts. Divide the mixture in half and spread to the marked-out circles on the paper. Sprinkle the remaining nuts over the top of the smaller circle. Transfer to the oven and immediately lower the temperature to 150°C/300°F/gas 2. Bake for 1 hour, then turn the oven off and leave the meringues in the oven, undisturbed, for a further 1 hour. Remove and cool on wire racks before removing the baking papers. Place the larger meringue base-side up on a serving dish.

Beat the cream to a soft, floppy consistency, then gently fold in the raspberries. Spread the filling on the base round and put the smaller meringue, right-side up, on top. Cover and chill until ready to serve. Just before serving, dust with icing sugar.

To prepare ahead: *The baked, cooled meringue can be wrapped carefully in foil and kept in an airtight container for 2 weeks. Or the finished meringue torte can be covered and kept in the fridge for up to 8 hours. Dust with icing sugar before serving.*

To freeze: *The finished meringue torte can be carefully wrapped with clingfilm then sealed in a freezer container to protect it from damage in the freezer. Label, then freeze for up to 1 month.*

To thaw: *Remove from the freezer container and thaw overnight in the fridge.*

To cook in a fan oven: *Pre-heat the oven to 160°C. When the meringue torte is put in to bake, immediately lower the temperature to 130°C and bake for 45 minutes. Turn the oven off and leave the meringue in the oven for a further 1 hour. Remove, then follow the recipe above.*

To cook in the Aga: *Place one meringue on its baking sheet on the grid shelf on the floor of the roasting oven with the cold plain shelf on the second set of runners for about 3 minutes or until a very pale cream, then transfer to the centre of the simmering oven. Now place the second meringue on the grid shelf on the floor of the roasting oven with a new cold plain shelf on the second set of runners for 5 minutes as before, transferring to the simmering oven on the floor. Both meringues will need about a further 55 minutes or more in the simmering oven until firm. Turn them round half-way through cooking time. Allow to become cold before removing the baking papers.*

ⓥ Chocolate and Orange Pavlova

SERVES 8–10

A luxury pavlova of light, crisp meringue filled with a rich chocolate and orange mixture.

For the meringue	
3 egg whites	1 teaspoon white wine vinegar
175 g (6 oz) caster sugar	1 teaspoon cornflour
For the filling	Grated rind of 1 small orange
100 g (4 oz) plain good chocolate	1 tablespoon orange juice
50 g (2 oz) caster sugar	300 ml (10 fl oz) double cream,
3 tablespoons water	chilled
3 egg yolks	
To decorate	8 Maltesers
150 ml (5 fl oz) whipping cream	A little icing sugar, sifted

You will need a 23 cm (9 in) circle drawn out on a piece of non-stick baking parchment. Turn over and use to line a baking tray.

Pre-heat the oven to 160°c/325°F/gas 3.

Put the egg whites in a large grease-free bowl and, preferably using an electric beater, or otherwise using a balloon whisk, whisk the whites until stiff but not dry. Now start adding the measured sugar slowly, a teaspoon at a time, whisking at full speed between each addition. When about two-thirds of the sugar has been added the process can be speeded up; in total it should take about 8 minutes (2–3 minutes with one of the newest mixers). Mix the vinegar and cornflour in a small bowl, then fold into the meringue. Spread the mixture to just within the boundary of the marked circle, making the shape slightly hollow in the centre and higher around the sides. Transfer to the oven and immediately lower the temperature to 150°c/300°F/gas 2. Bake for 1 hour or until firm to touch and a pale biscuit colour. Turn off the oven and leave the meringue inside the oven, without disturbing it, for a further 1 hour.

Carefully peel the baking parchment away from the base, then place the meringue on a serving dish. Cover and leave aside while making the filling.

Break the chocolate into sections and drop into a processor. Process for 1 minute or until just a few pieces remain in the otherwise powdery chocolate. Alternatively you can finely grate the chocolate. Combine the sugar and water in a small pan and heat gently until the sugar has dissolved, stirring occasionally. Now turn up the heat and boil briskly for 3–4 minutes to obtain a thin syrup. Set the processor containing the chocolate running and pour in the hot syrup through the funnel on to the chocolate so it melts and becomes liquid. Add just a little more boiling water if some unmelted chocolate remains. Next add the egg yolks, process for a few seconds then add the orange rind and juice. If you are not using a processor, beat the ingredients together with a wooden spoon.

In a separate bowl, beat the cream to a soft, floppy consistency, then fold in the chocolate mixture. Pile the filling into the meringue then transfer to the fridge to chill for 2 hours.

Just before serving, decorate the pavlova by beating the whipping cream until stiff enough to hold a firm shape, then fit a piping bag with a 6 or 8-point star nozzle and pipe 8 rosettes around the edge of the set chocolate, or use 2 teaspoons to form neat blobs. Top each rosette with a Malteser, then dust with sifted icing sugar and serve.

To prepare ahead: *The filled meringue can be made and kept in the fridge for up to 24 hours. Decorate just before serving straight from the fridge.*

To freeze: *Leave the filled meringue on the baking tray and cover both with clingfilm. Store in the freezer where nothing can rest or fall on it. Alternatively, wrap the filled meringue in clingfilm then seal inside a freezer box by turning the box upside-down; sit the meringue on the lid and replace the box on top, making sure it is sealed. Label clearly with 'Store this way up' and the usual details of contents and date. This method by-passes the tricky business of lifting a fragile thing out of a deep container. Freeze for up to 3 months.*

To thaw: *Unwrap and put on to a serving dish. Cover with foil and thaw overnight in the fridge. Decorate just before serving.*

To cook in a fan oven: *Pre-heat the oven to 160°c. When the meringue is put in to bake, immediately lower the temperature to 130°c and bake for 40 minutes. At this stage the meringue will be a pale biscuit colour, dry and crisp on the surface but soft underneath. Turn the oven off and leave for a further 1 hour. Remove and follow the recipe.*

To cook in the Aga: *Bake in the simmering oven for 1½–2 hours or maybe more or until a pale biscuit colour. Remove from the oven and follow the recipe.*

Hazelnut Meringue Torte Filled with
Raspberries and Cream (page 187).

Ⓥ
Exotic Fresh Fruits

Fresh fruit prepared and well presented can look simply stunning. Of course the fruits I have suggested below can be altered according to your tastes and their availability. You can also experiment with the style in which the fruits are served. I sometimes line the plate with grape or blackcurrant leaves, or arrange the fruits on a large glass plate then, just before serving, sift a light dusting of icing sugar over the top. You can give free rein to your artistic talents, but my advice is generally to prepare the fruit in a way that helps people to help themselves, at the same time making the arrangement look fresh and pretty.

1 ripe melon
1 paw paw
1 small ripe pineapple
1 ripe mango
Several rambutan or lychees
225 g (8 oz) strawberries
1 small bunch of black grapes
1 small bunch of white grapes

Chill all the fruits for several hours beforehand.

Halve and remove the seeds from the melon. Cut into slim wedges and remove the peel, leaving the wedges intact. Peel the paw paw, halve and remove the seeds and cut into wedges. Leaving the top on the pineapple, thinly peel the fruit then, with a sharp knife, cut out the brown eyes. These run in slightly spiral lines around the pineapple and cutting them out, following the lines, emphasises this effect. Now slice the pineapple in rings and reassemble to its former shape. Peel the mango, cut a thick slice from either side of the stone, then cut the flesh into wedges. Cut an equatorial line through the skin around each rambutan or lychee so that the top half can be lifted off to show the white flesh beneath. Leave the strawberries and grapes whole, making sure they are clean and perfect.

To arrange the fruits on a serving platter, arrange each type of fruit grouped together, leaving a space in the middle for the strawberries and grapes. Stand the pineapple upright at the back of the platter. Cover with clingfilm and chill until ready to serve. Just before serving, put the strawberries and grapes in the centre.

To prepare ahead: *The arranged plate, minus the strawberries and grapes, can be covered with clingfilm and kept in the fridge for up to 6 hours.*

To freeze: *Not suitable.*

(V) Gratin of Exotic Fruits

SERVES 6

This is a store-cupboard fall-back recipe that relies on three tins and one or two cartons. If it really is an emergency, you might not have time to chill the pudding sufficiently. Don't worry, push it into the freezer to speed things up; it will only need about 30 minutes. Then the sugar can go on and the pudding can be grilled. Just make sure you put the fruit into the sort of dish that can stand the change in temperature! You could use UHT long-life cream if you want to make this entirely from store-cupboard ingredients.

1 × 425 g tin mango slices
1 × 420 g tin mandarin slices
1 × 425 g tin lychees
600 ml (1 pint) double cream
100 g (4 oz) light brown muscovado
sugar

You will need a shallow flameproof dish.

Empty the tins of fruit into a colander and drain thoroughly, then tip out on to several sheets of kitchen paper to mop up any remaining moisture. Arrange the fruit to cover the base of a shallow, flameproof dish and gently press the fruits down to even them out and level the surface. Lightly whip the cream until it is floppy, then spread over the fruits to the edge of the dish. Chill for at least 2 hours; the cream needs to be very cold and firm. Leave the dish in the fridge right up to the last moment. If short of time put the cream-topped pudding in the freezer for about 30 minutes or until the cream is firm.

Pre-heat the grill to maximum.

Spread the sugar evenly over the cream and grill for about 1–2 minutes or until the sugar becomes liquid and darkens. Watch the pudding constantly as it caramelizes; the process happens so rapidly it can blacken and easily burn unless you are careful. Give the caramel 1–2 minutes to cool and become brittle, then serve.

To prepare ahead: *Have the pudding ready, topped with cream but not sugar, and keep covered in the fridge for up to 48 hours. Add the sugar just before grilling, then follow the recipe above.*

To freeze: *Not suitable.*

To cook in the Aga: *Top with broken caramel (see Frozen Pineapple Parfait, page 174).*

Ⓥ
Raspberries in Jelly with Boozy Syllabub

MAKES 6 × 274 ML (9 FL OZ) GLASSES

Setting the raspberries in jelly has the effect of prolonging their keeping. Nearly everyone nowadays is interested in cutting down on calories, so I have used one of the new sugar-free jellies which are now available in shops and supermarkets. The low-calorie jelly helps the topping seem a little less sinful! It is based on Elizabeth David's Everlasting Syllabub, so the cream will not spoil, sink or separate; which all adds up to a delicious dessert that can be made ahead with no fuss. It will not freeze, but you can't have everything!

For the jelly
450 g (1 lb) raspberries, fresh or
   frozen
1 sachet sugar-free raspberry jelly
450 ml (15 fl oz) water

For the syllabub
150 ml (5 fl oz) ruby port
Juice of 1 lemon
65–75 g (2½–3 oz) caster sugar
250 ml (8 fl oz) double cream

To decorate
Fresh raspberry leaves
Shortbread or thin biscuits

You will need 6 × 275 ml (9 fl oz) glasses.

If using frozen raspberries, put them in a large plastic sieve over a bowl and leave to thaw and drain for several hours.

Make up the jelly according to the instructions on the sachet, but using a maximum of 450 ml (15 fl oz) water. Also use any juices drained from frozen raspberries to make up the 450 ml (15 fl oz). Leave the jelly until syrupy, then gently stir in the raspberries and spoon an equal quantity into each glass. Put the glasses on a small tray and transfer to the fridge to chill and set.

SMART PUDS

Desserts in stem glasses look very pretty if they are served on plates lined with blackcurrant or vine leaves.

Pour the port into a bowl and stir in the lemon juice and sugar. Give the sugar a little time to dissolve before stirring in the cream. Whisk until the cream just holds a shape, then spoon into the glasses. Chill lightly until ready to serve. The glasses look very attractive if served on small plates lined with fresh raspberry leaves and accompanied with shortbread or thin biscuits.

To prepare ahead: *The made dessert can be kept in the fridge for up to 2 days.*

To freeze: *Not suitable.*

Mango Passion

SERVES 6

Very easy to make and, unusually, both rich and refreshing to eat. This dessert is better when made ahead as it allows the flavours of mango and passion fruit to develop in the cream and yoghurt, and the dark sugar topping has time to liquify and sweeten each spoonful as you eat. Delicious.

> *1 large, ripe mango*
> *3 ripe passion fruit*
> *1 × 500 g carton Greek yoghurt*
> *150 ml (5 fl oz) thick single cream*
> *75 g (3 oz) light muscovado sugar*

You will need 6 stemmed glasses or syllabub cups.

Slice the flesh from each side of the flat mango stone (see diagram **1**, page 186). Remove the peel and cut the flesh in cubes. Try and remove as much flesh as possible from around the stone (see diagram **2**, page 186) then peel and cube this too. Using a teaspoon, scoop the seeds and flesh from the passion fruit into a bowl then mix with the yoghurt and cream.

Put an equal quantity of the mango in each glass then fill with the yoghurt mixture. Chill for up to 8 hours. An hour or so before serving, sprinkle with sugar and return to the fridge until ready to serve.

To freeze: *Not suitable.*

Barbecues
and Grills

BARBECUES
AND GRILLS

We visited our son when he was working in Australia, and there they have barbecuing down to a fine art. Of course they have the weather, but in every public area, or in parking places off main roads, they have tables, benches and barbecues with fuel (usually wood). In larger places they even have coin-operated electric barbecues. On these barbecues they cook the food on a flat metal sheet, so I've adapted the idea, and now cover half of my barbecue with an old heavy baking sheet. It's useful for things that might drip on to the coals.

Giving a barbecue party is one of my favourite ways of entertaining these days. It's a very relaxed way of feeding your friends, and so much of the organization and food preparation can be done well in advance. Any foods to be grilled taste better when marinated, and the oils in the marinade can help protect the food, as well as cut down on the need for extra oil. This makes grilling and barbecuing very healthy cooking techniques.

Last summer, we organized a barbecue for 100 in order to raise money for our local church. I served butterflied legs of lamb – ten of them for those 100 people – which had been marinating for at least a day in advance. Even the vegetables I served were prepared ahead of time: I oven-roasted peppers, courgettes, aubergines and onions during the two days before the party and, as they were done, I put them on top of each other in a new washing-up bowl or bucket. Stored in the fridge, they lasted well.

We have a built-in barbecue at home, but I also like those kettle barbecues with a lid that run on portable gas; they heat up immediately, you can cook 'inside' outside, and they can be used even if it is raining (it's *you* who gets wet, not the food!). So far as inside grilling is concerned, I like my ridged cast-iron grill pan to

PREVIOUS PAGE
Alternately from left: Mediterranean Vegetable Kebabs (page 205);
Marinated Seafood Kebabs (page 202).

go on the hob – this doesn't use much oil, grills things wonderfully, and leaves lovely charred lines on the meat or fish.

To test for charcoal readiness and cooking temperature, hold the palm of your hand over the fire at roughly the height the food will be. If you have to pull your hand away on a count of one, the fire is ready; if you can last until a count of three, the fire is medium; a count of five means the heat is low. If flames are high, possibly caused by fat dripping on to the coals, spray them briefly with water from a plant or laundry spray. And add fragrance to the food above the coals by burning sprigs of the tougher herbs such as rosemary, marjoram or thyme. Even the dried stalks of fennel can create an aromatic smoke which is particularly good for fish.

To save time when barbecuing or grilling, you can pre-roast or grill certain foods, and then just re-heat and brown them on the coals or under the grill at the last minute. You could do this with the Minted Lamb Kebabs, Butterflied Lamb in Lemon Marinade and the Barnsley Chops with Onion Gravy. Chicken pieces would be much more reliably done this way, especially if you're catering for large numbers, as would Judy's Thighs. I think the latter would be lovely for a child at a barbecue (and much nicer for supper than a hamburger). Serve them with some barbecued baked beans (spice ordinary beans up with some ketchup, soy sauce, Worcestershire sauce and a drop of Tabasco). They might also enjoy sausages by themselves, and for barbecues I always ask my butcher to make me double-length sausages – they cook so much better.

Have large bowls of salads to accompany the barbecued or grilled foods, be they meat, fish or vegetable kebabs, lamb legs or chops, or whole fish. Dipping sauces are good for many grilled foods, and a nice bread would be welcome (see the Honey-glazed Walnut Bread on page 236). If you are having an outside barbecue, offer plenty of paper napkins, and it's all easier with paper plates; have a large basket handy lined with a bin liner to take the debris. Lastly, organize people to help you. Men always seem to like tending a barbecue, so let them. Get someone else to carve if necessary, someone to pour, and your barbecue party, large or small, should be a roaring success.

This sign indicates recipes that are suitable
for vegetarians, but please note that some of them
include dairy products.

Pan-seared Salmon and Vegetables with Thai Dressing

SERVES 6 AS A STARTER OR 3 AS A MAIN COURSE

This dish can be prepared well ahead of time and is excellent served with warm Honey-glazed Walnut Bread (see page 236). If you are keen on oriental food it could be that you have sesame oil and rice wine vinegar in the cupboard. By all means use 1 tablespoon of sesame oil to substitute for one of the tablespoons of olive oil (sesame oil has such a strong flavour), and rice vinegar can be used instead of white wine vinegar, but please do not rush out and buy these ingredients specially for this recipe; it simply is not worth it. Sesame oil has a particularly short shelf life, so keep it in the fridge once opened. Thai paste has a very hot flavour. If trying it for the first time, you might like to use just 1 teaspoon.

For the Thai dressing

6 tablespoons olive oil	*1 tablespoon caster sugar*
3 tablespoons white wine vinegar	*2–4 teaspoons red Thai curry paste*

---

3 × 200 g (7 oz) salmon tail fillets, skin on	*3 red or yellow peppers*
Olive oil	*1 medium aubergine*
Sea salt and freshly ground black pepper.	*2 tablespoons chopped fresh coriander*

First make the Thai dressing by combining all the ingredients together in a screw-top jar. Screw the lid on firmly and shake well to mix. Leave the jar in the fridge to allow the flavours to develop while you prepare the remaining ingredients.

Cut the salmon tail fillets in half from the wide end towards the point of the tail. Brush the fish pieces all over with olive oil and season with sea salt and pepper. Cut a cap from the stem and base of each pepper and remove the seeds and central core. Slit the peppers and open out into long strips. Trim away the inside ribs and cut the flesh into strips about 5–10 mm (¼–½ in) wide. Put into a bowl. Similarly, cut the stem and base from the aubergine, then slice into strips the same size as the peppers. Put into a separate bowl. Add 2 teaspoons of oil to each bowl, season well with salt and pepper, then mix with your hands to coat the vegetables completely.

To grill: To cook the salmon and vegetables, you can use either a cast-iron, ridged, stove-top grill pan, or a medium weight, non-stick frying-pan. Pre-heat over a moderate to high heat for 5 minutes. Sear the salmon slices for about 2 minutes on each side. To test if the fish is fully cooked throughout, make a small slit in the thickest part of the salmon. The flesh should be a matt pink throughout, not translucent. Remove the salmon pieces to a shallow serving dish and drizzle a spoonful of dressing over each piece. Return the pan to the heat for 2–3 minutes before adding the peppers. Continue to cook over a moderately high heat for about 4 minutes or until the strips are well coloured. Return them to the bowl and fry the aubergine strips in the same manner. When browned, add them to the bowl with the peppers, pour in the remaining dressing and add the coriander. Gently mix and add more salt and pepper, if liked. Spoon into the serving dish alongside the salmon. Cover closely and chill in the fridge until ready to serve. Bring back to room temperature before serving.

To prepare ahead: *The fully prepared dish can be arranged on a serving dish, covered with clingfilm and kept in the fridge for up to 24 hours before serving.*

To freeze: *Not suitable.*

To cook in the Aga: *Cook in a ridged grill pan on the fast boiling plate with a lid half on the pan.*

Grilled Sea Bass with Lemon and Lime Salsa

SERVES 4

Sea bass are now farmed and are surprisingly good, but if these are not available, two fat sardines or one trout per person could be substituted.

4 whole sea bass, about 350–375 g (12–13 oz) each, gutted and cleaned	A little olive oil
	Sea salt and freshly ground black pepper
8 sprigs of fresh tarragon	A little melted butter
½ lemon, cut into slim wedges	

For the lemon and lime salsa	Juice of 1 small lemon
2 tablespoons olive oil	Grated rind and juice of 1 lime
1 teaspoon white wine vinegar	1 tablespoon chopped fresh parsley
1 large courgette, quartered and thinly sliced	1 tablespoon chopped fresh tarragon
1 medium onion, finely chopped	2 tablespoons mango chutney

Start by preparing the salsa. Put the oil and vinegar in a small pan and sauté the courgette for about 2 minutes. Using a draining spoon, remove it to a bowl before adding the onion to the pan. Sauté again for about 2 minutes just until the onion loses its raw flavour, but retains its crispness. Add the contents of the pan and the remaining ingredients to the bowl of courgettes and mix well. Cover, cool and leave in the fridge for about 4 hours to allow the flavours to develop.

Prepare the fish by trimming off the fins with a pair of scissors. Slash the fish with 3 gashes in the thickest part of the body. Strip the leaves from the tarragon into a bowl, add the lemon wedges, a dribble of olive oil and some sea salt and freshly ground black pepper then toss together using your hands. Pack the mixture into the belly of the fish then brush with melted butter and sprinkle with seasoning.

To grill: Pre-heat the grill for about 5 minutes. Line the grill pan with foil, put in a grill rack and place the fish on top. Position the grill pan so the fish is about 10 cm (4 in) away from the heat source. Adjust the grill to a moderate heat and grill for about 8 minutes on each side. To test if the fish is cooked, use the sharp point of a knife to pierce the thickest part of the fish; the flesh should be flaky and opaque.

To barbecue: The timing will depend on the heat of the barbecue. Wait until the coals are hot and powdery. Grill as above.

To serve, remove the flavouring ingredients and serve the fish piping hot with the chilled salsa.

To prepare ahead: *The fish can be prepared for cooking, put on a plate and wrapped closely in clingfilm. It will keep in the fridge for up to 6 hours. The salsa can be kept covered in the fridge for up to 2 days, although the courgette will lose its bright green colour, so compensate by adding more chopped fresh parsley.*

To freeze: *Not suitable.*

To cook in the Aga: *Pre-heat a roasting tin containing a little butter on the floor of the roasting oven for 5 minutes. When the butter has melted, put the fish in, then slide on to the floor of the roasting oven for about 7 minutes on each side. Or fry on a pre-heated, ridged grill pan.*

Marinated Seafood Kebabs

MAKES 12 SKEWERS TO SERVE 6

The difficulty with kebabs is to get everything to cook in the same time. Choosing the right ingredients to cook together is the first step. The second is to cut them to the right size. Fish fillets have flesh that tapers away to nothing and so are not substantial enough to cook satisfactorily. It is much better to buy boned, skinned, thick fish steaks which can be cut into nice, large chunks of a similar size.

*450 g (1 lb) monkfish, boned and
    skinned*
*450 g (1 lb) salmon steaks, boned
    and skinned*
12 raw tiger prawns, heads removed
*8 baby courgettes, each cut in
    6 thick slices*
*Salt and freshly ground black
    pepper*

For the marinade
4 garlic cloves, crushed
Grated rind and juice of 1 lime
2 tablespoons good olive oil

To serve
*Lemon and Lime Salsa (see page
    201) or Dill Pickle Sauce (see
    page 215)*

You will need 12 skewers.

Cut each fish into 24 even-sized chunks. Combine the ingredients for the marinade in a large bowl, then gently turn the fish and prawns in the mixture. Cover and leave in the fridge for 1–1½ hours to marinate.

Thread 2 pieces of each kind of fish on each of 12 skewers, interspersing each piece with a slice of courgette and finishing with a slice of courgette and then a prawn. Season with salt and pepper.

To grill: Pre-heat the grill to maximum for 5 minutes. Turn the heat down to between medium and high. Position the kebabs on a grill rack in a grill pan about 10 cm (4 in) away from the heat source and grill for about 10 minutes, turning once or twice.

To barbecue: Wait until the charcoal has been alight for some time and the coals are grey. Arrange the skewers so they run at right angles to the grid on the barbecue and leave to grill for about 10–15 minutes, turning once or twice.

Serve warm with Lemon and Lime Salsa or Dill Pickle Sauce.

To prepare ahead: *The fish can be left to marinate for up to 8 hours in the fridge.*

To freeze: *Not suitable.*

To cook in the Aga: *Arrange the skewers lengthways on the large grill rack in a large roasting tin. Slide on to the top set of runners of the roasting oven for about 5 minutes. Turn the kebabs over and return to the oven for a further 3–5 minutes until the fish is tender. Or cook on a pre-heated, ridged grill pan.*

Mediterranean Vegetable Kebabs

Ⓥ

MAKES 12 SKEWERS TO SERVE 6

For the marinade
6 tablespoons good quality olive oil
1 tablespoon balsamic vinegar
2 generous sprigs of fresh thyme

2 fat garlic cloves
12 bay leaves
Freshly ground black pepper

4 peppers, all colours
2 large, mild onions
24 large button mushrooms

3 sweetcorn cobs
Salt and freshly ground black
*   pepper*

To serve
Minted Yoghurt Sauce (see page 214)

You will need 12 skewers.

Make the marinade. Spoon the oil and vinegar into a large mixing bowl. Bruise the thyme and garlic by tapping them with a rolling pin, then add to the oil with the bay leaves and some pepper.

Prepare the peppers by cutting a cap and base from each one, then slit and open out the peppers to a long strip. Discard the core and seeds and trim away the thick ribs. Cut each pepper strip into 6 rectangles to give 24 pieces. Peel and cut each onion into 6 wedges, then separate each wedge in half so they are not too thick. Trim and wipe the mushrooms, leaving them whole. Finally, slice each sweetcorn into 4 sections, discarding the tips. Mix all the vegetables in the marinade, season with salt and pepper and cover and chill for at least 1 hour. Arrange the vegetables alternately on 12 skewers. The kebabs are now ready to grill. If you prefer the vegetables a little blackened, then grill at a higher heat or closer to the heat source.

To grill: Pre-heat the grill to maximum for 5 minutes. Turn the heat down to medium. Position the kebabs on the grill rack in a grill pan about 10 cm (4 in) from the heat source. Grill for about 12 minutes, turning once or twice.

To barbecue: Wait for the charcoal to become hot and glowing without any flames. Arrange the skewers so they run at right angles to the grid on the barbecue. Grill for about 15 minutes, turning once or twice.

Serve warm with Minted Yoghurt Sauce.

Pan-seared Salmon and
Vegetables with Thai Dressing
(page 200).

To prepare ahead: *The vegetables can be left to marinate for up to 12 hours in the fridge.*

To freeze: *Not suitable.*

To cook in the Aga: *Arrange the skewers lengthways on a large grill rack in a large roasting tin. Slide on to the top set of runners in the roasting oven for about 10 minutes. Turn the kebabs over and cook for a further 8 minutes or until tender. Or cook on a pre-heated, ridged grill pan.*

Minted Lamb Kebabs

MAKES 16

This production-line method of making kebabs simplifies what can be a fiddly process, especially if you are catering for a crowd. If you intend to cook kebabs under a grill, soak the sticks in water so that they are less inclined to burn. My preference is to oven-roast. It creates far less smoke and smell, lessens the chance of the fat catching fire and, most important, produces a nicely browned, moist, well-flavoured kebab.

675 g (1½ lb) raw minced lamb	*1 teaspoon ground coriander*
1 onion, chopped in large pieces	*Salt and freshly ground black*
A good handful of fresh mint leaves	*pepper*
A handful of fresh parsley leaves	*A little vegetable oil for*
1 teaspoon ground cumin	*brushing*

For the glaze
2 tablespoons dark soy sauce
1 tablespoon clear honey

You will need 16 kebab sticks and a tin 16.5 cm (6½ in) square and 4 cm (1½ in) deep. Liberally brush the tin with oil.

Put the lamb in a food processor with the onion, herbs, cumin, coriander and a generous amount of salt and pepper. Process in short bursts until the mixture starts to form a ball around the central stem. Press the meat mixture firmly into the oiled tin and level with a palette knife (see **1**). Cover with clingfilm and chill in the fridge for a minimum of 1 hour.

Brush the work surface with a little oil. Run a knife around the inside edge of the tin to free the meat mix, then turn the tin over and give it a sharp rap on the work surface to turn out the kebab mixture. Using a large, broad-bladed knife, divide the mix in half across the width and part the halves slightly. Now divide each half lengthways into 8. Push a stick horizontally into each section until the tip just appears at the other end, then lift a section at a time from the surface with the aid of a palette knife (see **2**). Gently squeeze the meat into a rounded kebab shape (see **3**). Combine the soy sauce and honey and brush the kebabs with the mixture.

Pre-heat the oven to 230°C/450°F/gas 8 or pre-heat the grill to maximum or pre-heat the barbecue.

To oven roast: Arrange the kebabs on a baking tray. Cook in the top half of the oven for 10–12 minutes.

To grill: Pre-heat the grill. Arrange the kebabs on a foil-lined grill pan with the sticks extending over the edge of the pan and where they will not be in direct line of the heat. Grill for 10–12 minutes, turning once or twice and keeping an eye on them while they cook.

To barbecue: When the barbecue is hot, lay a double strip of foil on the barbecue. Arrange the kebabs so that the sticks are protected from the fire by the foil and the meat gets the full benefit of the heat. Barbecue for 10–12 minutes, turning once or twice.

Serve sizzling hot.

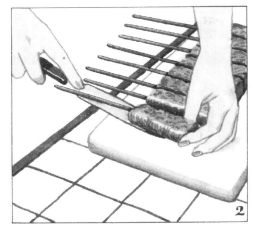

To prepare ahead: *The meat mixture in the tin, covered with clingfilm, can be chilled for up to 1 day. If kept longer than this, the fresh mint flavour deteriorates. Alternatively, assemble the kebabs, arrange in a single layer on a flat plate, cover with clingfilm and chill in the fridge for up to 8 hours. Brush with glaze just before cooking.*

To freeze: *Freeze the completed kebabs, well wrapped, for up to 1 month.*

To thaw: *Thaw overnight in the fridge.*

To cook: *Follow one of the methods given in the recipe.*

To cook in a fan oven: *Pre-heat the oven to 220°c. Cook the kebabs for 8–10 minutes.*

To cook in the Aga: *Cook on the top set of runners in the roasting oven on the grill rack in the roasting tin for about 10–12 minutes. Keep an eye on the kebabs.*

Butterflied Lamb in Lemon Marinade

SERVES 6

Get the butcher to bone out a leg of lamb to a butterfly cut. Butterflied lamb is a boned leg of lamb opened out flat which vaguely resembles the shape of a butterfly! The advantage of this cut is that being both thin and spread out it cooks quickly and there is lots of crispy meat for everyone. It can be grilled, barbecued or roasted. Some supermarkets are willing to bone a pre-packed leg if you give them a little time.

2–2.5 kg (4–5 lb) leg of lamb
(weight before boning)

For the marinade	*1 tablespoon mustard powder*
Juice of 3 lemons	*1 tablespoon coarse grain mustard*
3 large garlic cloves, quartered	*4 tablespoons clear honey*

You will need to start to prepare the dish a day ahead.

Mix together the marinade ingredients in a small bowl. Using 2 plastic bags large enough to contain the lamb, slip one inside the other. Put the lamb into the inner bag and pour in the marinade. Seal so no leakage can occur, then put in the fridge overnight.

The following day, take out the lamb and put into a large roasting tin. Leave covered to allow the meat to come up to room temperature.

Butterflied Lamb in
Lemon Marinade (above).

Pre-heat the grill or the barbecue to maximum.

To grill: Place the meat on a grill rack over a foil-lined grill pan and position it about 10 cm (4 in) from the heat source. Turn down the heat to between medium and high and grill for about 15 minutes on each side or until done to your liking.

To barbecue: Barbecue for about 15 minutes a side, depending on the heat of the barbecue.

To oven roast: Pre-heat the oven to 230°C/450°F/gas 8 and cook for about 15 minutes per 450 g (1 lb) boned weight. After 30 minutes strain the marinade and pour over the lamb.

To prepare ahead: *The meat can be left in the fridge, in the marinade, for up to 2 days.*

To freeze: *Not suitable.*

To cook in a fan oven: *Pre-heat the oven to 220°c. Roast the meat for 12 minutes per 450 g (1 lb) boned weight. After 30 minutes strain the marinade and pour over the lamb.*

To cook in the Aga: *Put the meat in the large roasting tin hanging on the lowest set of runners in the roasting oven. After 30 minutes strain the marinade and pour over the lamb. Transfer the meat to the simmering oven for a further 40 minutes.*

Barnsley Chops with Onion Gravy

SERVES 4

A Barnsley chop is a double chop, cut straight across the back of the lamb.

4 Barnsley chops
4 whole lambs' kidneys
Salt and freshly ground black pepper
4 teaspoons mint jelly

For the onion gravy
15 g (½ oz) butter
1 medium onion, grated
1 teaspoon plain white flour
1 teaspoon Dijon mustard
3–4 tablespoons beer or dry white wine
1–2 teaspoons mint jelly
300 ml (10 fl oz) Vegetable Stock (see page 58) or Chicken Stock (see page 14)

Trim the excess fat from each chop, then carefully cut around and remove the central bone. Snip the central core from each kidney using a pair of scissors. Curl the 'tails' of each chop around to enclose a kidney and use small skewers to hold the chop closed and keep the kidneys in position. Season with salt and pepper.

Pre-heat the grill to maximum for 5 minutes.

Position the chops in a foil-lined grill pan about 10 cm (4 in) away from the heat source. Grill for about 4 minutes, spread with half the mint jelly, then turn over and grill the other side for the same time. Spread with the remaining jelly and remove from the heat; cover and keep warm while you make the gravy.

Pour off any juices from the grill pan into a medium-sized frying-pan. Melt the butter in the pan and stir in the onion. Cook over a moderate heat for 5 minutes until softened and slightly coloured. Add the flour, stir in the mustard, beer or wine and mint jelly and when bubbling, pour in the stock. Bring to the boil and boil briskly until reduced by about a third. Taste and season, adding a little more jelly, mustard or salt and pepper to balance the flavours. Serve the chops with individual Pommes Anna (see page 138) and with the gravy spooned around.

To prepare ahead: *The boned, prepared chops enclosing the kidneys can be kept covered in the fridge for up to 24 hours.*

To freeze: *Not suitable.*

To cook in the Aga: *Pre-heat the ridged grill pan on the boiling plate, brush the chops with a little oil, then put them in the grill pan and partially cover with the tilted lid. Cook for about 8 minutes, turning once. Then spread with the jelly.*

Judy's Thighs

SERVES 4

This recipe is very popular with the family of a good friend. As far as I know it is the brainchild of her butcher, and that is all I know of its origins. Suffice it to say it is a straightforward, brilliant idea that is ideal for family suppers or barbecues. You take a chipolata, wrap a boned chicken thigh around it, and wrap a bacon slice around that. The simplest ideas are usually the best! Children love these with some good old tomato ketchup, but if you would prefer to be a little more adult serve with Tomato Passata Sauce (see page 215).

8 skinless, boned chicken thighs	*8 pork chipolata sausages*
Salt and freshly ground black	*8 long rashers rindless smoked*
pepper	*streaky bacon*
A little dried sage	*A little vegetable oil for brushing*

Pre-heat the oven to 220°c/425°f/gas 7.

Lie the chicken thighs flat, skinned-side down on the work surface. Season with salt and pepper and sprinkle with a little sage. Roll up a sausage in each thigh, then wind each roll around with a bacon slice. Brush a roasting tin with oil, sprinkle with a little salt and pepper and put the meat into the tin. Brush each roll with oil, then bake for about 25 minutes or until browned and cooked.

To barbecue: Heat the barbecue until medium hot, then arrange the rolls on the rack and cook for about 20 minutes, turning them so that they brown evenly

To prepare ahead: *The prepared thighs can be kept covered in the fridge for up to 1 day. Remove the meat so it can come up to room temperature before roasting.*

To freeze: *Arrange the prepared thighs on shallow plastic trays, slip into plastic bags, and seal, label and freeze for up to 4 months.*

To thaw: *Leave overnight in the fridge. Roast the following day, following the recipe above.*

To cook in a fan oven: *Pre-heat the oven to 200°c. Roast the thighs for 20 minutes.*

To cook in the Aga: *Cook in the roasting oven on the highest set of runners for about 25 minutes.*

(V)

Roasted Mediterranean Vegetables

SERVES 4–6

Serve cold as a salad, or hot without the balsamic vinegar and olives.

1 courgette	*1–2 tablespoons olive oil*
2 red peppers	*Salt and freshly ground black*
1 yellow pepper	*pepper*
1 bulb of fennel	*2 teaspoons balsamic vinegar*
4 garlic cloves, thinly sliced	*50 g (2 oz) pitted black olives in oil*

To serve
Fresh green salad leaves

First prepare the vegetables. Cut the courgette diagonally in 5 mm (¼ in) thick slices. Slice the top and base from the peppers and remove the seeds. Slit each pepper and open out to one long strip and cut into 5 mm (¼ in) sticks. Trim the stalks of the fennel level with the bulb, then cut in wedges like a cake. Put all the vegetables and garlic in a large bowl and combine with the oil and some salt and pepper.

To grill: Pre-heat the grill to maximum for 10 minutes. Arrange the vegetables on a grill rack. Grill for about 10 minutes, turning once. Or cook on a pre-heated ridged grill pan.

To barbecue: Use a ridged grill pan on top of the barbecue and pre-heat until very hot. Place the vegetables on the pan and grill for 10–15 minutes, turning once. If you do not have this type of grill pan, use an old wire metal cooling rack. Serve immediately.

To serve cold, allow the vegetables to cool, toss with balsamic vinegar and black olives and serve on a bed of fresh green salad leaves.

To prepare ahead: *If the vegetables are to be served hot they can be prepared and kept in a covered bowl in the fridge for up to 1 day. If they are to be served as a cold salad, they can be grilled or barbecued, mixed with balsamic vinegar and olives and kept covered in the fridge for up to 2 days.*

To freeze: *Not suitable.*

To cook in the Aga: *Spread the oiled vegetables over the base of the large roasting tin and cook on the floor of the roasting oven for about 5–10 minutes on each side until slightly charred.*

Ⓥ

Cucumber and Dill Pickle

MAKES 1.5 LITRES (2½ PINTS)

A crunchy, sweet pickle that is so more-ish it can be served on numerous occasions in different guises. It is excellent with hamburgers for barbecues and goes well with all manner of cold meats and smoked fish. A few pieces added to ham sandwiches gives them a good dill-flavoured crunch, and it makes an excellent swift sauce; just chop a couple of tablespoons of the pickle and add it to about 150 g (5 fl oz) Greek yoghurt and you have a delicious sauce to serve with grilled or baked chicken or fish.

4 cucumbers	*450 g (1 lb) onions, thinly sliced*
50 g (2 oz) salt	*2 teaspoons mustard seeds*
450 g (1 lb) sugar	*2 teaspoons dried dill*
300 ml (10 fl oz) white wine vinegar	*Plenty of freshly ground black*
5 tablespoons water	*pepper*

You will need 2 or 3 suitable storage jars, total capacity 1.5 litres (2½ pints).

Top and tail the cucumbers, but do not peel them, then halve them lengthways. Lay them cut-sides down on a chopping board, then slice across into pieces 3 mm (⅛ in) thick. As you work, transfer the slices to a glass bowl and sprinkle with some of the measured salt. When all the cucumber is sliced and all the salt added, cover and leave aside for 2 hours to allow the salt to drain water from the cucumbers. Then tip the contents of the bowl into a colander and rinse well with cold running water. Leave to drain.

Meanwhile measure the sugar, vinegar and water into a large pan. Heat slowly until the sugar has dissolved, then boil rapidly without a lid for 5 minutes. Add the drained cucumber, sliced onions, mustard seeds, dill and a generous amount of freshly ground black pepper and bring to a full boil. Pack into clean, hot storage jars then seal, label and store in a cool place for up to 2 months or in a fridge for 6 months.

Dipping Sauces

SERVES 4

These are for dipping or serving with grilled or barbecued foods. They could hardly be easier or quicker to prepare.

Minted Yoghurt Sauce

Particularly good with the Butterflied Lamb in Lemon Marinade (see page 208). A first-rate quick version is to add just 2 tablespoons concentrated mint sauce to a 150 g carton Greek yoghurt, stir and serve.

1 × 150 g carton Greek yoghurt	*3 tablespoons chopped fresh mint*
Grated rind and juice of 1 lemon	*Salt and freshly ground black*
1 garlic clove, crushed	*pepper*

Combine the first 4 ingredients in a small bowl, mix and season to taste with salt and pepper. Cover and chill in the fridge for at least 1 hour before serving.

To prepare ahead: *The made sauce can be kept covered in the fridge for up to 8 hours.*

To freeze: *Not suitable.*

Dill Pickle Sauce

1 × 150 g carton Greek yoghurt	1 tablespoon chopped fresh parsley
3 tablespoons drained Cucumber and Dill Pickle (see page 213), coarsely chopped	1–2 teaspoons vinegar taken from the dill pickles
1 garlic clove, crushed	Salt and freshly ground black pepper

Combine the first 5 ingredients in a small bowl, mix and season to taste with salt and pepper. Cover and chill in the fridge for at least 1 hour before serving.

To prepare ahead: *The made sauce can be kept covered in the fridge for up to 8 hours.*

To freeze: *Not suitable.*

Tomato Passata Sauce

MAKES ABOUT 600 ML (1 PINT)

This is an adaptable sauce which can readily be made more garlicky or hot by adding a dash or two of Tabasco sauce. Passata can be bought from supermarkets in cartons or tins. It is a thickish purée of tomatoes.

15 g (½ oz) butter	600 ml (1 pint) passata
1 medium onion, very finely chopped	1–2 teaspoons sugar
1 garlic clove, crushed	Salt and freshly ground black pepper

Melt the butter in a small pan, stir in the onion and garlic, then cover and cook over a low heat for about 10 minutes until softened but not coloured. Pour in the passata and add the sugar and some salt and pepper to taste. Bring to the boil and continue to cook for 3–4 minutes or until the sauce has reduced and thickened to your liking.

To prepare ahead: *The sauce can be made, quickly cooled, then stored in a sealed container in the fridge for up to 2 days.*

To freeze: *Pour the sauce into a freezer container. Cool, seal and label, then freeze for up to 3 months.*

To thaw: *Thaw in the fridge for about 3 hours.*

To re-heat: *Re-heat in a pan.*

Eats for Drinks

EATS FOR DRINKS

You're quite right in thinking that preparing those little nuggets of food to serve with drinks is fiddly. However, here you'll find a number of my time-saving techniques which will transform your life. And of course, as elsewhere, most of the preparation can be done well ahead of time.

The first consideration, though, is the type of party and the timing. If you're having a drinks party after which people will go on for dinner, you don't want to over-feed them. If they're coming to you straight after work, they might like something a little more substantial to go with the alcohol. I think about five items per person should be offered in general; a selection of hot and cold if possible. Scatter some bowls of crisps and olives around as well. To marinate my own olives, I drain olives in brine and refill the jar with olive oil, adding two peeled cloves of bruised garlic, a split fresh or dried chilli pepper, and a sprig of a fresh herb like rosemary, basil or coriander. Make sure, too, that there are plenty of paper napkins around, and dishes or plates for crumbs and cocktail sticks.

Eats for drinks should be the right size – you don't want to take a second bite. The pastry ideas, Blini and biscuits here are all small enough to present no difficulty when eating with the fingers. The Herb Cheese Toasts are particularly useful: French sticks cut in thin diagonal slices with butter and garlic cream cheese on top, they can be prepared three days in advance and kept in the fridge, or frozen. They take only about ten minutes to bake, straight from fridge *or* freezer. I always

PREVIOUS PAGE
Herb Cheese Toasts (page 220); Parmesan and
Paprika Nutters (page 221); Blini (page 226) topped with
soured cream and salmon and lumpfish roes; Danish-style
Open Sandwiches (page 237) topped with smoked salmon
and garnished with lemon slices and dill.

have these in stock in the freezer; at least then I've got something if people drop in unexpectedly.

The recipes here are for some of my favourite nibbles, but there are a host of other ideas that don't really need to be specified in such detail. Crudités are always welcome – sticks of carrot, celery, peppers, fennel, with some breadsticks as well perhaps. Many dips can be made from cream cheese or soured cream (or you can buy made-up salsas, hummus or taramasalata). Cubes of cheese look good and are very traditional. I like hard-boiled quails' eggs which, when shelled, can be dipped in celery salt and eaten in one go. Small grilled chipolata sausages on sticks are always popular, particularly with children. Serve them on a platter with cocktail sticks around a central bowl of tomato ketchup or a chilli tomato dip. For a change, roll grilled small sausages in a little finely chopped mango chutney, then in sesame seeds. Fresh chicken livers can be lightly fried in butter, then rolled in thin bacon to be re-heated quickly when you need them. Cooked button mushrooms are good with a topping of crème fraîche and snipped fresh chives. Fishy things like the Three-fish Pâté (see page 41) would be lovely spread on to an interesting base.

As for bases, never use toast or biscuits, as they get too soggy. Use celery pieces or little squares of fresh bread fried in oil or baked in the oven. And don't forget about little sandwiches, either open or 'closed'. These could be just the thing if people are hungry. Rye and pumpernickel breads – or my Honey-glazed Walnut Bread (see page 236) – can be topped with Cambazola and grapes or pâté with bits of crispy bacon and onions (you can buy the latter in jars nowadays). Prawns would be delicious, too, with a little mayonnaise or crème fraîche and chopped fresh dill.

Presentation is very important. Arrange your eats for drinks attractively on platters – I like using a plain black lacquer tray. And these can be decorated, too: use a fresh flower in summer, a tartan bow or holly at Christmas.

This sign indicates recipes that are suitable
for vegetarians, but please note that some of them
include dairy products.

Herb Cheese Toasts

MAKES ABOUT 18–24 INDIVIDUAL TOASTS

Simple and delicious, the sort of 'nibble' that everybody loves. My only advice is to make plenty!

---

1 long slim French loaf
Softened butter for spreading
1 × 125 g packet full-fat soft cream
    cheese with herbs and garlic
About 175 g (6 oz) Cheddar, grated
A little mild paprika

You will need 2 baking trays, lightly greased.

Pre-heat the oven to 220°c/425°f/gas 7.

Take a sharp bread knife and cut the loaf diagonally in 1 cm (½ in) thick slices. Thinly butter both sides of each slice, then spread the cream cheese on one side. Top each with a little grated cheese and a dusting of paprika. Arrange on the prepared baking trays and bake for about 8–10 minutes or until melted and golden brown.

To prepare ahead: *The toasts can be prepared before baking, arranged on the baking trays, covered in clingfilm and kept in the fridge for up to 3 days.*

To freeze: *Pack the uncooked made-up bread slices in a plastic freezer container, putting freezer tissues between the layers. Seal, label and freeze for up to 2 months.*

To thaw: *There is no need to thaw, simply remove the bread slices from the freezer and bake immediately.*

To cook: *Bake following the recipe above.*

To cook in a fan oven: *Pre-heat the oven to 210°c. Bake for about 8 minutes.*

To cook in the Aga: *Bake on the floor of the roasting oven for 8–10 minutes or until golden brown.*

ⓥ *Parmesan and Paprika Nutters*

MAKES ABOUT 40 BISCUITS

Quick and easy to make and utterly delicious. If you are nervous of using a piping bag, chill the mixture in the fridge until firm, then roll marble-size pieces of mixture between your hands instead. The result is just as good, but it does take a little longer.

100 g (4 oz) soft baking margarine, warm but not runny	*Salt and freshly ground black pepper*
50 g (2 oz) semolina	*1 teaspoon mild paprika*
85 g (3½ oz) self-raising white flour	*About 40 salted cashew nuts for topping*
75 g (3 oz) freshly grated Parmesan	

You will need 2 baking trays, greased, and a piping bag, fitted with a plain 1 cm (½ in) nozzle.

Pre-heat the oven to 180°C/350°F/gas 4.

Measure all the ingredients except the nuts into a large bowl and stir together until thoroughly mixed. This can be done in a processor, if you prefer. Transfer the biscuit mixture to the piping bag and pipe out small blobs of mixture, about 2 cm (¾ in), spacing them regularly on the baking trays. Press a nut in the centre of each biscuit. Bake for 12–15 minutes or until a pale golden brown, then cool on a wire rack.

To prepare ahead: *Prepare and freeze the biscuits (see below).*

To freeze: *Pack the freshly baked, cooled biscuits in plastic freezer boxes. Seal, label and freeze for up to 3 months.*

To thaw: *No need; simply take the biscuits from the freezer as and when they are needed and serve. If needs be, refresh them in an oven at 180°C/350°F/gas 4; taste and see first.*

To cook in a fan oven: *Pre-heat the oven to 170°C. Bake for about 10 minutes, but watch carefully towards the end of cooking time.*

To cook in the Aga: 2-DOOR: *Pipe the biscuits in the roasting tin, then hang on the lowest set of runners in the roasting oven with the cold plain shelf 2 sets above. Bake for about 10–12 minutes, watching carefully, until pale golden brown.*
4-DOOR: *Hang the roasting tin on the lowest set of runners in the baking oven. Bake for about 10–12 minutes, watching carefully, until pale golden brown. Should the biscuits brown too quickly, slide the cold plain shelf on the second set of runners to prevent this.*

(V)
Watercroft Flaky Cheese Biscuits

MAKES ABOUT 3 DOZEN SMALL BISCUITS

This recipe was inspired by a certain type of bought cheese biscuit of which I am particularly fond. As it is very more-ish and rather expensive, I tried to devise a recipe that would produce a very similar biscuit and I have done rather well! These are ideal to serve with drinks as they are small, crisp and piquant and relatively cheap and easy to make in party quantities. The off-cuts of pastry can be re-rolled and cut into extra-long cheese straws which look sensational served in tall containers on a buffet table. If you prefer to make cheese straws only, the method for making the pastry is slightly different and is given at the end of the biscuit recipe.

*350 g (12 oz) mature Cheddar,
    finely grated
1 tablespoon mustard powder
1 teaspoon salt
1 teaspoon freshly ground black
    pepper
1 × 375 g packet frozen, ready rolled
    puff pastry, thawed*

You will need 2 baking trays, lightly greased.

Pre-heat the oven to 190°C/375°F/gas 5.

Put the grated cheese into a large bowl with the mustard, salt and pepper and toss lightly together until well mixed; divide into 4 equal portions. Position the roll of pastry parallel to the front edge of the work surface and unroll it away from you; the piece will measure about 35 × 23 cm (14 × 9 in). Sprinkle the top half of the pastry with a portion of cheese. Cut off the lower half and place directly over the top half to cover the cheese. Roll the pastry out until the strip regains its original size. Again sprinkle the top half of the pastry with a second portion of cheese, cut off the lower half and use it to cover the top. Roll out to the original size. Repeat, using the third portion of cheese, covering it with the bottom half of the pastry. This time do not roll it out but use your hand to firmly press the pastry and grated cheese layers together. Now sprinkle the remaining portion of cheese on the right hand half of the pastry, cut in half and cover the cheese with the left-hand side. You will now have a block of pastry/cheese measuring about 18 × 11.5 × 2.5 cm (7 × 4½ × 1 in). Press the layers together firmly.

Trim off any uneven or unmatched edges and keep the trimmings. Take a large, sharp knife and cut into 5 mm (¼ in) wide strips. Turn these flat on to the work surface and cut into 2.5 cm (1 in) long pieces. Transfer the pieces to the baking trays so the biscuits bake cut-side up. The last slice is difficult to cut, so don't bother; gather it together with the pastry trimmings and put on one side. Bake the biscuits for about 8 minutes, but I advise you to watch them carefully during the last 2–3 minutes. They should be a good orange/brown for maximum crispness and flavour, but ovens vary and these biscuits over-brown very quickly so until you know exactly how long they will take in your oven, watch them carefully, then after that, time them exactly!

Use a palette knife to remove the biscuits to a wire rack. You will need to bake several batches, so after removing the baked biscuits from a baking tray, wipe it with kitchen paper and leave it to cool before using again. Roll out the pastry trimmings to a long narrow strip slightly longer than your baking trays then cut the pastry lengthways into strips about 1 cm (½ in) wide. Gently twist each strip about 6 times and arrange down the full length of the baking trays. Bake as above.

To make Cheese Straws only

Follow the above method to the stage of sprinkling on the third portion of cheese and covering this with the lower half of pastry. Now continue to roll out the pastry to its original size, then sprinkle with the fourth and final portion of cheese. Cut in half and cover with the top half and roll out for the final time so that the pastry is 3–5 mm (⅛–¼ in) thick. Cut into strips as described above, making them as long as the length of the baking trays will allow. Bake as above, then leave on the trays for about 5 minutes before carefully removing to the wire rack to finish cooling. They are rather fragile.

To prepare ahead: *The made biscuits can be stored in an airtight container in the fridge for up to 1 week.*

To freeze: *Pack the freshly baked, cooled biscuits in plastic freezer boxes. Seal, label and freeze for up to 6 months.*

To thaw: *Thaw 15 minutes at room temperature.*

To cook in the Aga: *Cook in the roasting oven on the grid shelf on the floor for about 6–8 minutes, turning if necessary.*

Miniature Cocktail Quiches

MAKES ABOUT 60

This is a quick, easy way to make a party quantity of bite-size quiches and serve them hot. Making one large quiche in a baking tray then cutting it out into miniature rounds is far quicker and less fiddly than making individual tiny quiches, so for me the cutting-out technique wins hands down.

225 g (8 oz) shortcrust pastry (made
with 225 g/8 oz plain white
flour, etc.)

For the filling
12 rashers of streaky bacon, rinded   *3 eggs*
1 large onion, finely chopped   *Salt and freshly ground black*
300 ml (10 fl oz) double cream   *pepper*

You will need a large Swiss roll tin measuring 33 × 23 cm (13 × 9 in), lightly greased.

Pre-heat the oven to 190°C/375°F/gas 5. Put a separate, flat baking tray in the oven to heat.

Roll out the pastry thinly and use to line the base and sides of the Swiss roll tin. Trim away and discard the excess pastry from the top rim of the tin, then transfer the tin to the freezer while you make the filling.

Cut the bacon rashers across into thin strips. Heat a non-stick frying-pan and cook the bacon strips without browning them until the fat starts to run. Stir in the onion, cover and cook over a low heat for about 10 minutes, stirring occasionally, until the onion is softened but not coloured. Remove from the heat and leave to cool.

Combine the cream, eggs, bacon and onion together in a bowl and beat together with a wire whisk. Taste and season with salt and pepper.

Remove the pastry-lined Swiss roll tin from the freezer, prick the base all over with a fork and put it on top of the pre-heated baking tray in the oven. Carefully pour in the quiche filling, then bake for about 30 minutes or until puffed and golden. Leave the Swiss roll tin on top of a wire rack to cool. When ready, the quiche can be cut into rounds using a 3.5 cm (1¼ in) plain cutter. Arrange them on a baking tray and re-heat in the oven at 220°C/425°F/gas 7 for 10–15 minutes or until tinged golden and piping hot. Serve immediately.

Watercroft Flaky Cheese Biscuits
(page 222).

To prepare ahead: *The quiches can be prepared about 6 hours ahead of serving.*

To freeze: *After baking and cooling, enclose the Swiss roll tin in a freezer bag, seal, label and freeze for up to 1 month.*

To thaw: *Thaw for 4 hours at room temperature.*

To re-heat: *Stamp out the rounds and bake as in the recipe.*

To cook in a fan oven: *Pre-heat the oven to 170°c and put a flat baking tray in the oven to heat. Bake the Swiss roll tin containing the quiche on the baking tray for 20–25 minutes or until puffed and golden.*

To cook in the Aga: *Cook the quiche on the floor of the roasting oven with the cold plain shelf above after 10 minutes until the pastry is brown and the filling set, about 20–25 minutes. Cool and stamp out rounds as in the recipe. To re-heat the mini-quiches, place them on a baking tray on the floor of the roasting oven for 8–10 minutes.*

Blini

These are a Russian type of pancake traditionally served with caviar and soured cream. They are a little like Scotch pancakes but not as sweet and with a yeasty flavour. Traditionally blini are made with buckwheat flour, which is difficult to buy and gives a curious taste not to everyone's liking. I prefer to use a combination of plain and wholemeal flour for flavour, and for ease and speed, make the batter in a food processor. It is then left in a warm place to bubble away quietly for about 45 minutes, so you can then fold in a beaten egg white when you are ready. Here I have adapted the recipe to make miniature versions of blini with caviar. Rather than go mad making dozens of tiny pancakes, I make larger pancakes and use a plain cutter to quickly cut out neat, small circles. Topped with soured cream and salmon or lumpfish roe, or snippets of smoked salmon and dill, they look and taste wonderful.

CRUDITÉS

My suggestions for these are celery batons, pepper slices, strips of carrot, small sprigs of cauliflower or broccoli, radishes or, perhaps, discs of cucumber. Serve these with the Fresh Herb Sauce (page 266) as a dip

---

175 g (6 oz) plain white flour
50 g (2 oz) wholemeal flour
1 packet easy-blend dried
    yeast
1 teaspoon salt
1 teaspoon sugar
10 fl oz (300 ml) warm milk
1 egg, separated
1 tablespoon melted butter, or
    cream

To serve
Soured cream
Snippets of smoked salmon
Chopped fresh dill
Salmon caviar or lumpfish roe

Put the dry ingredients into a food processor, then set the machine in motion. Pour in the warm milk then add the egg yolk and process until the mixture forms a smooth batter. Pour into a mixing bowl, cover with clingfilm, then a folded tea towel and leave aside in a warm place for 45 minutes.

Whisk the egg white until stiff but not dry. Fold the melted butter, or cream, into the batter followed by the egg white.

If you have a conventional pancake griddle, this would be ideal. If not use a large, medium-weight, non-stick frying-pan. Put the pan on a low to moderate heat and leave for several minutes. Wipe the surface with a piece of kitchen paper moistened with oil. Now, using a tablespoon, pour the batter from the tip of the spoon into the pan. This technique helps to keep the pancakes in a neat, round shape. After 1–2 minutes holes will appear in the surface of the batter; use a palette knife to flip the pancakes over then press them down on to the surface of the pan using the flat blade of the palette knife, just for 1–2 seconds. Cook for a further 1–2 minutes until browned, then transfer to a baking tray lined with kitchen paper to cool.

Using a plain 3.5 cm (1¼ in) cutter, cut out baby blini rounds. Top with seasoned soured cream, then snippets of smoked salmon and dill, or a little salmon caviar or lumpfish roe. Arrange on serving trays and serve slightly chilled.

To prepare ahead: *The freshly cooked blini can be cut, cooled and sealed in plastic bags. They can then be stored in the fridge for up to 2 days.*

To freeze: *Pack the cooled blini, before cutting, in a plastic freezer container. Seal, label and freeze for up to 2 months.*

To thaw: *Transfer the box of frozen blini to the fridge. Release the lid but leave it in place to minimize the condensation. Thaw overnight. Once thawed, cut out rounds and continue as in the recipe.*

To cook in the Aga: *The blini can be cooked on the simmering plate. Lift the lid for 15 minutes to allow the plate to cool sufficiently, grease the plate and proceed as in the recipe.*

Salmon Puff Pastry Roulades

MAKES ABOUT 40 SMALL BISCUITS

These are thin slices of smoked salmon rolled up in puff pastry – a very quick 'bite' to make and have with drinks. Actually, I cheat a bit with these; I call them salmon roulades, but in fact often use the cheaper smoked trout as it is well nigh indistinguishable from smoked salmon when cooked.

*1 × 375 g packet frozen, ready rolled
   puff pastry, thawed
2 × 115 g packets smoked trout or
   salmon slices
8 spring onions, trimmed and very
   finely chopped
Freshly ground black pepper*

LAST-MINUTE EATS FOR DRINKS
*Cut bite-sized chunks of ripe melon and wrap them in thinly sliced
Serrano or Parma ham. Secure them with cocktail sticks and
serve chilled. As a variation, try using cubes of ripe
mango instead of melon.*

You will need 3 baking trays, lightly oiled.

Pre-heat the oven to 200°C/400°F/gas 6.

Roll out the pastry to a long narrow strip about 60 × 20 cm (24 × 8 in). Cut this in half so you have 2 rectangles 30 × 20 cm (12 × 8 in). Lie them side by side on the work surface. Arrange the strips of smoked fish over the pastry. Sprinkle with the onions and a generous amount of pepper. Roll up each piece from one long side, rolling them smoothly and firmly. Using a small, sharp knife, discard the ends of both rolls before cutting the rolls into slices 5 mm (¼ in) thick. Arrange these rounds on the prepared baking trays, then bake for 15–18 minutes or until the pastry is golden and has lost the greyness in the centre of each biscuit. Cool the biscuits on a wire rack before eating.

To prepare ahead: *The biscuits can be made, cooled and stored in a container in the fridge for up to 1 week.*

To freeze: *When cooked, place in a freezer container, seal, label and freeze for up to 2 months.*

To thaw: *Leave the opened container for 3 hours at room temperature.*

To re-heat: *Re-heat in a pre-heated oven 200°C/400°F/gas 6 for about 5 minutes until hot and crisp.*

To cook in a fan oven: *Pre-heat the oven to 190°C. Bake for 12–15 minutes.*

To cook in the Aga: *Bake on the floor of the roasting oven for about 15 minutes, watching the biscuits carefully towards the end of the cooking time. Turn them over if they are not brown enough underneath.*

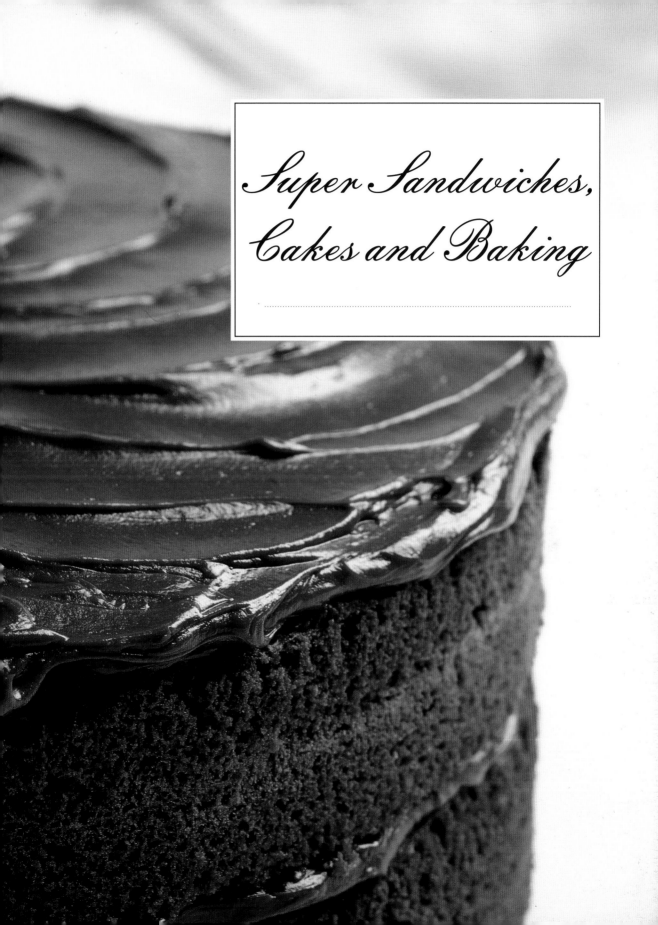

Super Sandwiches, Cakes and Baking

SUPER SANDWICHES, CAKES AND BAKING

The recipes in this chapter are primarily designed for teas but they can, of course, be adapted for picnics, and many of them would make a delicious addition to a lunch box, whether a child's or an adult's. And all, true to the spirit of the book as a whole, can be prepared in advance, and some frozen. Even scones, which we all know are always best eaten freshly made, freeze well, and just need a little refreshing in the oven to become perfect again. At home, we open the garden in the summer for the National Gardens Scheme, and this year I'm going to offer cream teas. I shall make all the scones months ahead and put them in bags in the freezer. Then all I have to do on the day is organize clotted cream and home-made strawberry jam.

The Honey-glazed Walnut Bread is wonderful, even if I do say so myself. It's good for open sandwiches, perfect with cheeses, and delicious with something like Gravadlax on top (see page 38). If you're not a bread-maker, I urge you to try this one as it's so easy. Another savoury loaf uses a new ingredient now available to us – jars of mushrooms in oil – and this bread is best eaten warm (it's good served with grilled meats). Both breads freeze very well.

The Lemon Poppyseed Traybake is very like one of my classic cakes, but I encountered it in Australia where they take it to the beach – a cross between a pudding and a cake. Another cake uses the new dried cranberries, and my chocolate cake really is the best I know – excessively moist, very easy to make, and it keeps well.

Sandwiches, whether conventional (with two slices of bread) or open (with just one slice of bread) can be served for tea, but they're useful at any time. They can be prepared a little while in advance, sometimes the day before, and stored in the fridge with a damp tea towel or clingfilm on top. Choose the fillings carefully though, as some are wetter than others. You can also cut some sandwiches small to offer at a drinks party. (For ideas on quantities required for large parties, see page 23.)

PREVIOUS PAGE
Very Best Chocolate Cake
(page 241).

The Very Best Scones

MAKES ABOUT 20 × 6 CM (2½ IN) SCONES

The secret of good scones is not to handle them too much before baking, and to make the mix on the wet, sticky side. If catering for cream teas for a crowd you will need about 450 g (1 lb) strawberry jam and 675 g (1½ lb) clotted cream for every 20 scones – and this is slightly on the generous side.

675 g (1½ lb) self-raising white
*   flour*
3 rounded teaspoons baking powder
120 g (4½ oz) butter, at room
*   temperature*
75 g (3 oz) caster sugar
3 eggs
About 300 ml (10 fl oz) milk

Pre-heat the oven to 220°C/425°F/gas 7. You will need 2 baking trays, lightly floured.

Measure the flour and baking powder into a bowl. Rub the butter into the flour until it resembles a crumble mix. Stir in the sugar. Beat the eggs until blended, then put 2 tablespoons of the beaten egg aside in a cup for glazing the scones later. Pour the rest of the egg into the dry ingredients with the milk and stir to form a soft dough.

Turn the dough out on to a floured surface and flatten it out to a thickness of 1–2 cm (½–¾ in). Use a 6 cm (2½ in) fluted cutter or octagonal cutter to stamp out the dough by pushing the cutter straight down into the dough; do not jiggle or twist the cutter, then lift it straight out. This will ensure that the scones will be a good shape and rise evenly. Arrange them close together on the baking trays. Glaze with the reserved beaten egg then bake for 10–15 minutes or until well risen and golden. To test if they are done, break one open, lifting the top away from the base, to see if the middle is cooked. Cool on a wire rack covered with a tea towel to keep them moist.

To serve, cut in half, spread generously with strawberry jam and top with a good teaspoonful of cream.

VEGETARIAN RECIPES
With the exception of some toppings and fillings for sandwiches, the recipes in this chapter are suitable for vegetarians; some contain dairy products.

To prepare ahead: *Scones do not keep fresh for long after baking; they really ought to be eaten the same day. But they do freeze well, see below.*

To freeze: *Pack the cooked, cooled scones in plastic bags, seal, label and freeze for up to 6 months.*

To thaw: *Thaw in the plastic bags for 2–3 hours at room temperature.*

To re-heat: *Refresh in a pre-heated oven at 200°c/400°f/gas 6 for 3 minutes.*

To cook in a fan oven: *Pre-heat the oven to 200°c. Bake for about 10 minutes. To check if they are cooked, follow the recipe.*

To cook in the Aga: *Cook on the grid shelf on the lowest set of runners of the roasting oven for about 10–15 minutes.*

Mushroom and Garlic-stuffed Picnic Loaf

An easy bread that does not need any skill in the making or shaping of it. It is baked with a filling of mushrooms, garlic and chopped parsley and so is well flavoured and moist and needs no butter. The jars of wild mushrooms in oil can be found in the larger supermarkets or good delicatessens. Serve with a salad or just home-grown tomatoes dipped in sea salt. It is also good with grilled meats.

For the dough	*1 teaspoon salt*
350 g (12 oz) strong plain white flour	*1 teaspoon easy-blend dried yeast*
	200 ml (7 fl oz) warm water
For the filling	*3 garlic cloves, finely chopped*
1 × 290 g jar wild mushrooms in oil	
A good handful of parsley leaves, chopped	*Salt and freshly ground black pepper*
To glaze	*A generous pinch of salt*
1 egg	*About 1 tablespoon sesame seeds*

You will need a large baking tray.

Empty the jar of mushrooms for the filling into a sieve placed over a bowl and leave to drain. Save the oil to use in the recipe.

To make the dough, combine the dry ingredients in a large bowl. Pour in the warm water and add 2 tablespoons of the drained mushroom oil. Mix to a sticky dough. You can now either use a mixer fitted with a dough hook to knead the dough for 5 minutes, or flex your muscles and do it yourself. The dough will be sticky and hard to work at first, but keep kneading and try not to use any additional flour. It will take about 10 minutes, but it will develop into soft, smooth dough that leaves the work surface and your hands clean.

Dribble a little more of the mushroom oil into the empty mixing bowl; roll the dough around in it then leave the dough on the work surface covered with the upside-down bowl. Leave for about 2 hours to prove, or until it looks to have doubled in size. To bake 1 large loaf, shape the dough into an oval, then put on to a large baking tray and roll out to a large oval about 33 × 23 cm (13 × 9 in).

Mix together the drained mushrooms (keeping any remaining mushroom oil on one side), parsley, garlic and some salt and pepper and spread over half the dough from one long end to the other and to within 1 cm (½ in) of the edge. Fold the other half of dough almost over the filling, so a narrow border of it is left showing.

To make individual rolls, divide the dough into 8 and roll, or push out, to 12 cm (4½ in) rounds. Put a heaped dessertspoon of mushroom mixture on each one. Fold as described for the single loaf and put on to a baking tray.

Beat the egg with a generous pinch of salt then brush on the bread. Sprinkle with the sesame seeds. Slip the baking tray into a large plastic bag, tuck the ends under the tray and leave in a warm place for 30–45 minutes or until the dough has doubled in size.

Pre-heat the oven to 200°C/400°F/gas 6.

Bake the loaf for 15–20 minutes, the rolls for 10–15 minutes, or until browned. It is difficult to tell when this bread is cooked because of the filling, so timing is the best indication. Remove from the oven and use a palette knife to transfer the loaf or rolls to a wire rack; brush the bread liberally with the remaining mushroom oil then leave to cool before eating, if you can resist it!

To prepare ahead: *Not suitable.*

To freeze: *Wrap the freshly baked, cooled bread in foil, then seal in a plastic bag. Label and freeze for 1 month.*

To thaw: *Thaw in the bag at room temperature overnight.*

To re-heat: *Loosen the foil wrapping, sprinkle the loaf with a little water and warm in a pre-heated oven at 180°C/350°F/gas 4 for 10–15 minutes.*

To cook in a fan oven: *Pre-heat the oven to 190°C. Bake the loaf for 12–15 minutes. The rolls will take 8–10 minutes.*

To cook in the Aga: *Bake the loaf on the grid shelf on the floor of the roasting oven for about 15 minutes, rolls for about 10 minutes. If the bread is getting too dark and is not done, slide the cold plain shelf above on the second set of runners. Continue to cook until the bread is done.*

Honey-glazed Walnut Bread

MAKES 2 × 20 CM (8 INCH) ROUND LOAVES

This recipe makes very good bread, very quickly! It needs mixing, shaping and only rising once before baking; about 1¼ hours altogether. Use walnut oil instead of olive oil if you wish, but I have not called for it in the recipe because I consider it a rather expensive 'specialist' ingredient which all too soon passes its sell-by date and most of it ends up being thrown away. Like scones, it is always better to have a bread dough on the wet side rather than dry, so if it sticks to your fingers it is a good sign. The recipe makes sixteen rolls instead of loaves, if preferred – and by the way this bread makes the best toast ever.

100 g (4 oz) walnut pieces	*1 tablespoon black treacle*
350 g (12 oz) Granary flour	*500 ml (17 fl oz) warm milk (1 part*
350 g (12 oz) strong white flour	*boiling to 2 parts cold)*
1 packet easy-blend dried yeast	*2 tablespoons good olive oil*
2 teaspoons salt	*100 g (4 oz) sunflower seeds*

To glaze
1 tablespoon beaten egg
1 tablespoon clear honey

Grease 2 baking trays. Briefly process the walnuts, or coarsely chop by hand, taking care to keep the pieces quite large. Put on one side until ready to use.

Combine the flours, yeast and salt together in a large bowl. Then add the treacle, milk and olive oil. Stir to form a dough, adding a little more milk if necessary to form a dough slightly on the sticky side. Turn the dough out on to a lightly floured surface and knead for about 10 minutes. Alternatively use a mixer fitted with a dough hook and leave running for about 5 minutes. When ready, the dough should be smooth and elastic and leave the bowl and the hands clean. Reserve about 2 tablespoons of sunflower seeds, then work the rest of the seeds and the nuts into the dough. Divide the dough in half, then shape each piece into a smooth round and place centrally on the baking trays. Enclose each tray inside a large plastic bag, sealing a little air inside so that the plastic is not in contact with the bread. Leave aside in a warm place for 30–45 minutes or until doubled in bulk. If your kitchen is cool this may take as long as 1–1½ hours.

Pre-heat the oven to 200°C/400°F/gas 6.

To glaze the loaves, mix together the egg and honey and brush gently over the surface of the dough. Sprinkle with the reserved sunflower seeds, then bake for 20–25 minutes or until the loaves are a good conker brown and sound hollow when tapped on the base. Leave on a wire rack until cold.

To freeze: *Seal the freshly baked bread in plastic bags, label and freeze for up to 6 months.*

To thaw: *Remove the bread from the freezer and thaw in the plastic bag for 5–6 hours at room temperature.*

To re-heat: *The bread is best served warm, so refresh in a pre-heated oven at 160°C/ 325°F/gas 3 for about 15 minutes.*

To cook in a fan oven: *Pre-heat the oven to 190°C. Bake for 20–25 minutes.*

To cook in the Aga: *Bake on the grid shelf on the floor of the roasting oven for 20–25 minutes. If the top is getting too brown, slide in the cold plain shelf above on the second set of runners.*

Danish-style Open Sandwiches

It can seem a daunting task to produce a large quantity of sandwiches. With every shape, size and variety now available in stores and supermarkets, how can you compete, given the usual limitations of time, space and budget? My answer is to make the Danish style of *smörrebrod*, as they call it, or open sandwich. This style of bread base with a variety of ingredients arranged on top gives a very attractive looking sandwich, with not too much bread. The Danes use mostly a range of rye breads for the sandwich bases, but this can be adapted according to the occasion, available breads, and your tastes.

If the occasion is one where people are able to sit and eat, then thinly sliced bread can be served with quite elaborate toppings. These can be eaten with a knife and fork. But the basic idea works just as well should guests be standing and eating out of doors. For this you would need a firmer bread base, such as pieces of halved French baguette, and a less elaborate topping that will stay in place whilst it is eaten. Just see that your guests are well supplied with generous-sized napkins so that no cutlery or plates are needed.

Experience has taught me a few basic rules for sandwich making. The first is to decide on three different types of sandwich, one of which should suit vegetarians. Know how many people you are to feed and make that number of each type of sandwich. This allows three sandwiches per person. There are a couple of items which are a great help. Have several large trays on hand that will fit in your fridge, as this will enable the easy movement of sandwiches in and out of the fridge and to wherever they are to be served. Arrange the sandwiches in rows on the trays and have an angled palette knife or fish slice available for guests to help themselves.

BREAD BASE

For a light lunch, use the denser types of bread that will slice thinly, such as light, medium or dark rye bread, pumpernickel, grain or Granary breads and Honey-glazed Walnut Bread (see page 236).

For outside eating, use a more robust, thicker bread. Brown and white baguettes, sliced in half lengthways and cut into 9–10 cm (4–5 in) chunks are ideal. Small pitta breads, or larger ones halved are also good; some types are available cut open into a neat pocket and so are easier to prepare.

SPREADS

There are alternatives to using butter. Low-calorie mayonnaise or low-fat yoghurt or light cream cheese are appreciated by many people. Otherwise a soft goats' cheese, pesto, or French mustard can help to make a flavourful sandwich.

TOPPINGS

These can be anything you choose. My favourites are listed below.

1 A spread of pesto, topped with sliced Mozzarella, sliced tomatoes, black olives and basil, drizzled with vinaigrette.
2 A spread of lemon-sharp mayonnaise topped with slices of smoked salmon, garnished with paper-thin slices of lemon and fresh dill.
3 Chopped hard-boiled eggs added to curry-flavoured mayonnaise, spread on a lettuce leaf base, each topped with sliced hard-boiled egg, mango chutney and coriander leaves.
4 Slices of Cambazola cheese with black grapes and flatleaf parsley.
5 Prawns mixed with a little herb-flavoured mayonnaise, arranged on lettuce leaves and topped with thin slices of lemon.

PREPARATION

The sandwiches can be prepared in the morning, assembled on the trays with all but the final garnishes, like sliced lemon or coriander, to add. Cover the trays with clingfilm and chill. They will keep up to 4 hours. Just before serving, add the final garnishes to the sandwiches and decorate the trays with fresh herbs, lemon and salad leaves.

HARD-BOILED EGGS WITHOUT TEARS
It is a strange thing to say: don't buy eggs too fresh when you need to hard-boil them. Nowadays they can be so fresh, they are impossible to peel, so use week-old eggs for hard-boiling.

Honey-glazed Walnut Bread (page 236).

'Proper' Sandwiches for Picnics and Teas

Closed sandwiches, with two slices of bread enclosing a filling, are still one of the best ways to feed people in some instances, and usually they are needed in some quantity. Here is the way I go about this task. Use brown or white bread, thinly sliced. The loaves average about 23 slices. Allow two slices of bread per sandwich and one sandwich per person, and a choice of two fillings. Always *taste* the filling before you put it in the bread. Flavour is very important – cucumber needs plenty of pepper, for instance.

SUGGESTED FILLINGS

EGG, MAYONNAISE AND MUSTARD AND CRESS: Finely chopped hard-boiled eggs mixed with mayonnaise and a little curry powder, mango chutney and salt and pepper. Spread on a bread slice, then scatter with mustard and cress before covering with the second slice.

CUCUMBER: If making the day before, use slightly thicker slices of cucumber and lemon-flavoured butter.

SARDINES: Bone the sardines and mash with mayonnaise, vinegar and a little French mustard.

SMOKED SALMON: Buy the cheaper salmon pieces, finely chop and add black pepper and lemon juice. If the salmon is rather salty, mix with a little cream cheese or use unsalted butter.

CHEESE AND PICKLE: Grate a well-flavoured Cheddar and sprinkle on top of bread spread with, preferably, a home-made chutney.

CREAM CHEESE: Season and mix with chopped walnuts and watercress leaves.

PÂTÉ AND PICKLE: Spread the bread with chicken liver pâté and top with chopped Cucumber and Dill Pickle (see page 213).

Have the fillings of your choice ready, and some soft butter. You will need a butter knife and a large, very sharp knife. The sandwiches can be made the night before, or in the morning before an afternoon event.

Butter the bread, fill and stack no more than 6 sandwiches on top of each other. Put them, uncut, on large trays, cover completely with clingfilm, then a damp tea towel. Transfer to the fridge.

No more than 2 hours before serving, trim the crusts from the bread using a very sharp knife, then cut each sandwich into 4 triangles or 4 domino shapes. For a buffet, arrange each plate or tray with one kind of sandwich, but if handing around, arrange a selection of all the sandwiches on large plates. Garnish fish flavours with lemon slices and parsley. Other types of filling can be garnished with mustard and cress or fresh herbs.

Very Best Chocolate Cake

MAKES 6–8 SLICES

Whatever your chocolate cake recipes, this will become your favourite; it is the best. It is speedily made in a processor or mixer, and the easy filling doubles as an icing. The cake is moist with a 'grown-up' chocolate flavour. Please try it and see if I am not right.

50 g (2 oz) cocoa, sifted	175 g (6 oz) self-raising white flour
6 tablespoons boiling water	1 rounded teaspoon baking powder
3 eggs	100 g (4 oz) soft baking margarine
120 ml (4 fl oz) milk	275 g (10 oz) caster sugar

For the icing and filling
3 tablespoons apricot jam
135 g (5 oz) plain chocolate, broken
    into sections
150 ml (5 fl oz) double cream

You will need 2 × 20 cm (8 in) sandwich tins, 4 cm (1½ in) deep, greased. Line the bases with circles of greaseproof paper and grease the papers.

Pre-heat the oven to 180°C/350°F/gas 4 and position the shelves in the oven so both filled sandwich tins can bake evenly at the same time.

Put the cocoa in the processor or mixer, set the machine in motion and carefully spoon in the boiling water. Blend for 1–2 minutes, then scrape down the sides of the bowl and add the remaining cake ingredients. Process again until the mixture has become a smooth, thickish batter. Divide the cake mix equally between the prepared tins and bake for 25–30 minutes. When baked, the cakes will be risen, fairly firm in the centre and show signs of beginning to shrink away from the sides of the tins. Remove the cakes from the oven and leave them sitting on a wire rack for 5 minutes. This allows them time to cool and firm up. Now use a knife to make sure the cake mix is free from the sides of the tins, turn out on to an oven-gloved hand, strip off the base papers, then immediately flip over, back on to the wire rack and leave until cold.

Warm the apricot jam in a very small pan, then spread a little over the base of one cake and the top of the other. Combine the chocolate and cream together in a heatproof bowl and stand the bowl over a pan of simmering water for about 10 minutes or just until the chocolate has melted. Remove the bowl from the heat and stir the chocolate mixture to make sure it is fully melted and smooth. Leave to cool until it is on the point of setting, then spread on top of the apricot on both cakes. Stack the top cake on the base one and use a small palette knife to decorate the top, drawing S shapes from the centre to give a swirled effect. Keep in a cool place until ready to serve.

To prepare ahead: *The cake keeps moist, but it is best eaten within 3 days.*

To freeze: *The cake is best frozen in a round plastic freezer container about 2.5 cm (1 in) bigger than the diameter of the cake. Sit the cake on the inside of the lid and place the container over the top. Seal, label and freeze, wrong side up, for up to 1 month. If the cake is frozen iced, it will not be quite as shiny once thawed.*

To thaw: *Release the lid but leave in position and thaw for 4 hours at room temperature.*

To cook in a fan oven: *Do not pre-heat the oven. Bake at 170°C for about 30 minutes.*

To cook in the Aga: 2-DOOR: *Cook on the grid shelf on the floor of the roasting oven with the cold plain shelf above on the second set of runners for about 20–25 minutes.* 4-DOOR: *Cook on the grid shelf on the floor of the baking oven for about 20–25 minutes. If getting a little too brown, slide the cold plain shelf on the second set of runners above.*

Cranberry and Apricot Fruit Cake

MAKES 1 × 23 CM (9 IN) CAKE

A light, moist, fruity cake with a good flavour without being heavy or too sweet. It is robust enough to pack for a picnic and not suffer from any amount of squashing or jogging, and also makes a good alternative Christmas cake. Dried cranberries are relatively new to the dried fruit sections of supermarkets. If they have not reached your area, substitute the same weight of washed and quartered glacé cherries.

1 × 227 g tin pineapple in natural juice	*75 g (3 oz) ground almonds*
350 g (12 oz) ready-to-eat dried apricots	*350 g (12 oz) sultanas*
	Finely grated rind of 2 lemons
100 g (4 oz) whole blanched almonds	*250 g (9 oz) self-raising white flour*
	250 g (9 oz) caster sugar
350 g (12 oz) dried cranberries	*250 g (9 oz) soft baking margarine*
	5 eggs

To decorate
50 g (2 oz) whole blanched almonds

You will need a 23 cm (9 in) deep, round cake tin, greased. Line the base and sides with a double thickness of greaseproof or silicone paper and grease the paper.

Pre-heat the oven to 150°C/300°F/gas 2.

Drain the pineapple, discarding the juice. Coarsely chop, then dry very thoroughly on kitchen paper. Snip the apricots into pieces and coarsely chop the almonds. Combine all the fruits, nuts (chopped and ground) and lemon rind in a large bowl and mix together well.

Put the remaining ingredients in a large mixing bowl and beat together for 1 minute until smooth. Fold in the fruit and nuts, then spoon the mixture into the prepared tin. Level the top with the back of a spoon and decorate the top with concentric circles of regularly spaced blanched almonds. Bake for about 2½ hours or until the cake is nicely browned. If it shows signs of becoming too browned before it is cooked, cover the top loosely with foil. When cooked, the cake should show signs of shrinking away from the side of the tin and a skewer inserted into the centre of the cake should come out clean. Leave to cool in the tin for about 30 minutes, then remove from the tin but leave the greaseproof paper in place.

To prepare ahead: *Like most fruit cakes, this improves on storing. Leaving the lining paper in place, wrap the cake closely in clingfilm and store in an airtight container for about 1 week.*

To freeze: *Wrap closely in clingfilm as above, seal inside a plastic bag (this takes up less space than a plastic freezer box), then label and freeze for up to 3 months.*

To thaw: *Thaw fully wrapped in the fridge overnight, or remove from the plastic bag and thaw for 8 hours at room temperature.*

To cook in a fan oven: *Do not pre-heat the oven. Cook at 130°C for 2½–2¾ hours. To make sure the cake is cooked, test as in the recipe.*

To cook in the Aga: 2-DOOR: *Stand the grill rack in the large roasting tin and place the cake on the top. Slide the roasting tin on the lowest set of runners in the roasting oven. Slide the cold plain shelf above, on the second set of runners. Bake the cake for about 30 minutes until a perfect pale golden brown, then carefully transfer the roasting tin and cake to the simmering oven and cook for a further 2½ hours or until a skewer comes out clean when inserted into the cake.*
4-DOOR: *Bake on the grid shelf on the floor of the baking oven for about 40–50 minutes until a perfect golden colour. Carefully transfer to the simmering oven and cook for a further 2 hours.*

Is Sifting flour Really Necessary?
Here is an admission: I rarely sift flour. The manufacturers spend millions of pounds on machinery to do that for me. The only time I do sift flour is when I am folding it into a whisked, fat-less sponge, when the sifting helps to combine the flour evenly into the mix. I certainly do not sift flour for one-stage mixes.

Lemon Poppyseed Traybake

MAKES 12 SQUARES

This was a recipe I brought back from Australia. It was the all-time favourite with tea and coffee. They always served it warm, not hot, heating the squares in a microwave for just a few moments.

For the cake

120 g (4½ oz) soft baking
   margarine
120 g (4½ oz) caster sugar
175 g (6 oz) self-raising white flour
2 eggs

1½ teaspoons baking powder
3 tablespoons milk
Finely grated rind of 1 lemon
25 g (1 oz) poppy seeds

For the topping

100 g (4 oz) sugar
Juice of 1 lemon

You will need a 4 cm (1½ in) deep roasting tin that measures 30 × 23 cm (12 × 9 in) from inside edge to inside edge at the top. Turn the tin upside down and mould a strip of foil around the base and sides. Turn the tin the right way up, drop the foil into the tin, then brush with a little oil.

Pre-heat the oven to 180°C/350°F/gas 4.

Measure the cake ingredients into a large bowl and beat for about 2 minutes until smooth. Turn the mixture into the lined tin and level the top with the back of a spoon. Bake for 20–25 minutes or until the cake is golden brown and shows signs of shrinking away from the sides of the tin. Press the centre lightly with your fingertips; it should be slightly resistant to the pressure. Remove the cake from the oven.

Mix together the sugar and lemon juice for the topping and brush over the surface of the hot cake. Leave the cake in the tin until barely warm, then use the foil lining to lift it from the tin on to a wire rack. Cut into 12 pieces and serve warm or cold.

To prepare ahead: *Wrap the uncut, baked, cooled cake, still with the foil lining attached, in clingfilm. Chill for up to 1 week.*

To freeze: *Remove the foil lining from the cooled cake and wrap closely in clingfilm. Seal inside a plastic bag, label and freeze for up to 3 months.*

To thaw: *Remove from the plastic bag and thaw for 3 hours at room temperature. Or thaw in the wrapping overnight in the fridge.*

To cook in a fan oven: *Pre-heat the oven to 160°C. Bake for about 20 minutes.*

To cook in the Aga: 2-DOOR: *Hang the small roasting tin on the lowest set of runners in the roasting oven and slide the cold plain shelf on to the second set of runners. Bake for about 20–25 minutes, turning once during cooking.*

4-DOOR: *Hang the small roasting tin on the lowest set of runners in the baking oven for about 20–25 minutes, turning once.*

Anzac Crunch Biscuits

MAKES ABOUT 36 BISCUITS

I fell in love with these biscuits in Australia. They are a crisp combination of oats and coconut, and very easy to make.

100 g (4 oz) butter	*75 g (3 oz) rolled oats*
2 tablespoons golden syrup	*135 g (scant 5 oz) plain white flour*
120 g (4½ oz) sugar	*1 teaspoon bicarbonate of soda*
75 g (3 oz) desiccated coconut	*1 tablespoon hot water*

You will need 2 baking trays, lightly greased.

Pre-heat the oven to 180°C/350°F/gas 4.

Melt the butter and syrup in a medium-sized pan. Remove from the heat and stir in the sugar, coconut, oats and flour. Mix the bicarbonate of soda and hot water in a cup, then immediately pour into the pan and stir well until thoroughly mixed. Form into small balls about the size of walnuts and arrange on the baking trays, leaving space around each biscuit for it to expand during cooking. Bake for 8–10 minutes or until the biscuits are a rich golden brown. Remove the trays from the oven and leave the biscuits for about 5 minutes before removing them with a palette knife to finish cooling on a wire rack.

To prepare ahead: *These are good keeping biscuits as they stay crisp for about 1 week if stored in airtight containers. They probably keep a lot longer, but I have never had a chance to find out; they are always eaten!*

To freeze: *Pack the freshly baked, cooled biscuits in plastic freezer boxes. Cool, seal and label, then freeze for up to 6 months.*

To thaw: *Thaw for 15 minutes at room temperature.*

To cook in a fan oven: *Pre-heat the oven to 170°C. Bake for about 8 minutes.*

To cook in the Aga: 2-DOOR: *Cook on the grid shelf on the floor of the roasting oven with the cold plain shelf on the second set of runners above for about 8 minutes. Keep an eye on them as they get to the last few minutes of baking.*

4-DOOR: *Cook on the grid shelf on the floor of the baking oven for about 8 minutes.*

Buffets and Large Parties

BUFFETS AND
LARGE PARTIES

I love organizing, cooking for, and giving large parties. Although there is obviously quite a lot of work involved, most of it can be done well ahead, and then all can be simply assembled attractively on a buffet table, work surface or wherever on the day itself. What you *do* need for large numbers is that large surface space, which must be situated in a convenient spot, preferably with space behind if someone is carving. If it's a table, it could be covered with an attractive cloth. Arrange the food and utensils on the surface in the order people will approach it (think of going through the acts of a play) – perhaps plates first, then food graduating from starters through to puddings, then cutlery and napkins. The details depend on your room and the numbers you're catering for. Think of colours too, as the look of the whole table will whet the appetite for the flavours to come.

Depending on numbers again, I would offer a couple of starter dishes (the Designer Mushrooms on Field Mushrooms on page 32 or the Mushroom and Goats' Cheese Tiers on page 31 perhaps), and two or possibly three main courses, both hot and cold. I'd have a large bowl of salad and a couple of vegetable dishes. Baked potatoes are delicious and easy to cook, but they're difficult to eat and cut standing up. My solution is to cook baby new potatoes, three to four per person, which are easily divided with a fork, and look very inviting tossed with a little butter. Breads would appear on my buffet table as well, particularly the Honey-glazed Walnut Bread (see page 236) – it's *so* easy and delicious – and perhaps a garlic bread (prepared well in advance and frozen in its foil).

The majority of the recipes here are for ten people, but they can be doubled to serve larger groups of guests. One word of warning, though. Although it sounds

PREVIOUS PAGE
Mosaic of Salmon en Croûte
(page 261).

silly, I have been told that the more people you have, the less they eat (some ten per cent less pro rata)! Many of the recipes, though, are for more, and the Baked Ham in Guinness will feed fifteen to twenty people. A ham or a turkey (boned, as in my Celebration Boned and Stuffed Turkey) would be a good centrepiece for a larger party, and handy too, because they *have* to be cooked the day before. I also like to serve something hot such as Mosaic of Salmon en Croûte or a vegetarian lasagne (using aubergines instead of meat as in the Aubergine and Spinach Lasagne). If you like the idea of serving curries, they will actually improve in taste if left to 'mature' overnight. But do be careful with food cooked in bulk; it must be cooled quickly after cooking – divide into two pots or dishes perhaps to speed the process – and then keep them in the fridge (use your neighbours' fridges as well if necessary).

Puddings are lovely at large parties, and the recipes for these are all in the puddings chapter (see pages 146–95). As for any party, I think I would serve something rich, creamy and delicious, with a large bowl of fruit salad. These should always be cold, and you should choose your recipe to suit the dishes you have available – two large bowls full of a trifle and fruit salad, say, with perhaps a few individual glasses or small pudding dishes or bowls with mousse, jelly or something creamy in them. Mousses are lovely in demitasse coffee cups.

It's nice to be able to sit down to eat, but at a buffet party this isn't always possible. If you're short of seating, remember that young people will probably be quite happy squatting on the floor, or on big cushions, and you could ask your nearest neighbours or friends if they could bring along a couple of folding or garden chairs. It's also a good idea to let those same friends know where you would like plates stacked (as near the dishwasher as possible probably, but don't forget the garden!); and someone helping you clear up as you go along is an absolute necessity.

Have your drinks table separate from the food if possible. Always offer soft drinks as well as alcohol, and if serving a cold drink, be it wine or beer, it *must* be cold. See pages 278–83 for more advice on drinks for parties large and small.

This sign indicates recipes that are suitable
for vegetarians, but please note that some of them
include dairy products.

Steak and Kidney Pie

SERVES 8–10

If you have a flameproof casserole then all the frying and cooking can be done in the one pot. If not, use a frying-pan, transferring the ingredients to a larger pan to cook. Make two pies for a party or double up if you have a larger pie dish.

For the filling

900 g (2 lb) beef skirt
450 g (1 lb) beef kidneys, cores removed
50 g (2 oz) plain white flour
1 teaspoon salt
Freshly ground black pepper
About 5 tablespoons sunflower oil

2 large onions, chopped
175 g (6 oz) smoked streaky bacon, rinded and cut in strips
300 ml (10 fl oz) red wine
300 ml (10 fl oz) Beef Stock (see page 14)
225 g (8 oz) brown chestnut mushrooms

For the topping

500 g (1 lb) puff pastry
1 egg
Salt

Preferably start this dish the day before it is served.

You will need either a shallow, rectangular pie dish, preferably one with a 5 mm (¼ in) wide rim, 28 × 23 cm (11 × 9 in) and 1.5 litre (2½ pint) capacity or a 23 cm (9 in) round, shallow dish of the same capacity.

Cube the beef, then cut the cored kidneys in thick slices. Mix the measured flour and salt with plenty of pepper. Heat the oil in a flameproof casserole or frying-pan. Toss about a third of the meat in the seasoned flour, then fry over a moderate to high heat until evenly browned. Use a draining spoon to remove it to a plate, then flour and fry the next batch in the same manner, adding a little more oil to the casserole when it is needed. Continue in this way until all the meat and kidneys have been browned. Now stir in the onions and bacon and cook over a low to moderate heat for 10 minutes or until lightly browned. Stir in any remaining seasoned flour and cook for a further 5 minutes, allowing the flour time to brown. Gradually stir in the red wine and stock and bring to simmering point. Return the meat and kidneys to the casserole with any juices, then cover and cook over a low heat for 1 hour or until the meat is tender.

Add the mushrooms to the casserole, cover and cook for a further 15 minutes, then remove from the heat and leave to cool. Chill overnight.

The following day, make the pie. Pre-heat the oven to 200°c/400°f/gas 6.

Place a handle-less cup or pie funnel in the centre of the pie dish ready to support the pastry. Spoon the cold meat mixture in around the pie funnel. Roll the pastry out to the size that is about 2.5 cm (1 in) larger than the top of the pie. Beat the egg with a generous pinch of salt, then brush this on the rim of the dish. Cut a strip from around the outside of the pastry and press this on to the rim of the dish. Brush the pastry strip with more beaten egg, then cover the pie with the remaining sheet of pastry, pressing the edges together all around the rim. Trim away the excess pastry from the rim, then pinch the edges together to form a tight seal so no juices can escape. Re-roll any pastry trimming to decorate the pie if you wish, then glaze all over with beaten egg. Make a steam hole in the centre of the pie, then transfer to a baking tray and bake in the oven for about 35 minutes or until the pie is a pale golden brown. Now lower the oven temperature to 180°c/350°f/gas 4 and continue baking for about 15 minutes or until the pie is piping hot and perfectly browned. Serve immediately.

To prepare ahead: *The meat filling can be cooked and kept in the fridge for up to 2 days. The pastry-covered but unglazed pie can be covered with clingfilm and kept in the fridge for up to 1 day. Allow the pie to come up to room temperature before glazing and baking following the recipe.*

To freeze: *Open freeze the pastry-covered uncooked pie, then cover with foil, seal, label and freeze for up to 2 months.*

To thaw: *Thaw for up to 12 hours at room temperature.*

To cook: *Bake in a pre-heated oven at 200°c/400°f/gas 4 as in the recipe.*

To cook in a fan oven: *Do not pre-heat the oven. Bake at 190°c for 30 minutes or until the pie is a pale golden brown, then lower the oven temperature to 170°c and continue baking for a further 15 minutes or until the pie is piping hot and perfectly brown.*

To cook in the Aga: *Stand the pie dish in a roasting tin. Cook in the roasting oven, hanging the tin on the lowest set of runners, for about 30 minutes or until golden. Then slide the cold plain shelf above and continue cooking until bubbling hot.*

STORING LEFT-OVER WINE
Decant small quantities of wine into a small bottle (with a top) or a screw-topped jar. Make sure there is no space between the wine and the top of the container and keep in the fridge. Longer term, and if you have more wine, it can be frozen for up to 2 months.

Nasi Goreng
with Tiger Prawn Kebabs

SERVES 10–12

This Indonesian rice dish is a very good way of using up cooked rice or the last of a roast chicken. If you boil the rice specially, do it the day before then keep in the fridge overnight. The idea of serving the dish with prawn kebabs came from a recent trip to Australia and it works very well for a party, but my husband still prefers the really traditional way of serving nasi goreng with a fried egg on top.

---

450 g (1 lb) easy-cook/par-boiled
   long-grain rice

For 2 flat pancake-like omelettes
3 eggs, beaten
Salt and freshly ground black
   pepper
A little butter

For the nasi goreng

9 rashers of smoked streaky bacon, rinded and chopped	*9 tablespoons dark soy sauce*
About 8 tablespoons olive oil	*Salt and freshly ground black pepper*
3 large onions, chopped	*9 spring onions, chopped*
4 garlic cloves, crushed	*75 g (3 oz) blanched, split almonds, toasted or fried*
½ teaspoon chilli powder	*2 × 250 g packets of frozen, raw tiger prawns, thawed*
3 heaped teaspoons medium curry powder	*About 3 tablespoons French Dressing (see page 129)*
3 boned, skinned chicken breasts, cubed, or cold, cooked chicken	

To serve
Prawn crackers

Bring a large pan of generously salted water to the boil. See the instructions on the rice packet for the quantity of water. Stir in the rice, then cover and simmer for 12–15 minutes. Drain the rice in a large sieve and rinse well by holding the sieve under the hot tap. Turn into a large bowl, cool, cover and chill overnight in the fridge.

To make the omelettes, beat the eggs with a little salt and pepper in a bowl. Heat a large, empty frying-pan, add a nut of butter, then use half the egg mix to make a thin, flat omelette. Turn it out on to a board to cool, then make another omelette with the remaining mixture and leave to cool. Roll the 2 omelettes together and shred in fine strips. Put on a plate, cover and leave aside until ready to use.

Heat a large, deep, non-stick frying-pan. Sprinkle in the bacon bits and heat until the fat runs. Pour in the olive oil then, when hot, stir in the onions and garlic. Cover and cook over a low heat for about 20 minutes or until softened but not coloured. Now stir in the chilli and curry powders and cook for a few minutes before stirring in the chicken, raw or cooked. Cover and cook for about 5 minutes, then uncover and add the soy sauce and the rice. Taste and season with salt and pepper. Arrange in a shallow dish. Finally, sprinkle in the shredded omelette, spring onions and almonds. Stir well, cover and keep warm in a low oven. Pre-heat the grill to maximum.

While the grill is heating, thread prawns on to short skewers; there should be sufficient to serve 3 prawns per person. Arrange them on a foil-lined grill pan and brush with the French dressing. Grill for about 2–3 minutes, then turn, brush with more dressing and grill until pink and cooked.

Turn the rice mixture into a large, warmed serving dish. Surround with the prawn crackers and arrange the prawn kebabs on top of the rice. Serve with a crisp green salad.

To prepare ahead: *The rice part of the dish can be made, omitting the addition of the shredded omelette and chopped spring onions. It can be kept covered in the fridge for up to 2 days. Have the prawns ready to grill.*

To freeze: *Not suitable.*

To re-heat: *Spread the rice mixture in a buttered shallow ovenproof dish or 2 dishes and put in a pre-heated oven at 200°C/400°F/gas 6 for 30 minutes, stirring from time to time, to heat and get crisp. Fork in the onion and shredded omelette and cook just sufficiently to warm through, about another 5 minutes.*

To cook in the Aga: *Cook nasi goreng and re-heat as above on the grid shelf on the floor of the roasting oven for a little shorter time. Cook kebabs in the top of the roasting oven for about 6 minutes in all.*

SERVING RICE

Allow 25–50 g (1–2 oz) per person, so for 12 people use 350–450 g (12 oz–1 lb). It can be prepared ahead; to re-heat plain boiled rice, put in a lightly buttered, shallow dish, cover with lightly buttered foil, then re-heat in a pre-heated oven at 180°C/350°F/gas 4.

Traditional Indian Curry with Coriander Naan Bread

SERVES 10–12

A curry is an excellent way to feed a crowd. Here is one that makes use of that wonderful cheap and flavoursome cut of meat, beef skirt, to make an ideal party curry that is not overpoweringly strong, that looks rich and authentic and yet is surprisingly easy to make. For twelve people allow about 450 g (1 lb) of rice – more if they are hungry.

4 tablespoons sunflower oil	2 × 227 g tins peeled tomatoes
4 large onions, chopped	4 rounded tablespoons tomato
4 fat garlic cloves, crushed	purée
A peeled piece of fresh root ginger, the size of a large walnut, grated	1.8 kg (4 lb) beef skirt, cubed
4–6 level tablespoons medium curry powder	About 3 teaspoons salt
	600 ml (1 pint) water

For the coriander naan bread
2 packets of 2 naan breads
175 g (6 oz) butter
2 garlic cloves, finely chopped
8 tablespoons chopped fresh
    coriander

Heat the oil in a large pan and stir in the onions. Cook over a low heat for about 25–30 minutes. This may seem far too long, but it is the time it takes for the onions to become nicely browned. For the first 15 minutes they will only need occasional stirring but they will need increasingly more attention as time goes on. Stir in the garlic and ginger, followed by the curry powder and carry on cooking for a further 3–4 minutes. Now add the tomatoes and tomato purée, then the meat. Stir, then cover and cook for 15 minutes. Uncover, add the salt and water and bring to the boil. Adjust the heat to a gentle simmer, then cover and cook for about 2½ hours or until the meat is tender. Alternatively the curry can be cooked in a low oven at 150°C/300°F/gas 3 (140°C in a fan oven).

To prepare the bread, spread one side of each naan bread generously with butter. Sprinkle the butter surfaces with the garlic and coriander, then stack them together and wrap in a neat, leakproof foil packet. Bake in a cool oven for about 20 minutes, separate the breads and cut each one in 3, then serve with the hot curry.

Traditional Indian Curry with
Coriander Naan Bread (above).

To prepare ahead: *The curry can be made, cooled, covered and stored in the fridge for up to 3 days. The bread can be prepared, wrapped in foil and kept in the fridge for up to 1 day.*

To freeze: *Pack the cooled curry into a plastic freezer container or a double thickness of freezer bags. Seal, label and freeze for up to 2 months.*

To thaw: *Thaw for 4 hours at room temperature.*

To re-heat: *Transfer the curry to a casserole and place in a pre-heated oven at 200°C/400°F/gas 6 for 20–30 minutes, removing the lid for the last 10 minutes.*

To cook in the Aga: *Cook the curry in the simmering oven for about 3 hours until tender. The naan will take about 30 minutes in the same oven.*

(V)

Garden Vegetable Curry

SERVES 6

Another simple, cheap curry to make and serve to friends, you can combine it with the coriander-buttered naan in the previous recipe. It is unlikely that you would want to make this for twelve; serve it as an alternative. It is easy enough to double the recipe.

900 g (2 lb) mixed, prepared vegetables, such as cauliflower, potatoes, turnip, carrots, leeks	*½–¾ teaspoon chilli powder*
4 tablespoons sunflower oil	*1 × 400 g tin chopped tomatoes*
2 large onions, chopped	*1 × 170 ml tin pineapple juice*
2 fat garlic cloves, finely chopped	*150 ml (5 fl oz) Vegetable Stock (see page 58)*
5 cm (2 in) fresh root ginger, peeled and finely chopped	*Salt*

Cut the cauliflower into sprigs, cube the potatoes and turnip, dice the carrots and thickly slice the leeks. Heat the oil in a large pan and add the chopped onions. Cook over a low heat for about 25 minutes, stirring occasionally, until the onion is nicely browned; do not allow it to burn. Stir in the garlic and ginger and cook for a further 5 minutes. Stir in the chilli powder, tomatoes, pineapple juice and stock and bring to a simmer. Add the vegetables. If you are using carrots, they take the longest to cook so they should go in first, 10 minutes ahead of the rest of the vegetables. Bring up to a gentle simmer, then cover and cook for 15 minutes. Uncover and test the vegetables. They will probably need a further 5–10 minutes cooking until tender, depending on the size of the pieces. Taste and add salt if necessary. Serve hot.

To prepare ahead: *The curry can be made, cooled, covered and kept in the fridge for up to 2 days.*

To freeze: *Not suitable.*

To re-heat: *Heat the curry in a large pan until boiling and thoroughly heated through.*

ⓥ Aubergine and Spinach Lasagne

SERVES 8

Made with vegetarian Cheddar, this would satisfy most strict non-meat eaters. If you do not like aubergines, this is also excellent made with 450 g (1 lb) sliced button mushrooms quickly fried in butter. Don't forget to season each part of the dish carefully before it is assembled. An easy recipe to double up.

550 g (1¼ lb) aubergines	*1 teaspoon sugar*
Salt	*Freshly ground black pepper*
About 3 tablespoons oil	*500 g packet of frozen whole leaf*
1 large onion, chopped	*spinach, thawed*
2 fat garlic cloves, crushed	*About 150 g (5 oz) lasagne, no*
25 g (1 oz) plain white flour	*pre-cooking required*
2 × 400 g tins chopped tomatoes	*300 g (10 oz) mature Cheddar,*
1 teaspoon dried basil	*grated*

For the sauce

900 ml (1½ pints) milk	*100 g (4 oz) butter*
1 bay leaf	*75 g (3 oz) plain white flour*
2 sprigs of fresh thyme	*Salt and freshly ground black*
½ teaspoon black	*pepper*
peppercorns	*1 teaspoon Dijon mustard*

You will need an ovenproof baking dish about 30 × 20 cm (12 × 8 in).

Pre-heat the oven to 200°C/400°F/gas 6.

Top and tail the aubergines, then cut into sugar-cube sized pieces. Put them in a colander and toss with a rounded teaspoon of salt. Leave aside to drain for about 30 minutes. Turn the cubes out on to a double thickness of kitchen paper and pat dry.

To start the sauce, measure the milk into a pan, add the bay leaf, thyme and peppercorns and heat to just below boiling point. Cover and leave aside to infuse for about 30 minutes.

Heat the oil in a large frying-pan and stir in the onion. Cook over a moderate heat for about 5 minutes until the onion is beginning to soften and colour, then add the aubergines and cook for a further 5 minutes. Add the garlic and cook for 1–2 minutes. Sprinkle the flour into the pan, stir and cook for 1 minute, then pour in the chopped tomatoes, basil and sugar and bring to the boil, stirring. Taste and season with salt and pepper. Remove from the heat and leave aside until ready to use.

Squeeze all the excess moisture from the thawed spinach, then tease out into small pieces. Season with a little salt and pepper, then put on one side until ready to use.

To finish the sauce, melt the butter in a medium-sized pan and stir in the flour. Gradually stir in the strained, infused milk and bring to the boil, stirring all the time. Season to taste with salt, pepper and mustard.

Now you are ready to assemble the lasagne. Spread one-third of the tomato and aubergine mixture across the base of the ovenproof baking dish, then dot a third of the spinach over the top. Cover this with a third of the sauce and grated cheese. Lay half the pasta sheets over the surface and up to the edges, then continue the layering as before starting with the tomato and aubergine mixture, then the rest of the pasta. Layer again, finishing with the sauce and cheese. By the time you add the final layer of sauce it may have cooled and thickened somewhat. This doesn't matter, just be firm and ease it over, then sprinkle with the remaining cheese. Bake for about 35–40 minutes or until golden brown and bubbling hot. If possible leave the lasagne to rest and 'set' for 5–10 minutes before serving.

To prepare ahead: *Cover the prepared lasagne with clingfilm and keep in the fridge up to 24 hours.*

To freeze: *Cover with clingfilm, then foil. Label and freeze for up to 3 months.*

To thaw: *Thaw overnight at room temperature.*

To cook: *Bake in a pre-heated oven at 200°c/400°f/gas 6 for 35–40 minutes.*

To cook in a fan oven: *Do not pre-heat the oven. Bake at 190°c for about 30 minutes.*

To cook in the Aga: *Cook towards the top of the roasting oven for about 30–35 minutes.*

MUSHROOM VARIATION
*Replace the aubergines in the Aubergine and Spinach Lasagne
with 450 g (1 lb) button mushrooms. Include the stalks
of the mushrooms*

Quick Cassoulet-style Sausages and Beans

SERVES 10–12

A proper French cassoulet is a magnificent dish, taking days to make in a very large casserole; a dish you might try to do properly once in a lifetime. By contrast, this recipe retains all the elements of good home cooking on a much more modest scale, with everyday ingredients.

350 g (12 oz) dried haricot beans, soaked overnight	2 tablespoons plain flour
2 teaspoons mixed, dried herbs or a fresh bouquet garni	2 × 400 g tins chopped tomatoes
3 tablespoons sunflower oil	2–3 tablespoons tomato purée
350 g (12 oz) smoked streaky bacon, rinded and cut in strips	2 bay leaves
350 g (12 oz) smallish onions, quartered	3 sprigs of fresh thyme
	Salt and freshly ground black pepper
	20 Toulouse or French sausages

To garnish
Chopped fresh parsley

Drain the beans and put them in a pan with plenty of fresh water to cover. Sprinkle in the mixed herbs or add the bouquet garni and bring to the boil. Adjust the heat to a gentle simmer and cook for about 30 minutes or until the beans are tender. Drain, reserving the cooking liquor.

Heat the oil in a large pan and fry the bacon until just beginning to crisp. Stir in the onions and continue to cook until the pieces start to brown around the edges. Sprinkle in the flour and stir and cook for a minute before adding the tomatoes, tomato purée, bay leaves and thyme. Add the cooked beans and 250 ml (8 fl oz) of the reserved liquor. Bring the mixture to the boil and add a little more bean liquor if you prefer, then taste and season with salt and pepper.

SPEED UP SOAKING BEANS
If time is short and soaking pulses overnight is not possible, put them in a pan with plenty of cold water to cover, bring to the boil then remove from the heat, cover and leave to stand for 1 hour. Cover with fresh water and press on with the recipe.

Pre-heat the oven to 200°C/400°F/gas 6.

Pour the bean mixture into a large shallow baking dish or 2 dishes and arrange the sausages on top. Cover with foil and bake for 20 minutes. Now remove the foil and bake for a further 20 minutes, turning the sausages once until the sausages are browned and the beans piping hot. Scatter with parsley and serve.

To prepare ahead: *The bean mixture can be made, cooled, covered and kept in the fridge for up to 3 days. If you keep it this long, add a further 150 ml (5 fl oz) of bean liquor.*

To freeze: *Not suitable.*

To re-heat: *Put in a covered casserole with the sausages on top and cook in a pre-heated oven at 200°C/400°F/gas 6 for 20 minutes. Uncover and cook for a further 20 minutes, turning the sausages so that they brown evenly.*

To cook in a fan oven: *Pre-heat the oven to 190°C. Bake for 20 minutes covered, then a further 20 minutes uncovered or until the sausages and beans are done to your satisfaction.*

To cook in the Aga: *Cook, covered, on the grid shelf on the floor of the roasting oven for 15 minutes. Then uncover for a further 10–15 minutes, turning the sausages to brown.*

Mosaic of Salmon en Croûte

SERVES 10

To be honest, this recipe takes a little time and effort but the result is scarcely less than spectacular in both appearance and taste. It is a long roll of puff pastry containing a mousse of dill-flavoured salmon, studded with nuggets of salmon wrapped in spinach; but this description hardly does it justice. It can be served hot, or cold with Fresh Herb Sauce (see page 266), which I prefer, and cuts well in both cases – a four-star buffet-party recipe.

1.5 kg (3 lb) single fillet of salmon, skinned	Salt and freshly ground black pepper
1 egg white	20–25 large spinach leaves
2 teaspoons chopped fresh dill	350 g (12 oz) puff pastry

To glaze
Salt
1 size 3 egg, beaten

Nasi Goreng with
Tiger Prawn Kebabs
(page 252).

Start the recipe the day before it is to be served.

You will need a large greased baking sheet. It would also help considerably to use non-stick lining material; the pastry can be rolled out on it and the pie fully assembled, then it is easily lifted on to the baking tray and baked on the lining material.

Trim the salmon fillet to a neat, long rectangle; don't be afraid of trimming away a fair quantity because you should have about 275 g (10 oz) of trimmings (see **1** right). Weigh the trimmings to make sure you have enough, then put them into a food processor with the egg white, dill and some salt and pepper and process to a smooth paste. Leave aside until ready to use. Cut the remaining salmon lengthways in 6 even strips (see **1** left).

Take each spinach leaf and pull off the stalk all the way along the back of the leaf so no slightly tough vein remains. Blanch for 1 minute in boiling, salted water. Drain and pour in cold water so that the leaves unfold. Carefully arrange each leaf flat on kitchen paper (see **2** right) and pat dry. Arrange a line of leaves along the work surface and put a strip of salmon fillet on top (see **2** left). Season with salt and pepper, then roll up neatly and fairly tightly in the leaves, trimming away any excess (see **3**). Prepare the remaining salmon strips in the same way.

Roll out the pastry thinly to a rectangle about 46 × 33 cm (18 × 13 in). Do this on non-stick lining material if you have it. If not, the next stage is to lift the pastry carefully, with the aid of the rolling pin, on to the baking tray. Spread half the salmon paste in a rectangle down the centre of the pastry. Carefully arrange 3 salmon strips on top (see **4**). Spread with the remaining paste then arrange the final 3 strips directly on top of the paste, to make a long, thin compact loaf shape.

Beat a generous pinch of salt into the egg, then brush the edge of the pastry. Bring both the short ends of pastry up and over the filling; brush the glaze down the folded pastry edge. Now bring the two long edges up to meet in the middle, down the length of the pastry. Press the edges together then, leaving a 1 cm (½ in) border of pastry standing, trim away the excess with scissors. Pinch the pastry edges together between thumb and forefingers to give an attractive, firm seal (see **5**). Brush the pastry all over with the glaze. Alternatively, seal the pastry without crimping it, then turn it over and after glazing use re-rolled pastry trimmings to cut out letters to spell SALMON along the top of the pie and brush them with glaze. Chill the pie in the fridge overnight. Re-glaze before baking.

Pre-heat the oven to 220°C/425°F/gas 7.

Bake the pie for 35–40 minutes or until a deep golden brown. If serving the pie hot, allow it about 10 minutes to settle. I think it is best served cold because it holds its shape well.

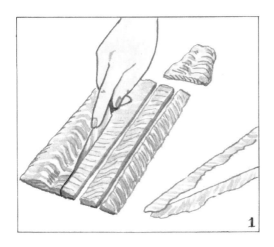

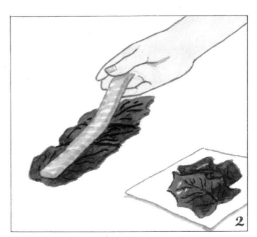

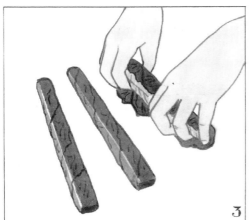

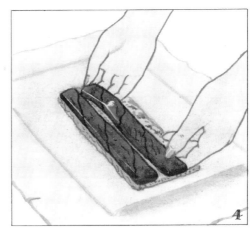

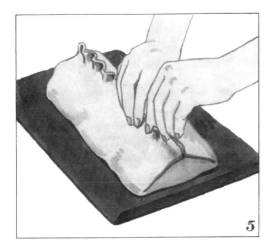

To prepare ahead: *Chill the unglazed pie for up to 24 hours before baking; brush with glaze just before putting it in the oven. Once baked and cooled, the pie can be kept chilled for up to 48 hours before serving, but the appearance of the puff pastry is not quite as good.*

To freeze: *Seal, label and freeze the uncooked pie for up to 2 weeks.*

To thaw: *Thaw at room temperature for 8 hours.*

To cook: *As soon as the pie has thawed, bake promptly following the recipe.*

To cook in a fan oven: *Do not pre-heat the oven. Bake at 210°C for 35 minutes or until a deep golden brown.*

To cook in the Aga: *Bake on the floor of the roasting oven for 30 minutes, sliding the cold plain shelf in if the pastry becomes too dark.*

Chilled Celebration Salmon with Fresh Herb Sauce

SERVES 10–12

A magnificent cold salmon makes a marvellous centrepiece for a cold buffet. But even an enthusiastic cook is unlikely to have a metre-long poaching pan in which to cook the fish. Home cooks are far more likely to have a preserving pan or large stock pot, so here is a recipe, blissfully simple, that uses a round pan to give the salmon a semi-circular curl. The method guarantees perfectly cooked salmon and a four-star presentation.

---

2 kg (4½ lb) whole salmon, gutted

To poach the salmon
About 7 litres (12 pints) water
1 tablespoon salt
1 tablespoon peppercorns
2 bay leaves
Pared zest of ½ lemon
½ lemon, cut in wedges

To garnish
1 small cucumber, thinly sliced
20 whole, cooked prawns, peeled,
*   leaving the heads on*
Generous bunch of fresh dill or
*   fennel*
12 wedges of lemon

You will need a large stock pot or preserving pan about 30 cm (12 in) diameter, 22 litres (4–5 gal) capacity. Fold a strip of foil to a 2.5 cm (1 in) broad band. Put this into the pan in a north–south direction, the strip following the shape of the pan down the side, across the base and up the other side. Put a tea plate upside down in the centre of the base of the pan on top of the foil. Now put in a second, similarly folded, foil strip, in the same way as the first, but in an east–west direction, over the top of the plate.

Put all the poaching ingredients into the pan, cover and bring to a full boil. For the next stage you might find it helpful to wear rubber gloves to protect your hands from the hot water. Turn the salmon belly-side up and hold on to the head with one hand and the tail with the other. Move your hands towards each other to bring the salmon round into a gentle curl. Hold that position and put the fish into the pan, belly-side up, so it curls around the shape of the pan. The foil should be between the fish and the pan. Take a good look at the shape. If your fish is on the small side it might not have a tight enough curl. This is easily solved by inserting 2 or 3 tea plates behind the foil, between the fish and the pan. Bring the water back to a full, rolling boil over a high heat, then boil gently for 2 minutes. Remove the pan from the heat. Cover with a lid and leave aside for about 2½ hours or until the salmon has cooled just sufficiently to handle. I have found that the hotter it is, the easier it is to peel off the skin. Again, you might find it helpful to wear rubber gloves to retrieve the salmon from the poaching water and it helps to have 2 people to lift the salmon out with the aid of the foil strips. Place the salmon straight on to a serving tray or plate in the position it is to be served.

Working fairly quickly, skin the salmon from head to tail whilst it is still hot, removing fins from the side and central back. Trim the tail fin into a neat shape with scissors. The skinned salmon should be a uniform, unblemished colour. Clean the serving plate carefully before starting to garnish the fish.

Arrange a line of halved cucumber slices down the backbone of the fish and around the base of the salmon, on the plate. Interlink the tails of the prawns and arrange 1 pair on the head of the salmon and 1 pair on the tail. Use sprigs of dill laid in the same direction to cover the base of the serving dish, and sprigs to garnish the head, centre back and tail. Now use the remaining prawns, cucumber slices and lemon wedges to garnish the plate and make it look as fresh and attractive as possible. Serve lightly chilled soon after garnishing. Each person should be given a serving of fish, 2 prawns, a lemon wedge and some cucumber accompanied by Fresh Herb Sauce (see overleaf).

To prepare ahead: *The cooked, skinned salmon can be closely covered with clingfilm on the serving dish and kept in the fridge for up to 24 hours before garnishing and serving.*

To freeze: *Not suitable.*

Fresh Herb Sauce

MAKES ABOUT 1.2 LITRES (2 PINTS)

This sauce is perfect with salmon or any other hot or cold, poached or grilled fish. It improves in flavour if it is made the day before as this gives the herbs time to develop and infuse the sauce.

2 tablespoons snipped fresh dill	1 × 200 g carton Greek yoghurt
2 tablespoons snipped fresh chives	300 ml (10 fl oz) low-fat
2 tablespoons torn fresh mint leaves	mayonnaise
2 tablespoons small sprigs of fresh	Salt and freshly ground black
parsley	pepper
1 × 200 g carton half-fat crème	2 teaspoons sugar
fraîche	Juice of 1 lemon

Put the herbs into a food processor and process for a second or two to chop them. Add the rest of the ingredients and blend to a smooth sauce. If you do not have a processor simply finely chop the herbs and combine with the rest of the sauce ingredients. Taste and season with more salt and pepper if necessary, then pour into a serving boat (not silver, it will discolour) cover with clingfilm and chill in the fridge until ready to serve.

Baked Ham in Guinness

SERVES 15–20

Before ham is cooked it is known as gammon. It helps with the carving if the joint is boned; smoked or green (unsmoked) the choice is yours. Ask for the main bone to be removed but the last bone to be left in. This means there is something to hold on to when carving. Ask the butcher or supermarket whether the joint needs soaking. My butcher suggests soaking for 48 hours in cold water.

SUPERMARKET FRESH HERBS IN POTS

After buying potted herbs and snipping them to bits I found that if shown a little care and attention by being re-potted in a sunny window box or in the garden, they will recover and keep on producing leaves to the end of the season.

---

*4.5 kg (10 lb) piece of half a
    gammon, hock end, boned
1 × 330 ml bottle of Guinness
2 tablespoons brown sugar
1 teaspoon ground allspice*

For the coating
*3 tablespoons thick honey
3–4 tablespoons coarse grain
    mustard*

You will need a large roasting tin and 2 long, wide strips of foil.

Pre-heat the oven to 200°C/400°F/gas 6. Place the foil strips across the roasting tin in a north–south and east–west direction. Put in the gammon. Combine the Guinness, sugar and allspice and pour over the joint, then bring up the foil over the top and fold the ends together to seal. Insert a meat thermometer if you have one. Put the joint into the oven and lower the oven temperature to 160°C/325°F/gas 3. Bake the ham for about 4 hours. By this time the ham should be cooked and the thermometer should register 75°C/167°F. Remove the gammon from the oven and leave until cool enough to handle.

Adjust the oven temperature to 220°C/425°F/gas 7.

Discard the cooking juices and remove the skin from the joint; it should peel off fairly readily. Score the top with a sharp knife with lines about 5 mm (¼ in) apart around the circumference of the joint. Combine the honey and mustard and spread it over the fat. Replace in the oven and cook for a further 10 minutes or until the coating is well browned and rather crisp. Serve hot or cold.

To prepare ahead: *Cool as quickly as possible after cooking, wrap loosely in foil and keep for up to 1 week in the fridge.*

To freeze: *Not suitable.*

To cook in a fan oven: *Pre-heat the oven to 200°C, then turn down to 150°C when the gammon is put in. Bake for about 3½ hours, or until a meat thermometer registers 75°C/ 167°F. Bake the coated gammon at 210°C for about 10 minutes or until well browned and crisp.*

To cook in the Aga: *Cook in the simmering oven for 5–6 hours. Agas do vary, so the time could be considerably longer. A meat thermometer is a great help here. After coating in mustard, etc., brown in the roasting oven for 10 minutes.*

Cool Minted Chicken

SERVES 6

For more years than I care to remember, a recipe called Coronation Chicken – which came from the Constance Spry cookery book – has appeared on buffet tables. It is a wonderful recipe but, dare I say it, perhaps a little too rich for today's tastes? My version is a little lighter and fresher in flavour, is very easy to prepare, and is improved if it is made the day before.

350 g (12 oz) freshly cooked
   chicken
150 ml (5 fl oz) half-fat crème
   fraîche
150 (5 fl oz) light mayonnaise
2 tablespoons chopped fresh mint
1 spring onion, finely chopped
Juice of ½ lemon
¼ teaspoon sugar
Salt and freshly ground black
   pepper

To garnish
Sprigs of fresh mint

Cut the chicken into bite-sized pieces, removing all the skin and bone. Mix together the remaining ingredients except the salt and pepper, fold in the chicken pieces, then taste and season carefully. Cover and chill in the fridge for 12 hours or overnight.

When ready to serve, taste and check the seasoning once more, then spoon out on to a dish and decorate with fresh mint. Serve with hot garlic bread and salad.

To prepare ahead: *See recipe above.*

To freeze: *Not suitable.*

Baked Ham in Guinness (page 266).

Celebration Boned and Stuffed Turkey

SERVES 12–15 AS PART OF A BUFFET

This contains a stuffing of herbed sausagemeat marbled with gammon, pistachio nuts and chicken livers. It carves easily, looks good and is literally packed with flavour.

1 × 5.5 kg (12 lb) oven-ready dressed turkey
25 g (1 oz) butter, melted
Salt and freshly ground black pepper

For the stuffing
50 g (2 oz) butter
2 large onions, chopped
200 g (7 oz) fresh breadcrumbs
900 g (2 lb) pork sausagemeat
50 g (2 oz) sprigs of fresh parsley, chopped
A handful of sprigs of fresh thyme, chopped

Rind and juice of 1 lemon
1 × 100 g packet shelled pistachio nuts
2 eggs, beaten
1 × 225 g carton frozen chicken livers, thawed
Salt and freshly ground black pepper
4 thick slices raw gammon

You will need a roasting tin just big enough to take the turkey. A very snug fit helps the turkey to keep its shape whilst roasting. If you choose too large a tin the turkey will become squat and wide during cooking! You will also need 2 long, wide sheets of foil.

The first thing is to bone the turkey. If you have bought it from a local butcher it is possible, if you ask him nicely, that he will bone the turkey for you. If not, it is not the complicated job it may seem to bone the bird yourself. Start by putting the turkey breast-side down on the work surface. Using a small, sharp knife remove the parson's nose. Now make a cut along the backbone from stem to stern (see **1**). Working down one side at a time, separate the flesh from the bone, gradually working round the rib cage of the bird. When you arrive at the wing and leg joints, cut through the ball and socket joints at the junction with the rib cage (see **2**). Now work on the leg bone, scraping the flesh back gradually to expose the thigh bone that joins the drumstick. When it is free of flesh, cut it away from the drumstick (see **3**). Similarly, work your way down the first bone of the wing, then cut it off. The bones and parson's nose can be kept to make stock if you wish. Repeat these procedures on the other side of the bird until you come down to the point of the breastbone. This is the only difficult bit, because here the skin lies close to the bone. Separate the two very carefully so as not to puncture the breast skin of the bird. Now lift the body cage free and put into the stock pot, if you wish. The turkey is now ready for stuffing. Cover the bird and put aside while making the stuffing.

In a large pan, heat the 50 g (2 oz) butter. Stir in the onions then cover and cook over a low heat for about 10 minutes until softened but not coloured. Remove from the heat and stir in the breadcrumbs; leave to cool a little. Put the sausagemeat, herbs, lemon rind and juice, nuts and beaten eggs into a large mixing bowl and squeeze the ingredients together with your hands to mix. As soon as the onions and breadcrumbs are cool enough, work them into the stuffing. Drain and dry the chicken livers on kitchen paper then cut into small nuggets with the turkey liver, if available, and gently work them into the stuffing mixture without breaking them up. Season with salt and pepper. Have ready the gammon slices, trimmed of rind, cut into finger-thick lengths.

Now to stuff the turkey. The aim is to use the stuffing to replace the bones that have been removed so eventually the turkey can be re-formed to almost its original shape. Take about 50 g (2 oz) of the stuffing and mould it into something like a cone shape. Insert this where the leg bones have been removed (see **4**). Do this on both sides. With the turkey spread

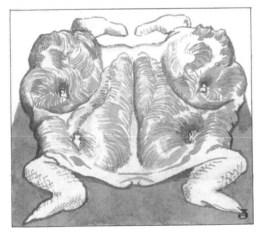

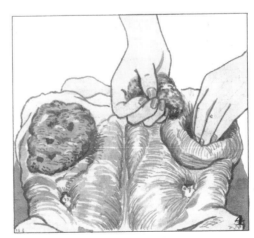

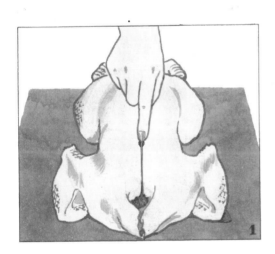

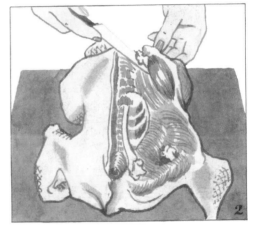

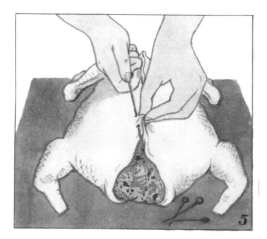
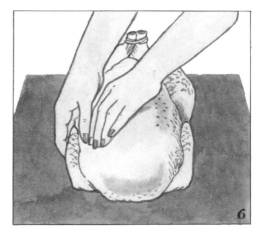

out, legs and arms akimbo, pat a layer of stuffing in the centre. Lay some of the gammon strips on top, down the length of the bird, then go on building up layers until the gammon and stuffing are all used. Now you start to re-form the bird. Bring the sides of the bird up around the central stuffing and use small skewers in running-stitch fashion through the skin to hold the two sides together along what was the backbone. You can do this from the leg end or the wing end; I find it easiest from the wing end (see **5**). Turn the turkey over, breast-side up and, rather like plumping a cushion, squeeze the bird into a turkey shape. Tuck the wing tips under the body so they hold the breast skin in place. The turkey should now look its normal self (see **6**).

Pre-heat the oven to 180°C/350°F/gas 4.

Line the roasting tin with 2 very long strips of foil, one in a north–south direction, the other east–west. Sit the turkey neatly in the roasting tin, brush with the melted butter and season with salt and pepper. Bring the ends of the first strip of foil up to meet in the middle and loosely pleat together, then do likewise with the second strip so the turkey sits inside a foil tent. Transfer to the oven to cook for 3 hours. About 30 minutes before the end of cooking, undo the foil so the turkey has a chance to become a good, golden brown. When the cooking time has elapsed, remove the bird from the oven and leave to cool. Cover and chill for 24 hours before serving.

For a buffet, arrange the turkey on an oval plate and carve about 8 slices from the breast end. Arrange these on the plate in front of the turkey and leave a carving knife and fork handy for people to help themselves later on.

Celebration Boned and Stuffed Turkey
(page 270).

To prepare ahead: *The stuffed, cooked turkey can be covered and kept for up to 3 days in the fridge.*

To freeze: *If you have used a fresh oven-ready bird and all fresh ingredients, the prepared, uncooked turkey can be sealed, labelled and frozen for up to 3 weeks.*

To thaw: *Thaw at room temperature for 48 hours.*

To cook: *Cook, following the recipe.*

To cook in a fan oven: *Do not pre-heat the oven. Bake at 170°c for 3 hours. About 20 minutes before the end of cooking, unwrap the turkey so the skin has a chance to brown.*

To cook in the Aga: *Squeeze the turkey into the small roasting tin, double-foil lined, and cook in the roasting oven on the grid shelf on the floor for about 2½ hours, removing the top foil for the last 30 minutes.*

Golden Parsleyed Smoked Salmon Roulade

SERVES 6–8

A parsley and carrot flavoured roulade, perfectly offset by a filling of fromage frais and smoked salmon. It is just the right sort of food for a picnic: moist, fresh-flavoured, it travels well and eats easily. I usually take the roulade already cut in slices, then if I forget to take a knife, it is not a disaster! For twelve or more people, make two.

For the roulade	4 eggs, separated
40 g (1½ oz) butter	Salt and freshly ground black
2 tablespoons water	pepper
450 g (1 lb) carrots, coarsely grated	
For the filling	100 g (4 oz) smoked salmon
250 ml (8 fl oz) low-fat fromage	trimmings or rough pieces,
frais	chopped
Salt and freshly ground black	25 g (1 oz) flatleaf parsley leaves,
pepper	chopped

You will need a large Swiss roll tin 33 × 23 cm (13 × 9 in). Grease the tin, then line with greased greaseproof paper.

Pre-heat the oven to 220°C/425°F/gas 7.

Heat the butter and water together in a large frying-pan or a large, shallow pan. Stir in the grated carrots, then cover and cook over a low to moderate heat for 5 minutes, stirring occasionally. Uncover and cook for about 2 minutes or until the pieces of carrot are tender and most of the moisture has evaporated. Transfer the carrots to a large bowl and leave to cool.

Mix the egg yolks into the cooled carrots and season well with salt and pepper. Put the egg whites in a clean, grease-free bowl and whisk until they form peaks. Stir a heaped tablespoon of the whites into the carrot mix, then carefully fold in the rest. Spread quickly in the prepared tin and bake near the top of the oven for 10–12 minutes or until firm to the touch and lightly browned. Leave to cool in the tin.

Turn the roulade out on to a large sheet of greaseproof paper and spread the fromage frais to within 1 cm (½ in) of the edges. Season with salt and pepper, then sprinkle thickly with the chopped smoked salmon and parsley. Starting from one long side, form the roulade into a firm roll, Swiss-roll style, using the greaseproof paper to lift and guide the carrot base into a compact roulade. Leave the paper wrapped around the roll, and chill in the fridge until ready to serve.

For a lunch, the roll can either be sliced and arranged on a large serving plate, garnished with flatleaf parsley; or the slices can be served on individual plates surrounded with a green salad as a starter. For picnics, slice, re-form the roll and wrap closely with clingfilm, ready for people to help themselves.

To prepare ahead: *The roulade can be made a day ahead, covered in clingfilm and kept in the fridge.*

To freeze: *Not suitable.*

To cook in a fan oven: *Pre-heat the oven to 200°C. Bake for about 10 minutes.*

To cook in the Aga: *Cook on the grid shelf on the floor of the roasting oven for about 8–10 minutes.*

A Few Drinks

A Few Drinks

It seems to have become a forgotten art, the making of squashes and cordials at home, but it's something I enjoy doing a great deal, and they can be very useful in a number of ways.

Two of the drinks I suggest here can actually be made from hedgerow fruits and flowers. Elderflowers blossom in abundance in the early summer before the rich, dark berries arrive, and they are incredibly fragrant. (Try to choose flowers from trees and bushes that are away from main roads.) To preserve their fragrance, you can either make them into Elderflower Cordial straightaway, macerating them in a syrup, or you can freeze them whole, just when they are newly open, so they are instantly available as and when you want to use them. (Don't, however, let the flower heads thaw after freezing, as they will turn brown; plunge the perfect heads, straight from the freezer, into the hot syrup.) The wonderful result of this can be diluted with sparkling or still water for a refreshing drink, or it can be used as part of the liquid for a fruit salad.

The other 'free' liquor you can make is Sloe Gin. Sloes are a *Prunus*, so are related to the apricot, cherry, peach, nectarine and plum, and they are very sour indeed. After macerating with sugar and gin for up to six months, though, the liqueur is a warm red in colour, with a rich flavour somewhere between black-currants and cherry brandy, with just a hint of their *prunus* relative, the almond. (Sloes can also be made into a sharp jelly, ideal for accompanying game dishes.)

The other recipes here are for hot or cold wine or cider cups or punches, the sort of mixtures that help a party get off to a very cheerful start. The Winter Mulled Wine in particular is like a Glühwein, reminding me of skiing holidays, and it is

---

PREVIOUS PAGE
A selection of drinks with, in the centre, Iced Wine Tea (page 282) and,
on the right, Sparkling Wine Cup (page 281).

very warming, the perfect welcome for a guest just arrived in from the cold and icy outdoors. The Iced Wine Tea, on the other hand, is the best possible drink to have on a hot summer's day, full of flavour and very thirst-quenching.

When you are serving cold drinks, of whatever variety, they must be *cold*. To ensure this, you should have a good supply of ice, or you must have pre-planned well, with the fridge full and at its coldest. If you're catering for a larger party, for instance, a fridge with twelve bottles of white wine in it will take very much longer to get properly cold. I always make lots of blocks of ice in advance of such an occasion. (Lots of people won't have the space for this, but you can buy ice from your local off-licence.) I fill ice-cream boxes with water and freeze them; then I decant them into my sink or bucket, and set the bottles of wine or water amongst them to keep cool. Be careful with wine bottles, because the labels can come off while they're chilling – a disaster if you've got them on sale or return! The answer is to put the bottles in plastic bags before chilling.

These days many people are being very careful about alcohol, and especially about drinking and driving, so you must take their needs into consideration. I always have a selection of soft drinks on offer, whatever sort of party I am giving. There are some very good quality juices in cartons, and I sometimes make up my own mixture of these, diluting them with carbonated water, and adding some pieces of ice, fruit and a sprig of borage. These look lovely in an attractive glass, and the recipient will be suitably grateful. It's very nice to be thought of if you're the poor person doing the driving.

And as for how much drink to offer per person: this is quite difficult, as it really depends on the length of the party and whether you will be serving food. If it's a wine-all-night affair – a barbecue, for instance – I would think in terms of at least three-quarters of a bottle of wine per person, roughly 4½ glasses. And don't forget that you can borrow glasses free of charge (you only pay for breakages) from your wine merchant or supermarket when you buy the wine.

INTERESTING ICE CUBES
For clear ice cubes use boiled, cooled water or bottled water. Pour into ice cube trays and insert tiny sprigs of mint or strips of orange or lemon peel, removed with a zester.

Winter Mulled Wine

SERVES 12

For an extra kick on a winter's day, add a sherry glass of brandy just before serving.

4 lemons	*16 cloves*
2 large oranges	*2 cinnamon sticks*
2 bottles red wine	*100–175 g (4–6 oz) caster*
1.2 litres (2 pints) water	*sugar*

Peel the zest very thinly from 2 lemons and 1 orange. Thinly slice the remaining orange and 1 whole lemon, then quarter the slices, put on a plate, cover and reserve for a garnish. Squeeze the juice from the remaining 3 lemons and zested orange.

Pour the wine, water and citrus juices into a large pan and add the cloves and cinnamon sticks. Bring to simmering point, then cover and keep just below that heat for 1 hour. Stir in sugar to taste, then strain and serve hot with the reserved orange and lemon slices floating on top.

To prepare ahead: *The mulled wine can be made, strained, cooled and kept in covered jugs in the fridge for up to 3 days. Re-heat and add the quartered slices of lemon and orange just before serving.*

Cider Punch

MAKES 14 GLASSES

Chill everything well beforehand. For a slightly less alcoholic and very refreshing drink, omit the brandy and add a litre bottle of chilled lemonade.

1 litre (1¾ pints) medium dry cider	*1 wine glass brandy, about 150 ml*
1 bottle dry white wine	*(5 fl oz)*
1 wine glass medium sherry, about	*1 lemon, thinly sliced*
150 ml (5 fl oz)	

SUMMER DRINKS
If serving drinks such as Pimms or fruit cup on a hot day, put the fruit and ice straight into the glasses arranged on a tray. It is then much easier to pour the liquid into the glasses and serve.

To serve
1 red-skinned apple, sliced
1 small thin-skinned orange, sliced

Combine all the liquid ingredients together in a large glass jug. Have the glasses ready assembled with the fruit divided amongst them. Pour and serve.

To prepare ahead: *The drink can be made and kept covered in the fridge for up to 1 day.*

Sparkling Wine Cup

MAKES 18 GLASSES

Make sure that all bottles and fruit are chilled well ahead of time. If no liqueurs are available, brandy is an acceptable alternative. There is no sugar added to this recipe as the lemonade sweetens the drink.

½ ripe melon, seeded and cubed	*1 litre (1¾ pints) lemonade*
225 g (8 oz) fresh strawberries, hulled and sliced	*1 wine glass orange liqueur, such as Cointreau, Curaçao, or Grand Marnier*
24 ice cubes	
2 bottles Sauternes, chilled	*Juice of 1 lemon*

To serve
18 sprigs of fresh mint

Put some of the fruit in a large glass jug with 6 ice cubes and divide the rest of the fruit and ice between the glasses. Pour the chilled wine, lemonade, liqueur and lemon juice into the jug, stir and serve. Pop a sprig of mint into each glass just before handing them to your guests.

To prepare ahead: *This drink is best drunk freshly made when it has some fizz.*

ICED COFFEE
For the very best iced coffee, use Camp coffee diluted to taste with ice-cold milk, semi-skimmed if you prefer. Add cream or ice cubes, if liked. I usually keep a jug of iced coffee made up in the fridge in very hot weather.

Iced Wine Tea

MAKES 10 GLASSES

An excellent thirst-quencher. I usually use Entre-deux-Mers for this, and serve it on a hot afternoon instead of tea, adding a sprig of mint to each glass. It is essential to serve it very cold.

2 teaspoons Darjeeling tea
600 ml (1 pint) water
1 bottle dry white wine
A few parings of orange rind
A few sprigs of fresh mint
Ice cubes (optional)

Warm the teapot in the usual way, then spoon the tea into the pot. Pour in the freshly boiled water. Stir, cover and leave to brew for 2–3 minutes. Strain the tea into a jug, cool, then chill in the fridge.

Combine the tea and wine in a chilled jug and add the orange parings and fresh mint. Serve with ice if you wish.

To prepare ahead: *The made drink can be kept covered in the fridge for up to 1 day.*

Elderflower Cordial

MAKES ABOUT 2.9 LITRES (5¼ PINTS)

Making this delicious drink need not be restricted to the short flowering season of the elder. I have discovered that the elderflowers can be successfully frozen in plastic bags. The heads are then added, still frozen, to the *hot* syrup to make a cordial tasting exactly the same as one made with fresh flowers. Citric acid is no problem; the white crystals, resembling sugar, can be bought from all chemists.

ICED TEA

Iced tea is not too fattening, is thirst quenching and very easy to make.
Use a fragrant loose tea and make a rather weak infusion by stirring
the leaves into a jug of cold water. Leave overnight in the fridge,
then strain. Lemon juice and sugar can be added just before serving.
For extra chill, freeze some of the tea in ice-cube trays.

1.5 kg (3 ½ lb) sugar
1.5 litres (2 ½ pints) water
3 lemons

About 25 elderflower
heads
50 g (2 oz) citric acid

To serve
Chilled carbonated water
Ice cubes

Measure the sugar and water into a large pan, bring to the boil, stirring, until the sugar has dissolved. Remove from the heat and leave to cool. Slice the lemons thinly either by hand or using the thin slicing disc in a processor; put the slices in a large plastic box or glass bowl. Add the elderflower heads and citric acid and pour in the cool sugar syrup. Cover and leave overnight.

The following day, strain the syrup, decant into bottles, seal and store in the fridge. To serve, dilute to taste with chilled carbonated water and serve with ice.

To prepare ahead: *The cordial can be made, bottled and stored in the fridge for 4–6 weeks.*

Sloe Gin

Sloes are the fruit of the blackthorn and are like very small damsons with a bloom like black grapes. They need to be picked when they are ripe in the autumn, but you don't have to start making the sloe gin there and then because the fruits can be frozen and used when it suits you.

Wash the sloes, remove the stalks and snip or prick each sloe to make the juices run. Take a clean, empty gin bottle, or similar, and fill two-thirds full with snipped sloes. To each bottle, add 225–275 g (8–10 oz) caster sugar, then fill the bottle up with gin. Put the lid on and shake well.

Put on one side for at least 2 months before using, shaking the bottle once or twice a week. In theory you should not drink it for at least 6 months to experience the flavour at its rich and redolent best! After 6 months, strain the sloes from the gin and discard them.

Serve in small glasses as an after-dinner drink.

To freeze: *Freeze the clean, dry sloes in a plastic box for up to 1 year.*

To thaw: *Leave the box for 6 hours at room temperature before using to make sloe gin. The berries will not need pricking, just pack them into bottles with any juices that have accumulated during thawing.*

Specialist Suppliers and Useful Addresses

Aga-Rayburn
Station Road
Telford
Shropshire
YF1 5AQ
Tel: 01952 642000

For Leeds Creamware,
e.g. candlesticks,
bowls, jugs
Hartley Greens and Co.
PO Box 46
Selby
North Yorkshire
YO8 5ZR
Tel: 01757 213556

For white ovenware and
Berndes non-stick pans
ICTC
3 Caley Close
Sweet Briar Rd
Norwich
Norfolk
NR3 2BU
Tel: 01603 488019

For all manner of
kitchen equipment
Lakeland Ltd
Alexandra Buildings
Windermere
Cumbria
LA23 1BQ
Tel: 015394 88100

Particularly for heavy
baking sheets, but also
for general catering
equipment
Nisbets
1110 Aztec West
Bristol
BS32 4HR
Tel: 01454 855525

For Lift-Off Baking Paper
(previously known as
Magic Paper)
NKS
Dogcraig House
Peebles
Scotland
EH45 9HS
Tel: 01721 729824

For tartan apron and
gauntlets
Treadlers Ltd
Auchinleck Est
Auchinleck
Ayrshire
KA18 2LR
Tel: 01290 551517

For Victorinox
kitchen knives
Burton McCall Ltd
163 Parker Drive
Leicester
LE4 0JP
Tel: 01162 344646

For specialist kitchen
equipment
Divertimenti
45–47 Wigmore St
London
W1U 1PS
Tel: 020 7935 0689

For barbecues and
barbecue equipment
Outdoor Chef UK Ltd
Mill Road
Barton St David
Near Somerton
Somerset
TA11 6DF
Tel: 01458 851234

Our thanks to Aga-Rayburn for lending the Aga module for the television series; and to Michael Whitaker of Traditional Interiors Fitted Furniture Ltd, 74 Baddow Road, Chelmsford, Essex CM2 7PJ.

Index

Page numbers in *italic* refer to the illustrations